Toronto Medieval Texts and Translations 6

Hetoum: A LYTELL CRONYCLE

Richard Pynson's Translation (c 1520) of *La Fleur des histoires de la terre d'Orient* (1307)
Edited by Glenn Burger

La Fleur des histoires de la terre d'Orient was written about the year 1307 by the Armenian aristocrat Hetoum. Dedicated to Pope Clement v, *La Fleur des histoires* was intended to reawaken European interest in a crusade to the Holy Land. Hetoum had a unique view of crusade history and politics. As a member of the Armenian royal family he had close ties with both the European West and the Mongol East; moreover he was a first-hand observer of many of the events and places he describes. *La Fleur des histoires* gives a distinctive and generally accurate account of the new geopolitical realities in the Near East in the years following the rise of Mongol power and the fall of the Latin kingdom of Jerusalem. It opens with a brief historical and geographical survey of Asia, followed by a lengthy history of the Mongols, which focuses in particular on the conflicts between the Mongol ilkhans of Persia and the Moslem sultans of Egypt. The work concludes with a detailed and pragmatic plan for a new crusade involving an alliance of European, Armenian, and Mongol forces.

La Fleur des histoires enjoyed a great popularity throughout the later medieval and early modern period, and it continues to be an important source for modern historians of the Crusades. Richard Pynson's translation, entitled *A Lytell Cronycle*, published about 1520, is still the only complete English version. Besides being accurate and readable, it is an attractive witness to the survival of the idea of the crusade and of the taste for exotic and chivalric literature in the Tudor period. This edition presents a corrected text with extensive introduction, notes, and glossary that explain the work in late medieval and early modern contexts.

GLENN BURGER is a member of the Department of English, University of Alberta.

The title-page of Richard Pynson's translation of *A Lytell Cronycle* c 1520.
By permission of the Newberry Library, Chicago

HETOUM

A Lytell Cronycle

Richard Pynson's Translation (c 1520)
of *La Fleur des histoires*
de la terre d'Orient (c 1307)

EDITED BY GLENN BURGER

UNIVERSITY OF TORONTO PRESS
Toronto Buffalo London

© University of Toronto Press 1988
Toronto Buffalo London
Printed in Canada
ISBN 0-8020-2626-5

Printed on acid-free paper

Canadian Cataloguing in Publication Data

Hethum, Prince of Korghos, ca. 1235-ca. 1314.
[La fleur des histoires de la terre d'Orient.
English]
A lytell cronycle

(Toronto medieval texts and translations, ISSN
0821-4344; 6)
Includes index.
Bibliography: p.
ISBN 0-8020-2626-5

1. Asia – History – Early works to 1800. 2. Tatars
– Early works to 1800. 3. Cilicia – History –
Armenian Kingdom, 1080-1375 – Early works to 1800.
4. Crusades – Early works to 1800. I. Burger,
Glenn, 1954-   . II. Pynson, Richard, c. 1530.
III. Title. IV. Title: La fleur des histoires de
la terre d'Orient. English. V. Series.

DS33.5.H413 1988   956.4   c88-093462-x

The maps on pages lxiii–lxvi are reproduced by permission of University of Wisconsin Press from *A History of the Crusades* gen ed Kenneth M. Setton, vol v, maps 12, 1, 6, and 7, compiled by Professor Harry W. Hazard.

This book has been published with the help of grants from the Calouste Gulbenkian Foundation and from the Canadian Federation for the Humanities, using funds provided by the Social Sciences and Humanities Research Council of Canada.

Contents

Abbreviations

BL   British Library
BN   Bibliothèque Nationale
EETS OS   Early English Text Society, Original Series
Fr   French
ME   Middle English
MED   *Middle English Dictionary*
OED   *Oxford English Dictionary*
P   Pynson's *A Lytell Cronycle* or its translator
P1   Bodleian Library, Auct QQ supra II 24
P2   BL 148.c.1
P3   BL G.6789
R   *The Floure of Histories* (BL, MS Royal 18.B.26) or its translator
RHC Arm   *Recueil des historiens des croisades: Documents arméniens*
RHC Occ   *Recueil des historiens des croisades: Documents occidentaux*
STC   *Short-title Catalogue of Books Printed in England, Scotland, & Ireland, and of English Books Printed Abroad, 1475–1640*
var   variant

Acknowledgments

Grateful acknowledgment is made to the Newberry Library for permission to reproduce the woodcuts forming the frontispiece and endpiece to the Pynson edition; and to Professor Harry Hazard and the University of Wisconsin Press for permission to reproduce the maps from their *History of the Crusades*. I would also like to thank the Social Sciences and Humanities Research Council of Canada for grants in aid of this project, and the Canadian Federation for the Humanities and the Calouste Gulbenkian Foundation for grants in aid of publication. I have worked at the British Library and the Bodleian Library, and owe much to the kindness and efficiency of their librarians. I am also grateful for permission to reproduce the selections from BL MS Royal 18.B.26 found in the appendix (pp 163–202).

I take great pleasure in acknowledging particular debts of gratitude: first to my parents without whose interest and help this edition would not have been undertaken; to Douglas Gray, who first suggested the project and whose criticism and advice over the years have been invaluable; to Denton Fox and René Graziani for reading the text; and to Gordon Barthos, Philip Knight, and the Federation readers for their helpful comments.

GLENN BURGER

Introduction

La Fleur des histoires de la terre d'Orient, written by the Armenian aristocrat Hetoum about the year 1307, contains a brief historical and geographical survey of Asia, then an account of the rise of the Mongols and subsequent conflicts between the Mongol rulers of Persia and the Moslem sultans of Egypt, and finally, a proposal for a new crusade involving the Mongols and Latin and Armenian Christians. Hetoum's narrative is distinctive and compelling for the range and depth of his knowledge. He was a first-hand observer of many of the events he describes, a nephew of the great King Hetoum I. As a Cilician Armenian with strong ties to the Mongols and Latin Christians, Hetoum was uniquely positioned to comment on the contemporary military and political situation in the Middle East.

La Fleur des histoires enjoyed a great popularity throughout the later medieval and early modern period. It was a basic source for parts of *Mandeville's Travels* and it continues to be used by modern historians of the Crusades. Unfortunately this important medieval work is largely unknown by the general reader today. The only modern edition of the original French and Latin texts is buried in a collection of Armenian documents relating to the Crusades. No complete English translation is currently available. The present edition is intended to fill this gap by publishing two anonymous English translations dating from the first quarter of the sixteenth century – the whole of Richard Pynson's early printed edition and selections from the anonymous British Library manuscript Royal 18.B.26. These translations, accompanied by introduction, notes, and critical apparatus, will make Hetoum's work more readily accessible.

1

Hetoum's Text

Authorship and Composition

Hetoum himself states that he dictated his history in French to a scribe named Nicolas Falcon while at the papal court in Poitiers in 1307.[1] Later in the same year, Falcon translated the work into Latin at the request of Pope Clement v.[2] Whether Falcon's duties as scribe to Hetoum were as wide-ranging as Rustichello of Pisa's for Marco Polo is impossible to tell. But according to Shinobu Iwamura, Rustichello's work 'seems to have been that of arranging the various portions of the story in order, to knit the different chapters and divisions into a suitable form for a book, to insert opening and closing lines, etc., and, finally, to translate Marco's Venetian dialect into Franco-Italian commonly used for such popular works.'[3] However, Hetoum's general accuracy about dates, his own claim to have been an eye-witness of events after 1263, and the reliability of his description of Mongol history and culture all indicate a major, if not definitive, role for him in the composition of La Fleur des histoires. There is, as well, a record of historical composition in Hetoum's family. His uncle, Sempad the Constable, in addition to translating the Assizes of Antioch into Armenian, is credited with one of the most famous of thirteenth-century Armenian chronicles.[4] Hetoum himself is traditionally supposed to have written an Armenian chronicle, although its authorship may have been assigned to him on the basis of La Fleur des histoires.[5]

Manuscripts, Early Printed Editions, and the Popularity of a Genre

Hetoum's work is not very well known today. The only modern edition of the French and Latin versions of *La Fleur des histoires* remains that of C. Kohler et al, in *Recueil des historiens des croisades: Documents arméniens*, II, published in Paris in 1906.

Yet the number of extant manuscript copies of Hetoum's work testifies to its popularity during the later Middle Ages. Kohler lists fifteen manuscript copies of the original French text and thirty-one copies of the Latin.[6] The Latin text was later translated back into French: anonymously in BL Cotton Otho. D.V, and then in 1351 by the monk Jean Le Long, as part of a collection of eastern travel literature and works relating to the Mongols.[7] Except for the English translation in BL MS Royal 18.B.26, the only other known vernacular manuscript translation is in Spanish, Escurial Z.I.2, commissioned by Juan-Fernandez Herdia, Grand Master of the Order of St John of Jerusalem (1377–96).[8]

Hetoum's work enjoyed a great popularity with the early European printers. There were three undated, early sixteenth-century printings of the French text, under the title *Sensuyrent les fleurs des histoires de la terre Dorient*: first in Paris by Philippe Le Noir, second in Paris by Denys Janot after Le Noir, and third in Lyon, also after Le Noir, for Benoist Rigaud. These editions show that Hetoum was considered more than a historical curiosity, for Le Noir attempts to bring Hetoum's text up to date by replacing the original Book IV and its plan to reconquer the Holy Land with a new book entitled 'des Sarrazins et des Turcz depuis le premier iusqus aux presens q'ont conqueste Rhodes Hongrye et dernierement assailli Austriche.' Also, in 1529, Jehan St Denys printed Jean Le Long's French translation under the title *L'Hystoire merueilleuse plaisante et recreative du grand Empereur de Tartarie*. Editions of the Latin text were published in 1529, 1532 (twice), 1537, 1555, 1585, and later. Books I and II were translated again into English in the seventeenth century, and included in the collection of travel texts by Samuel Purchas entitled *Haklvytus Posthumus, or Purchas his Pilgrimes* (London 1625). In the sixteenth century there were also numerous editions in the major European languages: German (1534), Italian (1559, 1562 [twice]), Spanish (1595), Dutch (1563, and three more times in the late seventeenth century). Ironically, *La Fleur des histoires* was not translated into Armenian until 1842.[9]

The continued popularity of Hetoum's work long after his death reflects the heightened interest in works connected with Asian travel, geography, and history throughout the later Middle Ages and into the early modern period. Hetoum himself wrote during the first great period of European travel in Asia, made possible by the *pax mongolica* (c 1250–1350).

For a time, European traders and missionaries made regular and frequent use of the land-routes across Asia, and their reports greatly widened Europe's vision of the world and stimulated its appetite for such exotic literature.[10] Hetoum's geography and history of Asia, and especially his first-hand descriptions of the Mongols, would thus have an obvious appeal. Such accounts of far-off places and strange peoples and customs achieved an immense circulation in the later Middle Ages. Around 250 manuscript copies survive of *Mandeville's Travels* (which makes use of parts of *La Fleur des histoires*) and at least seventy of *Marco Polo* and Oderic of Pordenone's *Descriptio orientalium partium* (another work included by Jean Le Long in his collection of translations).[11] The frequency and popularity of pilgrimages to the Holy Land, and the continued interest in the crusade well into the fifteenth century, also helped to maintain interest in the East.[12]

But by the middle of the fourteenth century the Black Death, the rise of Ottoman power in the Middle East, and the fall of the Mongol dynasties in Persia and China combined to disrupt the peaceful flow of people and goods overland across Asia. As the valuable trade in spices came to be monopolized by the Venetians and Egyptians, other European nations were forced to turn their attentions to the discovery of a sea route to the Indies, either around Africa or directly west across the Atlantic. The modern mind tends almost unconsciously to separate the men who made these voyages – Vasco da Gama, Columbus, and others – from those who read the popular medieval travel literature. The former are pictured as dedicated to pure scientific discovery ushering in the modern era and free from the gullible beliefs of their contemporaries. Thus it is often forgotten that Prince Henry the Navigator, for example, founder of Portuguese Atlantic exploration, was an ardent crusader who hoped by these voyages to discover the legendary Prester John and to unite with him in a new crusade.[13] And not only did Columbus possess an early printed copy of *Marco Polo* (and perhaps also of *Mandeville's Travels*),[14] but he used it as his guide in reckoning the distance to Asia across the Atlantic.[15] Even after Columbus' death in 1506 – when it was becoming generally accepted that the new lands he had discovered formed a completely new continent – European explorers continued for the next fifty years and more to search for a north-west passage rather than explore the resources of this new continent. What remained of central importance for them was what had motivated Marco Polo and his contemporaries two centuries earlier, the exotic appeal and riches of the East.[16]

Throughout this period the new medium of print kept the European public informed of these discoveries almost as soon as they occurred.[17] Nor were older travellers' tales neglected by the early printers. Thirty-five incunabula editions of *Mandeville's Travels* and four of *Marco Polo* were produced, as well as the many translations and editions of Hetoum's work listed above. In England, Pynson published *Mandeville's Travels* in 1496 (*STC* 17246) and Wynkyn de Worde came out with his own editions in 1491 (*STC* 17247), 1503 (*STC* 17249), and 1510 (*STC* 17248).[18] Thus, in an age when travel literature, both old and new, was a best-selling item and when Europe was once more in touch with the Orient, it should not be surprising that *La Fleur des histoires*, which Sir Henry Yule has characterized as 'probably the best geographical summary of that continent which had yet been compiled,'[19] was thought relevant enough for translation and publication.

The Mongols and Cilician Armenia

For modern readers, however, the particular appeal of *La Fleur des histoires* surely rests in its vivid account of the remarkable convergence of cultures and races in the Middle East during the second half of the thirteenth century. Western Crusaders, Armenian Christians, Moslems, Persian Mongols, all forced together in this strategically important region, battle for supremacy or survival. And Hetoum's position as an Armenian – an independent Eastern Christian with strong ties to the West – makes him particularly well placed to illuminate both the strengths and weaknesses of the Christian states of Outremer at this time. For this was a particularly significant and often melancholy period for Christians in the Middle East. The second half of the thirteenth century saw the last crusade to the Holy Land undertaken by a European sovereign (Louis IX of France, 1248–54) and, with the fall of Acre in 1291, the disappearance of the last mainland Crusader state. Yet while this period witnessed the gradual erosion of the Crusader states, its beginning, paradoxically, promised much for the continued survival of the Latin states of Outremer. The arrival of the Mongols in Persia in the middle of the century, and with it the possibility of a Western-Mongol alliance, provided a chance to break out of the strategic impasse that had always plagued Outremer: its dependence on constant infusions of European men and aid, and its uneven position against the forces of the sultans of Egypt. While the kingdom of Cilician Armenia under Hetoum I quickly responded to the potential offered by an alliance with the Mongols, the refusal of the Latin Christian states in the area to follow Hetoum's example and adapt to changing conditions by allying themselves with the new Mongol empire must stand as one of the saddest of the many failures of Outremer.

Yet few people had been able to foresee in 1206, when an obscure Mongol chieftain named Temujin took the grandiose title of Genghis Khan or 'Universal Emperor,' that within forty years he and his successors would rule an empire stretching from the Pacific to the Crimea. The world had witnessed other spectacular eruptions of barbarian nomads move across Asia – the last had been the Turks two hundred years before. But previous invasions had been like plagues, destructive but temporary phenomena. The Mongols, however, had developed an unparalleled level of military organization and discipline. In the words of Denis Sinor, '... une stratégie de grande envergure et une organisation militaire qui ne seront dépassées que par les moyens employés dans la deuxième guerre mondiale. On demeure abasourdi en examinant le caractère "logistique" – pour employer un terme moderne – de la guerre mongole. L'organisation minutieuse des campagnes, l'utilisation à fond d'un service de renseignements, la coordination des mouvements de troupes s'effectuant souvent à des milliers de kilomètres les uns des autres, à une époque sans télécommunications – il y a de quoi forcer notre admiration.'[20] The Mongols also were fearsomely destructive conquerors if they did not receive total and unconditional submission to their rule. Whole cities were razed and entire populations slaughtered by Genghis Khan's armies. Yet Mongol government after Genghis Khan was, for its time, surprisingly tolerant, and interfered little in the day-to-day life of its citizens. This tolerance was due in large part to the set of rules laid down by Genghis Khan before he died. Called the *yasa*, these laws were intended to keep the Mongols a united ruling caste separate from their new subjects, forbidding intermarriage with the native peoples and conversion to their religions. Thus the Mongols did not identify themselves with any particular interest group within their empire, kept themselves above sectarian disputes, and allowed local institutions to flourish as long as they did not threaten Mongol authority. Mongol rulers were generally exceptionally open to foreign advisers and methods and continued to use the superior bureaucracies of the countries that they conquered. In this way the Mongols were able to evolve a highly efficient and stable political and economic framework for their heterogeneous empire. Indeed the security provided by Mongol control over the whole of Asia, combined with a remarkable 'pony express' communication network spanning the continent, meant that the trade routes from China to the West were safer than they had ever been before.[21]

To understand the reasons for Cilician Armenia's *rapprochement* with the new and immensely powerful Mongol empire, one must first understand the kingdom's unique historical position among the Christian states of Outremer.[22] When members of the First Crusade entered Cappadocia and Cilicia, they received unexpected assistance from native Christians living in the region. These Christians were Armenians, who for the most part had drifted south and southwest from Greater Armenia after its conquest by the Seljuk Turks following the battle of Manzikert in 1071. These Armenians found refuge in the Taurus and Anti-Taurus mountains, or in the cities of the Cilician plain and northern Syria. For nearly a century after their arrival the political situation of the Armenians was confused and frequently precarious. Those scattered throughout the cities of Cilicia and Syria were under direct Turkish rule or under the control of semi-autonomous governors of the Byzantine emperor. However, a few Armenian barons in the relative security of the Taurus and Anti-Taurus mountains managed to preserve varying degrees of independence. By the beginning of the twelfth century two of these baronial families were beginning to gain the ascendancy. The Hetoumids held the fortress of Lampron, thereby controlling the narrow western pass into Cilicia; the Roupenids, the wider eastern pass into the rich Cilician plain. While the Hetoumids remained loyal to their Byzantine overlords, the Roupenids aimed continually at the establishment of an independent Armenian kingdom in Cilicia. After 1120, when most Armenians living outside Cilicia were part of the newly established and powerful Crusader states, Roupenid attention focused on the Cilician plain and on Hetoumid territory to the west. Throughout the twelfth century Roupenid fortunes fluctuated wildly, usually in direct proportion to the strength or weakness of the Byzantine emperor and the Crusader states (especially the nearby principality of Antioch). Under Toros I (1100–29) and his brother Leon, the Roupenids extended their control over most of the eastern plain, only to lose all their gains to an invading Byzantine army in 1137. However, Leon's son Toros II made good these losses, and under Roupen III and his brother Leon I[23] the barony prospered throughout the last quarter of the twelfth century.

Only with Leon I, who succeeded his brother in 1187, did the kingdom of Cilician Armenia become a recognized political entity. Leon was a strong supporter of the Third Crusade, welcoming Frederick Barbarossa, the Holy Roman Emperor, and participating in the siege of Acre. Afterwards, as a result of his diplomatic missions to Pope Celestine III and to the German emperor, Henry VI, Leon achieved his long-held aim of a

king's crown. On 6 January 1198 he was crowned King Leon I by the
Armenian catholicus in the cathedral of Tarsus. Present were the
Armenian clergy and nobility, the Greek archbishop of Tarsus, the
Jacobite patriarch, and the caliph's ambassador. Archbishop Conrad of
Mainz, as the emperor's representative, brought the crown and bestowed
on Leon the other royal insignia. At the same time the Armenian church
submitted to the authority of the pope, although retaining its own liturgy
and creed. Leon's Latin crown intensified the growing westernization of
the new Armenian kingdom, and was a visible sign of Armenia's
importance as one of the stronger and more vital of the Christian states in
Outremer. For strategic reasons Leon also granted considerable territory
in the west of Cilicia to the Hospitallers and Teutonic Knights, in order to
free his forces for the struggle against Antioch and the Templars to the
east. As well, Leon began the tradition of intermarriage between
Armenians and the Frankish nobility of Outremer, most notably in 1214
with the marriage of his daughter Rita to John of Brienne, regent of the
kingdom of Jerusalem.

After Leon's death in 1219, his daughter Isabel succeeded to the throne.
She was quickly married off to Philip, fourth son of Bohemond IV of
Antioch, in the hope of maintaining internal stability and of easing
tensions on the insecure eastern border of the kingdom. Unfortunately
Philip's high-handed preference for Latin barons and the Latin ritual soon
alienated his new subjects and resulted in his deposition, imprisonment,
and murder in 1225. Constantine of Lampron, regent and head of the rival
Hetoumid clan, then forced the reluctant Isabel to marry his son Hetoum
in the following year, ending a century of dynastic and territorial
wrangling between the Roupenid and Hetoumid factions within the
kingdom.

The accession of Hetoum I marks the beginning of Cilician Armenia's
golden age. Throughout his reign the kingdom remained strong, free of
dynastic quarrels, and, for much of the time, free of foreign invasion.
Armenia's ties with the Franks widened, especially with the kingdom of
Cyprus. Hetoum's sister Stephanie married Henry I of Cyprus in 1237,
and, at the instigation of King Louis of France, Hetoum's daughter Sybil
married Bohemond VI of Antioch in 1254. Hetoum's brother, Sempad the
Constable, translated the Assizes of Antioch into Armenian, thereby
providing the new kingdom with a basis of Frankish feudal law. Hetoum I
appears to have been a wise and far-sighted ruler, genuinely liked and
respected by his contemporaries. His nephew, our author Hetoum,
speaks of him repeatedly with great fondness and admiration. And

Kirakos of Ganjak describes in glowing terms King Hetoum's reception of Armenian dignitaries on a visit to Greater Armenia:

He received them all with love, for he was a gentle man, wise and learned in the Scriptures. And he gave them presents in accordance with his means and sent them all away happy: he also gave sacerdotal robes for the adornment of the churches, for he greatly loved mass and the church. He received the Christians of all nations and besought them to live in love with one another, as brothers and members of Christ, even as the Lord had commanded.[24]

But Hetoum's most inspired action was his early recognition of the Mongol danger and the necessity for quick and far-sighted diplomatic action. By 1243 the Mongols had conquered the Seljuk kingdom of Iconium, devastating Greater Armenia and Georgia on their way. In 1247, facing the imminent demise of his kingdom at the hands of the apparently invincible Mongols, King Hetoum sent his brother Sempad on an official peace mission to the Great Khan's capital of Karakorum. Sempad returned in 1250 with a promise of autonomy for the Armenian kingdom, but only under Mongol suzerainty. Three years later Hetoum I himself undertook the long journey across Asia to submit in person to the Great Khan Mongke. As the first ruler in the West voluntarily to submit to and seek alliance with the Mongols, he received a warm welcome. Hetoum gives a rather ritualized account of this interview, with his uncle presenting seven demands to which Mongke formally and lengthily agrees. Mongke is then baptized by the king's chancellor, who just happens to be a bishop.[25] However, Kirakos of Ganjak in his account mentions only the guarantee of Hetoum's lands and the promise of religious freedom for all Christians living under the Mongols.[26] It must be remembered that *La Fleur des histoires* was written after the fact, an attempt to persuade Europeans of the worth of Mongols as allies. Mongol encouragement of Hetoum I may have extended to a promise to return Armenian land and to help in the reconquest of the Holy Land (witness Hulagu's invasion of Palestine in 1260, when both these things did occur).[27] But despite what our author says, neither Mongke nor his successors converted to Christianity.

Nonetheless, for Hetoum I, acceptance of Mongol suzerainty must have seemed an inspired way to ensure Armenian survival against the far more dangerous threat of Egyptian invasion. The Mongol yoke, if it could be called that, was light in comparison to the danger of annihilation by the Egyptians. The Mongols guaranteed Armenian autonomy and freedom of religion, and offered a chance to fulfil the Crusaders' dream of the reconquest of Jerusalem. Unfortunately the rest of Outremer did not share Hetoum I's enlightened viewpoint.[28] At this time Mongol expansion and power were reaching their zenith, and, because the Mongols believed their mission to be the total subjugation of the world, any future ally must first acknowledge their overlordship (as Hetoum I did in 1254). Such a condition was of course inimical to the feudal pride of the Latin states in Outremer. Their loyalty belonged to Europe and to the pope. Moreover, in the eyes of the West, the Mongols, who were seen initially as the fulfilment of the Prester John stories, on closer inspection now were viewed as semi-barbaric pagan hordes threatening Europe. Therefore, with the exception of the principality of Antioch, ruled by Hetoum's son-in-law, the Crusader states preferred the hostility of the Saracens, an enemy they knew, to the doubtful friendship and insulting claim to overlordship of the Mongols. It was not until twenty years later, when the situation in the Holy Land had grown more desperate and when Abaga, Mongol ilkhan of Persia, had dropped the demand for suzerainty, that the possibility of a general alliance between Mongols and the West could seriously be considered (notably by Edward I of England during his crusade of 1271). In King Hetoum's time, on the other hand, the principality of Antioch was roundly criticized for acknowledging Mongol authority and fighting with these enemies of Christendom.[29]

From an Armenian point of view, however, the Mongol alliance was a great success – at least initially. By 1260 the Mongols had destroyed the caliph of Baghdad and were in control of upper Mesopotamia. In the same year a combined Mongol force led by the Christian general Ketboge, and including Hetoum I and Bohemond IV of Antioch, invaded Syria, sacked Aleppo, captured Damascus, and occupied the Ayyubid principalities in Syria and Palestine. After the capture of Aleppo Hetoum I received territory in western Cilicia originally taken from the Armenians by the Turks, and Bohemond was given the port of Latakia (in return for his reinstatement of the Greek patriarch of Antioch). But the death of the Great Khan Mongke the previous year meant that Hulagu, ilkhan of Persia, had to divert his attention eastward to the disputed election of Mongke's successor. Thus, later that same year Kutuz, the Mamluk sultan of Egypt, was able to defeat Hulagu's small holding force in Palestine and to reoccupy most of Syria. This spelled the ruin of the Armenian cause, for it left Kutuz free to ravage much of Antioch and Cilician Armenia the following year. This see-saw pattern of sporadic Mongol aid in Palestine and subsequent Egyptian vengeance continued into the early fourteenth century until the collapse of the Mongol ilkhans in 1335. Unfortunately for Cilician Armenia, throughout this period the resources of the ilkhans were continually diverted to their northern border where they were threatened by the Mongols of the Golden Horde. Thus Mongol assistance to Cilician Armenia was often inadequate, despite the general goodwill of the ilkhans and their genuine desire to conquer Syria and Palestine. Indeed by singling out the Armenians, the Mongol alliance often served to focus the wrath of the Egyptians on the frequently isolated Armenian state.

Nor did King Hetoum's hope for the conversion of the Mongols ever materialize. An all-out cultural assault from the West would have been needed to bring the Mongols of Persia within a European and Christian sphere of influence and to counter the overwhelmingly Islamic tendencies of the Persian state. Yet by the time that Latin Christians were able to tolerate the idea of an alliance with the Mongols, Mongol power, and that of the idea of the Crusade to initiate actual military action, had so much declined that when joint efforts did occur (in the abortive expeditions of 1301 and 1303)[30] their effects were minimal. In the short term, Hetoum's diplomatic initiative with the Mongols successfully preserved the integrity and peace of his country, and his dream of an alliance between Mongols and the West remained official Armenian foreign policy until the fall of the ilkhans. But viewed in the light of history, his efforts were doomed and merely postponed the inevitable ascendancy of Islam in the region.[31] Nevertheless, Hetoum i was the first to realize that the status quo in the thirteenth century was not favourable in the long run to the Christian cause and that a new way had to be found to counter Egyptian power in Palestine and Syria. Partly because the Armenians considered strategic matters more from an Eastern point of view, partly because they were traditionally not averse to an absentee overlord, and partly because they were more directly affected by the Mongols, their foreign policy proved more adaptable and imaginative than that of the Latins. Despite various European missions to the Mongols, the Armenians possessed a realistic and practical picture of the Mongols much earlier than the West. The force of King Hetoum's vision, especially its pragmatism and openness, can be seen more than fifty years later in its influence on the subject matter of his nephew's history, and especially in the continued belief in a crusade combining Western, Armenian, and Mongol forces.

Hetoum: A Biographical Sketch

Very little information can be gleaned about Hetoum's early years. On the basis of *La Fleur des histoires,* where he claims that 'from the begynnyng of Albaga [ie, from 1263] ... I speke as he that was present in person,'[32] it would appear that he must have been born sometime around 1245. Certainly he would have had every advantage of birth; for his father, Oshin, lord of Korikos, Manioun, and Gantshi, was a younger brother of King Hetoum I and Sempad the Constable. Hetoum's elder brothers inherited their father's titles after his death on 26 December 1264: Oshin, the lordship of Gobidar and Gantschi, and Gregorios (?Toros), that of Korikos. Thus it was not until the death of his brother Gregorios (sometime after 1280) that Hetoum became lord of Korikos, the title by which he is generally known.[33] Around this time Hetoum married a Cypriot cousin, Isabel Ibelin.[34] At least six children resulted from the marriage: Leon; Guy, lord of Gantschi; Baudouin, lord of Simongla and governor of Tarsus; Constantine, lord of Lampron and constable of Armenia; Zabel (born 1282), wife of King Oshin I of Armenia; and Oshin, lord of Korikos and later regent of Armenia during the minority of King Leon IV.[35]

Given his close family connection to the royal house of Cilician Armenia and the successful careers of his children, one can presume that Hetoum played an important and dynamic role in the political life of the kingdom. If so, he could not have cut himself off from the dynastic struggles dividing Cilician Armenia between 1295 and 1305,[36] nor could he have failed to align himself with one or more of the feuding parties. But the exact nature of his role is unclear and has been much disputed. Throughout *La Fleur des histoires,* Hetoum characterizes himself as an Armenian patriot and a pious son of the Church. According to his own testimony he played a central role in restoring Armenia to some measure of internal and external calm during these years.[37] Only then, he says, could he fulfil his long-held vow of devoting himself to religion, which he does in 1305. However, the Cypriot chroniclers, from Amadi onwards, have always insisted that Hetoum's sudden departure for Cyprus in 1305 was the result, not of a long-held religious vow, but of his seditious activities against Hetoum II.[38] Kohler finds support for this accusation in Hetoum's suppression of any direct reference to Hetoum II in his history and in Hetoum's passionate support of the young King Leon III.[39] And when Hetoum returned to Cyprus in 1308 – Hetoum II and Leon III having been assassinated the previous December – he wasted no time in returning to Armenia and did not take up again the religious life in Cyprus that he claims to have desired so much. Certainly by 1305 Hetoum must have been an established and influential force in Armenian politics, and if hostile to Hetoum II, then one of his most powerful enemies. Hetoum may perhaps have moved to put an end to Hetoum II's regency and free Leon III (who would probably by this time have reached his early teens). Or possibly, with the military situation looking more hopeful, Hetoum II may have felt that this was an opportune time to rid himself of a longstanding thorn in his side.

Hetoum's position after 1305, supposedly as a canon regular of the Premonstratensian monastery of S Maria de Episcopia in Cyprus, is also ambiguous. The Cypriot chroniclers accuse Hetoum of being one of the principal agents in the insurrection of Amalric of Tyre against his brother, King Henry I of Cyprus. And Hetoum's arrival in Cyprus does coincide with the first secret plans made against Henry, which culminated in April 1306 with Amalric's self-appointment as governor of Cyprus (supposedly at the request of the Cypriot barons). While Kohler points out that Hetoum was not a signatory of the baronial brief accusing Henry of incapacity to govern, Hetoum's abbot was probably the 'frater Bartholomeus, abbas monasterii s. Mariae de Epyra' who did sign the brief ('Epyra' is likely a misreading of 'Episcopia').[40] Indeed the Cypriot chroniclers maintain that Hetoum's visit to the papal court in Poitiers a year later was as Amalric's official ambassador, sent to gain the support of the pope. While Amadi and the other chroniclers have probably exaggerated Hetoum's villainy, his role seems to have gone far beyond sending reports to Amalric concerning the disposition of the pope and the best way of winning him over to the prince's side, as Kohler believed.[41] Hetoum arrived in Poitiers some time late in 1306 and remained there at least until 8 February 1308, when he is mentioned in four papal letters. None of these letters concerns political matters: three deal with the affairs of monasteries in Cyprus and the fourth with an absolution sought by two Cypriots. Nor is Hetoum in them referred to as an ambassador of Amalric; instead he is called by his Armenian title 'dominus de Curcho' or by his monastic position, 'conversus monasterio sanctae Mariae de Episcopia.'[42] But a letter written between 7 April and 4 June by Raymond de Piis, papal legate to Cyprus, to Cardinal Rufati, referendary of Clement V, proves that Hetoum did play an important role behind the scenes on Amalric's behalf, involving the promise of money to at least one prominent member of the papal court. Raymond had been authorized by the cardinal to collect the ten thousand florins offered to him by Hetoum if the cardinal would help ensure papal recognition of Amalric's governorship. Amalric told Raymond 'that he was prepared ... to comply as far as the sum of the ten thousand florins was concerned for which I asked him in your name, and which the said lord of Curcus had promised you.'[43] But Amalric refused to pay the much larger sum of fifty or sixty thousand florins which Hetoum supposedly had offered to the cardinal on the pope's behalf. Later, when Raymond met with Hetoum in Armenia, 'the same lord of Curcus talked to me several times about these matters, and I to him; and ... he said that he had made you no promise concerning the person of our lord aforementioned [ie, Pope Clement], but had only made a promise for ten thousand florins payable to you (and to be paid within three years by the lord of Tyre), if our lord, through your good services, would confirm the same through a letter of his in his office of government.'[44] Whatever the exact details of the agreement, Hetoum clearly functioned as a trusted agent of Amalric while in Poitiers, intent on furthering the lord of Tyre's cause at the papal court.[45]

This financial manoeuvring by Hetoum need not provoke the moral outrage that one finds in the chroniclers. Financial incentive, after all, was a fairly common feature of contemporary diplomacy. And there is no reason to believe that Hetoum's espousal of Amalric's cause was primarily self-seeking. By all accounts Amalric had played an active role in attempts to stabilize Armenia and to oppose Egyptian dominancy in Syria. Furthermore, he had shown himself willing to co-operate with the Mongol ilkhans of Persia. From an Armenian viewpoint, his belligerent tactics in Cyprus would promise an aggressive Cypriot foreign policy and future support for the beleaguered Armenians.[46] Hetoum's diplomatic role might also suggest a political motivation, at least in part, for writing *La Fleur des histoires.* One of Clement's main reasons in opposing Amalric's insurrection was that civil unrest in Cyprus would hinder the chances for a new crusade. If Hetoum could show that the lord of Tyre's party was pro-crusade, and furthermore, more likely to have the strength to actively promote one, then Clement might be more inclined to favour Amalric's cause over Henry's.

Almost immediately upon his return to Cyprus in May 1308, Hetoum proceeded to Armenia – within six days according to Amadi.[47] His return was probably the result of the assassination of Hetoum ii the previous December. But the growing urgency of the Cypriot political situation and the desire for Armenian involvement in it may also have contributed to Hetoum's speedy return home. In June of 1308 Amalric exiled several of Henry's leading supporters to Armenia, and in 1309 took the extreme measure of placing King Henry in prison in Armenia under the guard of his brother-in-law King Oshin. It is perhaps this outright seizure of power that accounts for Amalric's vagueness about, and Hetoum's denial of, any promises of money to the pope, since the pope could hardly now recognize Amalric's blatant usurpation of his brother's throne. All signs point to a resumption by Hetoum of an active and influential role in the political life of his country, and about this time his daughter Zabel married King Oshin, successor to Leon III. Hetoum may have resumed his position as constable of the kingdom, if he is the 'Haytonus dux generalis' mentioned as present at the Council of Adana in 1314.[48] If this is so, then he was certainly dead by 1320 when his son Oshin, now lord of Korikos, became regent, for no mention is made of Hetoum's presence. If Hetoum is not the constable mentioned at the Council of Adana, then it seems probable that he died sometime between 1310 and 1314.

NOTES

1 *A Lytell Cronycle* (hereafter referred to as P), 85/25–34. Hetoum's name is spelled in a variety of ways, including 'Het'um,' 'Hethum,' 'Haiton,' 'Haytonus,' 'Haitonus,' 'Hayconus,' 'Haiconus,' 'Hétoum,' 'Ayton,' and 'Aiconus.'

2 Generally, the Latin and French versions are the same. But in Book III, Chapter 44 (*RHC Arm* II 326–31; cf P 59/34–60/36), two Latin manuscripts provide a much longer and more detailed account of Armenian history from the accession of Hetoum II in 1289 to our author's departure for Cyprus in 1305. In this version Hetoum also mentions an earlier pilgrimage to France, probably sometime in the 1290s (cf note 38 below). Kohler argues persuasively (*RHC Arm* II lxi–lxvii) that Book IV was not part of the first French version of the text, but was added as part of the Latin text prepared at the request of Pope Clement V. Later it was translated into French and added to the original three books.

3 *Manuscripts and Printed Editions of Marco Polo's Travels* (Tokyo 1949) 4

4 See *RHC Arm* I 605–98 for the Armenian text of the Chronicle with a French summary; also, S. Akelian *Chronicle of the General Sempad* (in Armenian: Venice 1956); and Serarpie Der Nersessian 'Armenian Chronicle of the Constable Smpad' *Dumbarton Oaks Papers* No 13 (1959) 145–68, for selective English translations and commentary. Cf also *The Cilician Kingdom of Armenia* ed T.S.R. Boase (New York 1978) 27–8.

5 See *RHC Arm* I 469–90 for the Armenian text with a French summary. The most recent editor of the Chronicle, A. Akopian, *Short Chronicles: XIII–XVIII Centuries* I (in Armenian: Erevan 1951) 65–73, assigns authorship to King Hetoum II. Cf Der Nersessian 'Armenian Chronicle' 162 n71.

6 See *RHC Arm* II lxxxv–cxxxi, for Kohler's detailed descriptions of the manu-

script copies and printed editions of Hetoum's texts and their translations. Kohler's edition is based on a collation of thirteen French and eight Latin manuscripts.

7 Five manuscript copies survive: listed by M.C. Seymour *Mandeville's Travels* (Oxford 1967) 277–8.
8 Ed Wesley Robertson Long *La Flor de las Ystorias de Orient* (Chicago 1934)
9 Trans Br P.M. Krtitch Avkerian [ie, Jean-Baptiste Aucher] (Venice 1842)
10 C. Raymond Beazley *The Dawn of Modern Geography* III (Oxford 1906) 15–409 provides a comprehensive survey of late medieval European travellers in Asia and of their writings. Sir Henry Yule *Cathay and the Way Thither* 2nd ed rev H. Cordier, The Hakluyt Society, Second Series, Nos 38, 33, 37, 41 (London 1913–16), 4 vols, gives translated extracts from many of the traveller writers of this period.
11 See Josephine W. Bennett *The Rediscovery of Sir John Mandeville* (New York 1954) 219–20, 265–334.
12 See A. Atiya *The Crusade in the Later Middle Ages* (London 1938), 155–230; *A History of the Crusades*, Vol 3, *The Fourteenth and Fifteenth Centuries* gen ed Kenneth M. Setton (Madison, Wisc. 1975); Boies Penrose *Travel and Discovery in the Renaissance 1420–1620* (Cambridge, Mass. 1952) 21–32.
13 See C.R. Beazley *Prince Henry the Navigator* (London 1895) 138–44, 154–9.
14 See Iwamura *Manuscripts of Polo's Travels* 7–8; Bennett *Rediscovery of Mandeville* 234.
15 See J.H. Parry *The Age of Reconnaissance* (London 1963) 150.
16 See R.A. Skelton *The European Image and Mapping of America A.D. 1000–1600* (Minneapolis, Minn. 1964) 19.
17 See Penrose *Travel and Discovery* 274–326 for a survey of European geographical literature in the sixteenth century.
18 See Bennett *Rediscovery of Mandeville* 230–43; also C.W.R.D. Moseley 'Mandeville's Travels: A Study of the Book and its Importance in England 1356–1750' Diss East Anglia 1971, 177–80, where he draws an interesting parallel between the rise in interest shown by a European country in exploration and the rise in the number of printed editions of *Mandeville's Travels* produced.
19 Yule-Cordier *Cathay and the Way Thither* I (London 1913), 168–9. Dorothee Metlitzki, in *The Matter of Araby in Medieval England* (New Haven 1977), suggests another powerful reason for the continued popularity of a work like Hetoum's: the importance of the 'matter of Araby' in the romantic imagination of the later Middle Ages and its presence in the subject matter, themes, and imagery of popular romances. See especially 220–50 for a discussion of *Mandeville's Travels* and romances.
20 '[The Mongols had developed] a strategy with great scope and a military

organization which would be surpassed only by the means employed during the Second World War. One can only gasp at the 'logistical' aspect – to use a modern term – of Mongol warfare. The minute organization of the campaigns, the thorough utilization of an intelligence service, the coordination of troop movements often carried out thousands of kilometres apart, in an age without telecommunications – this is what must win our admiration' (Denis Sinor 'Les Relations entre les Mongols et l'Europe jusqu'à la mort d'Arghoun et de Bela iv' *Cahiers d'Histoire Mondiale* 3 [1956–7] 46; rpt as No x in Sinor *Inner Asia and its Contacts with Medieval Europe* [London 1977]). For further information in English concerning the Mongols see J.J. Saunders *The History of the Mongol Conquests* (London 1971); E.D. Phillips *The Mongols* (London 1969); René Grousset, *Conqueror of the World* trans D. Sinor and M. MacKellar (Edinburgh 1967); Bertold Spuler *History of the Mongols, Based on Eastern and Western Accounts of the Thirteenth and Fourteenth Centuries* (London 1972); Claude Cahen 'The Mongols and the Near East,' in *A History of the Crusades* gen ed Kenneth M. Setton ii (Philadelphia 1962) 715–34; *Cambridge History of Iran*, v, *The Saljuq and Mongol Periods* ed J.A. Boyle (Cambridge 1968) 303–421.

21 Although the Mongols made the transition from military expansionism to imperial stability with remarkable ease, the loose dynastic organization of the empire made future discord almost inevitable. The Great Khans who succeeded Genghis continued to claim his status as the supreme ruler of all Mongols. But the personal kingdom of the Great Khans was centred in China and inevitably their attention focused more and more on the East. As the power of the Great Khans over the other Mongol kingdoms became increasingly nominal, the rest of the empire divided into three independent kingdoms ruled by the descendants of Bachu (the 'Golden Horde' of the Crimea), Hulagu (the ilkhans of Persia), and Chagatai (situated in the area to the north and east of Persia). Sources of friction between these three kingdoms were minimized only so long as the Mongols were united in acquiring new territory. After the zenith of Mongol expansion in the middle of the thirteenth century, personal animosities and regional interests came more and more in the way of that extraordinary discipline and unity which had characterized the early Mongol empire.

22 For further information on Cilician Armenia, see Serarpie Der Nersessian 'The Kingdom of Cilician Armenia' in Setton *History of the Crusades* ii 630–60; *The Cilician Kingdom of Armenia* ed Boase; Fr H. François Tournebize *Histoire politique et religieuse de l'Arménie* (Paris [1910]) 168–231; and *The Cambridge Medieval History*, iv, Part i, *Byzantium and its Neighbours* ed J.M. Hussey (Cambridge 1966) 628–37.

23 The numbering of the rulers of Cilician Armenia is varied and confusing. Although King Leon I is the second of that name in the Roupenid dynasty, he is the first to be crowned king. I have followed the numbering practice of W.H. Rüdt-Collenberg, *The Rupenides, Hethumites and Lusignans* (Paris 1963), but the other method of numbering is also found. See 'Appendix: The Rulers of Cilician Armenia,' *The Cilician Kingdom of Armenia*.

24 J.A. Boyle 'The Journey of Het'um I, King of Little Armenia, to the Court of the Great Khan Möngke' *Central Asiatic Journal* 9 (1964) 186; rpt as No x in Boyle *The Mongol World Empire 1206–1370* (London 1977)

25 P 37/16–38/39

26 Boyle 'The Journey of Het'um I' 181

27 Cf P 40/29–42/2

28 For relations between the Mongols and the West, see: Sinor 'Les Relations entre les Mongols et l'Europe'; Sinor 'The Mongols and Western Europe' in Setton *History of the Crusades* III (Madison, Wisc. 1975) 513–44; rpt as No IX in *Inner Asia and its Contacts with Medieval Europe*; J.A. Boyle 'The Last Barbarian Invaders: the Impact of the Mongol Conquests upon East and West' *Memoirs and Proceedings of the Manchester Literary and Philosophical Society* 112 (1970) 1–15, rpt as No I in *Mongol World Empire*; Boyle 'The Mongols and Europe' *History Today* 9 (1959) 336–43, rpt as No v in *Mongol World Empire*; Boyle 'The Il-Khans of Persia and the Christian West' *History Today* 23 (1973) 554–63, rpt as No XIII in *Mongol World Empire*; Jean Richard 'The Mongols and the Franks' *Journal of Asian History* 3 (1969) 45–57; J.P. Abel-Rémusat 'Mémoires sur les relations politiques des princes chrétiens et particulière-ment des rois de France, avec les empereurs mongols' *Mémoires ... de l'Acad-émie des Inscriptions et Belles-Lettres* 6 (1882) 396–469; 7 (1884) 335–438; Paul Pelliot 'Les Mongols et la papauté' *Revue de l'Orient chrétien* 23 (1922) 3–30; 24 (1924) 225–335; 28 (1931) 3–84; A. Bryer 'Edward I and the Mongols' *History Today* 14 (1964) 696–704.

29 See Steven Runciman *A History of the Crusades* III (Cambridge 1954) 307, 311–12.

30 Cf P 56/7–20

31 During the reign of Hetoum I's son, Leon II, the position of Cilician Armenia remained hopeful. But the years following the death of Leon in 1289 until the final demise of the kingdom in 1375 are ones of continued and steady decline in the fortunes of the country. Throughout this period, the king-dom was split by quarrelling between the Westernized, Catholic ruling class and Armenian nationalist and anti-Catholic factions. And this civil strife was often made worse by frequent disputes over the succession. Despite continued appeals to the West for aid, more often than not Cilician Arme-nia, like its neighbour the kingdom of Cyprus, was left on its own to battle

the increasingly ominous power of Mamluk Egypt. Cilician Armenia suffered notable Egyptian incursions in the periods 1274–1305 and 1319–23, and in 1337 and 1359. This period also saw a steady reduction in the kingdom's area. When Leon v, last king of Cilician Armenia, ascended the throne in 1373, the kingdom included only the cities of Sis and Anazarbus with their adjoining regions. In 1375, when the Egyptian forces finally achieved the complete destruction and occupation of Cilician Armenia, King Leon and his family were taken as prisoners to Cairo. Although Leon was eventually released in 1382, he spent the rest of his life in exile in Europe, dying in 1393 in Paris. With his death the title of king of Armenia passed to the kings of Cyprus, and eventually to the house of Savoy and the kings of Italy. However Cilician Armenia itself remained in Mamluk hands until its conquest by the Ottoman Turks in the sixteenth century. For further information about the history of Cilician Armenia in this period, see *The Cambridge Medieval History* IV, Part I, 634–7; *The Cilician Kingdom of Armenia* ed T.S.R. Boase, 28–33; Sir Harry Luke 'The Kingdom of Cyprus, 1291–1369' and 'The Kingdom of Cyprus, 1369–1489,' in Setton *History of the Crusades* III; and for full, reliable genealogies, W.H. Rüdt-Collenberg *The Rupenides, Hethumites and Lusignans* (Paris 1963).

32 P 61/8–10. Cf *RHC Arm* II xxviii, where Kohler suggests a birth-date somewhere between 1230 and 1245, 'et probablement plus près de la première de ces dates que de la seconde.' However, if Hetoum was born in 1230, he would have been in his early thirties before he began to participate fully in the military and political life of his country, and seventy-six when he went to Poitiers. A later date therefore seems more likely.

33 The spellings of Hetoum's title are as various as those of his name. The most common medieval form is a variant of the Latin 'Curcus.' The *STC* uses the less common 'Gorigos,' a spelling often adopted by modern writers. However, the city itself, formerly Corycos, is now generally referred to as Korikos.

34 Isabel's parents were Guy Ibelin, son of Baudouin, seneschal of Cyprus, 1246–50, and Marie of Armenia, daughter of Hetoum I. See Rüdt-Collenberg, *The Rupenides, Hethumites and Lusignans*, Table III, after p 48.

35 Ibid

36 These dates coincide with a period of civil war in Cilician Armenia between King Hetoum II and his brothers. In 1295–6 Hetoum II and his brother Toros were in Constantinople arranging the marriage of their sister Rita to Michael, son of the Byzantine emperor. During their absence Sempad seized power, possibly with the support of the catholicos Gregory VII and Pope Boniface VIII. Hetoum II and Toros were arrested and imprisoned by

their brother after an unsuccessful visit to the court of Ghazan, ilkhan of Persia, having been thwarted by a previous mission of Sempad. While in prison, Toros was strangled and Hetoum blinded by their brother. However, two years after in 1298, another brother, Constantine, deposed Sempad, only to be ousted in turn by Hetoum, who had by then partially recovered his sight. Both Sempad and Constantine were exiled to Constantinople under the care of their sister Rita, now wife of the emperor Michael IX. These conflicts were finally resolved in 1305 by the recognition of the son of Toros as King Leon III, and his uncle Hetoum as regent. Unfortunately the young king's reign was short-lived, for on 7 December 1307 both Hetoum and Leon III were treacherously assassinated by the Mongol general Bilarghu. After a brief attempt by Constantine to seize power, Oshin, another brother of Hetoum II, ascended the throne.

37 Cf P 60/17–25

38 See *Chronique d'Amadi* ed René de Mas Latrie *Collection de Documents Inédits sur l'Histoire de France,* Première Série (Paris 1891) 254. An earlier instance of piety on Hetoum's part is also open to varied interpretation. In a version of *La Fleur des histoires* III xli (found in only one French and eight Latin manuscripts), Hetoum tells of a pilgrimage he made 'apud Vallem Viridem' (probably to France between 1297 and 1299 – see *RHC Arm* II 330). This pilgrimage also took place during a time of civil strife and dynastic struggle in Armenia (see note 36 above). And here too Hetoum's pilgrimage might have been a disguise for a diplomatic mission (to add his voice to those urging a new crusade) or a polite term for an enforced exile.

39 *RHC Arm* II xxxvii–xxxviii

40 Ibid, xxxix and note 3

41 Ibid, xlii

42 *Regestum Clementis Papae V, Anni Secundus et Tertius* (Rome 1886) Nos 2434–7. On the other hand, a letter of 27 February 1308 (No 2469) does refer to one 'Iohanne Lombardi, ambasciatore Amaurici, domini Tyri, gubernatoris regni Cypri,' and deals with the more official business of marriage dispensations.

43 'Paratus erat ... usque ad summam decem milium florinorum per me ab ipso, vestro nomine, petitam et per dictum dominum de Curco vobis promissam complacere'; letter of Raymond de Piis, Papal Legate to Cyprus, to Cardinal Rufati, Referendary of Pope Clement V, Vatican Archives *Instrumenta Miscellanea* No 484; printed in Charles Perrat 'Un Diplomate gascon au xive siècle: Raymond de Piis, nonce de Clément V en Orient' *Mélanges d'Archéologie et d'Histoire,* xlive année (1927) 73.

44 'Idem dominus de Curco pluries super hiis fuit mihi locutus et ego secum; et ... diceret quod nullam promissionem personam dicti domini nostri con-

tingentem vobis fecerat, nisi solum de decem milibus florinis vobis dandis et in tribus annis solvendis per dominum Tirensem, si idem dominus noster eidem officium gubernationis, vobis procurante, per suas litteras confirmaret' (ibid). Nor had Hetoum's mission been a total failure. By referring to Amalric as 'gubernator Cypri' in his letters (cf *Regestum Clementis Papae V* No 2469) the Pope implies a *de facto* recognition of Amalric's new position. What Clement may have been hoping for in postponing any official decision until after his legate's visit was that some compromise could be worked out on the spot, contingent, that is, on receipt of Amalric's promised money.

45 Significantly, Raymond refers to Hetoum as 'nuncius dicti domini Tirensis' and to the stay at the papal court of 'dicto domino de Curco et aliis nunciis domini Tiri' (Pellat 'Un Diplomate gascon' 72, 73). As further proof that Hetoum functioned as a trusted ambassador of Amalric's, there is Amadi's claim (*Chronique d'Amadi* 280) that before returning on 6 May Hetoum went to Genoa to negotiate a treaty with that city on behalf of Cyprus. And, although Hetoum brought with him no definite reply from Clement, it is likely that he carried letters from the pope urging Amalric to begin proceedings for the suppression of the Templars in Cyprus. For on the 20 August 1308, Pope Clement v wrote in a letter to Philippe le Bel of France that he had received Amalric's acknowledgment of the pope's letter concerning the Templars, which Hetoum delivered to him in May. The letter is printed by S. Baluze *Vitae paparum Avenioniensium* (Paris 1693) II 103; and by V. Langlois *Revue de l'Orient* 3ᵉ Série 15 (Paris 1863) 105 note 2.

46 It is possible, as well, that Hetoum might have developed a personal relationship with Amalric during their campaigns together or even that Hetoum was repaying Amalric for past support in the twists and turns of Armenian politics.

47 *Chronique d'Amadi* 280

48 See *RHC Arm* II xlv for a discussion of the possible dates of Hetoum's death. Kohler favours a date after 1314.

2

Tudor Translations

Pynson's *A Lytell Cronycle*

Five copies of *A Lytell Cronycle* (*STC* 13256) have survived: Chicago,
Newberry Library, Case 5A 173; Oxford, Bodleian Library, Auct QQ supra
II 24 (used as the base text for this edition and referred to as P1); London,
British Library, 148.c.1 (P2 in this edition); London, British Library, G.6789
(P3 in this edition); and a copy in the private collection of Paul Mellon.[1] All
are printed in folio. In addition to the translation of *La Fleur des histoires*,
Pynson's edition contains a Latin Provincial found in four of the surviving
French manuscripts.[2] The Mellon and Newberry copies, along with P3,
contain forty-eight leaves gathered A–E^6, F–G^4, H^6, I^4, with leaf 38 (G4) a
genuine blank. P1 and P2 have the same collation formula, except that G4,
9.the blank leaf, is missing. P1 also lacks I4, which is reproduced in
facsimile.[3] The Mellon copy contains the bookplate of John Pierpont
Morgan, and the Newberry copy, that of Louis Silver (from whom it was
bought in the sale of 1964). P1 belonged to Horace Walpole, whose
bookplate it contains; on the endpaper at the beginning of this copy
Walpole has written 'bought at the sale of Mark Cephos Gutch 1786.' P3
belonged first to Richard Heber and then to Lord Grenville before passing
to the British Library.[4]

Throughout the book Pynson follows the contemporary English
practice of numbering the signatures of the first three leaves of each
gathering. In addition he numbers each folio after A2, and provides a
Table of Contents (A1^v–A2^v) which refers to these folio numbers. Pynson
also provides running titles throughout. There are generally forty-one
lines of text per page, printed in two columns. Each chapter begins with a
large initial capital, two, three, or five lines in height, or a space up to five

lines high with a guide letter left for such a capital. The first large capital (A3r) and one other (E2v) are seven lines in height and contain a fleur-de-lis. Three different watermarks are found in the paper used by Pynson: a capital 'P,' a unicorn, and an enclosed fleur-de-lis over a cross.[5] The title-page contains a large woodcut (155 × 132 mm)[6] first used by Pynson in his 1506 edition of the *Kalendar of Shepherdes* (and again in editions of 1516 and 1527). On the final page of *A Lytell Cronycle* there is a second woodcut, this time of Pynson's device. R.B. McKerrow lists the first use of this device as 1519 (in Horman's *Vulgaria*) but does not mention its occurrence in *A Lytell Cronycle*.[7] According to Henry R. Plomer, the device was taken up by Pynson after 1516 when his previous one had worn out.[8]

Pynson himself provides no date of publication for *A Lytell Cronycle*. The arrest and speedy execution of the duke of Buckingham for treason in 1521 makes it most unlikely that the book was printed after that date. The use of the woodcut from the *Kalendar of Shepherdes* means that it must have come after 1506. Also the fact that the printer's device used on the last page only came into use after 1516 suggests a publication date for *A Lytell Cronycle* sometime in the period between 1517 and 1520 (which coincides with the prominence of the idea of the crusade during these years). If the duke of Buckingham contributed part of the printing costs, a date earlier in this period might be likely, for the duke was under heavy financial obligations in 1519 (for the lavish entertainments staged at Penshurst for Henry VIII and his court) and in 1520 (for Buckingham's costly participation in the festivities surrounding the meetings between Henry VIII and Francis I at the Field of Cloth of Gold).[9]

The punctuation of Pynson's edition consists of virgules (conforming roughly to a modern comma) and full stops and capitals (conforming roughly to a modern semicolon, colon, and full stop). Paragraph marks begin each chapter and occur occasionally within the text. The punctuation is sometimes systematic and related to the general sense of the passage, but just as often it is inconsistent and may reflect the disjointed effects of a compositor working through the text bit by bit and unaware of an individual syntactic unit's relationship to the general context. For example, at the beginning of III, ii, 'How Cangius was elect emperour of the Tartas' (B5v), the punctuation of the first twelve lines reflects the syntax of the passage:

After that the Tartas ordayned a seat in the myddes of them all and putte there vpon the grounde a blacke carpet and made Cangius to syt therupon. And the vii.

captayns of the .vii. natyons reysed hym vp with the sayd carpet and set hym
vpon the seat. And named hym Can / and with knelinge dyde hym all honour
and reuerence as to theyr owne lorde.

This section of text has been taken (correctly) as one distinct unit, for the
next line begins with a paragraph mark. But what follows after shows a far
more arbitrary, piecemeal approach to punctuation, especially in the use
of capitals and full stops:

Of the solempnyte that the Tartas dyde to theyr lorde In that tyme sholde no man
maruayle of it / for peraduenture they coulde do no better or they had no fayrer
clothe to set hym on but for that they wolde nat change theyr first vsage. It is
marueyle seynge that they haue conquered so many landes and realmes and yet
they kepe theyr fyrst maner for they wyll chuse their lorde and twyse haue I ben at
thelectyon of the Tartas emperour / ...

Pynson's punctuation, then, while often adequate, does not demonstrate
any real consistency and often needlessly obscures the meaning of the text
for the modern reader. I have, therefore, punctuated according to modern
usage, trying whenever possible to give the feeling of Pynson's longer,
less rigid syntactical units. As for the capitalization of words within the
text, it is generally difficult to distinguish capitals intended as emphasis or
to mark proper names from a general tendency to indiscriminate capitalization. I have therefore followed modern practice, retaining original
capitals only in the few cases where the reason for their original
capitalization is in doubt, for example, 'Assassyn' (70/6) and 'Lices' (5/34,
62/5).

The British Library Manuscript

Royal 18.B.26 contains 256 folios and is of paper throughout, measuring
303 × 210 mm. The one exception is fol 1, a piece of vellum 110 × 140 mm,
containing various owners' names and other scribblings and bound with
the text. Gatherings begin at fol 2 and are by twelves which I number thus:
i, A^{11}, B–N^{12}, O^{14}, P–R^{12}, S^{11}, T–U^{12}, V^{3}. The twelfth leaf of s is cancelled, and
the original fourth leaf of v has also been cancelled or torn out. The
eleventh leaf of s (fol 229) is blank, and on it someone has made two ink
drawings of one of the two hand-star watermarks (Briquet Nos 10718,
11165) found on the paper used in the manuscript. The manuscript is
written in a loose, mobile Secretary hand with several Secretary graphs

(final -s, -g, -e, etc), long tapered ascenders and descenders, no horns, and a fair amount of splay in the writing of minims. The hand retains certain Anglicana graphs, for example, 'a,' long 'r,' and the '2–r' form,[10] and is generally consistent with the last quarter of the fifteenth and the first quarter of the sixteenth centuries.

The manuscript is a unified collection of translations of works connected with the Crusades, often with an English association. The collection begins with a general preface (fol 2r–v), followed by a brief history of the crusade activities of Robert, duke of Normandy (fols 3r–6r), then those of Godfrey of Bouillon (fols 6v–86v), Richard Coeur-de-Lion (fols 86v–129r), Edward I of England (fols 129v–143r), then Hetoum's *The Floure of Histories* (fols 143r–228v), and finally (following a blank leaf) an extensive explanatory index (in another hand) of people and places, compiled from the works in the collection (fols 230r–256r).[11] The collection contains no information that would provide a definite date for its composition. However, in the preface to Hetoum's text the translator speaks of the changes that have occurred 'in thise CC yeres' (fol 143v) since Hetoum wrote his history (ie, since 1307). Also, the reference to 'your highnes' and to contemporary plans for a crusade in the general preface, as well as the bias towards the crusading efforts of English princes in the contents of the collection, suggests that the work may have been intended for King Henry VIII. The fact that between 1516 and 1520 Henry VIII was likely to have wanted to appear interested in taking part in the projected crusade plans current at the time might suggest a date of composition sometime within this period for the Royal manuscript collection of crusade literature.

Various owners' names have been written on the manuscript at several points. The name of Laurence Howarde is most frequent, occurring on fols 1, 229, 256v. The manuscript later belonged to Richard Hanslepp, whose name occurs on fols 1, 2. Hanslepp then gave it to John Theyer, senior, on 21 August 1656 ('Ex dono Ricardus Hanslepp 21° Aug. 1656' is written at the top of fol 2r). Theyer's monogram and the name of his grandson Charles have been written in Theyer's hand at the top of fol 2r. Theyer's library, which probably contained around 334 books, was one of the last great accessions of the Royal Library, purchased after his death sometime around 1678.[12]

A table of contents precedes each book of Hetoum's history, and all the chapters are headed by their number and title from the table of contents. A running title occurs at the top of each page, and a catchword at the bottom of the verso side of the last leaf in a gathering. There is little in the way of punctuation in the text. Occasional virgules occur, which, depending on their context, could correspond to modern commas, semicolons, or full stops. The most frequent method of punctuation and of division within chapters is the use of capital letters to indicate syntactic units of varying lengths – from the length of a modern sentence to that of an entire paragraph. Except for the index, the manuscript has been corrected throughout sometime shortly after it was written by its scribe. These corrections are often made to improve the sense: correcting the spelling, substituting omitted nouns, verbs, etc, sometimes changing entire phrases.

Motives for Translation into English

THE DUKE OF BUCKINGHAM

Edward Stafford, third duke of Buckingham, was one of the richest and most powerful men in England. Through Thomas Woodstock, duke of Gloucester, whose daughter married Thomas, third earl of Stafford, Buckingham was a direct descendant of King Edward III[13] and thus a possible claimant to the crown of England. In addition to this royal lineage, Buckingham claimed descent from Godfrey of Bouillon and the legendary Knight of the Swan (through Eleanor de Bohun, wife of Thomas of Woodstock). Because of his Bohun ancestry the duke also claimed the chivalric title, constable of England, which he mistakenly thought to be an hereditary office.[14]

Not only did Buckingham possess and lay claim to an exalted pedigree and chivalric background, but he was also eager to seize every opportunity for displaying his wealth and position. His chivalric and genealogical pretensions led him in 1512 to commission the translation and printing of the romance *Helyas, Knyght of the Swanne*. For, according to its translator, the Duke of Buckingham desired

cotydyally to encrease and augment the name and fame of such as were relucent in vertuous feates and triumphaunte actes of chyualry. and to encourage and styre euery lusty and gentell herte by the exemplyficacyon of the same hauyng a goodli booke of the highe and miraculous histori of ... Helyas the knight of the swanne of whome linially is dyscended my sayde Lorde. The whiche ... hath of hys hie bountie bi some of his faithful and trusti seruauntes cohorted mi mayster wynkin de worde to put the said hystori in printe.[15]

The duke also played a prominent role in the many tournaments and ceremonies that marked the early Henrician court, outdoing all but the king with the lavishness and cost of his costumes and entourage.[16] And in 1511 Buckingham undertook the rebuilding of Thornbury Castle in Gloucestershire as his main country seat.

Four great towers were to command the new west front, and the graceful southern range, with its elegant and finely proportioned windows, testified to a taste and confidence which was royal. Over the west gateway, the many heraldic devices, mantle of Brecknock, swan and antelope of the Bohuns, knot of the Staffords, recall an overpowering pride of ancestry.[17]

Although work stopped with the duke's death in 1521, what remains bears witness both to his grandiose intentions and to the orthodoxy of his late-medieval taste in architecture.

Buckingham appears to have been well educated and always sympathetic to poor students, clerks, musicians, etc: 'A Welsh harpist, an Irish poet, gypsies and choristers all shared Duke Edward's largesse. So did friars, scholars and preachers whom his piety and love of learning attracted to his household.'[18] Standards of education for those boys in his care seem to have been high,[19] and the books in the duke's library ranged from 'practical treatises on cosmology, natural history, medicine and theology to texts by the early fathers, biblical commentaries and recent editions of the classics.'[20]

The picture that emerges, then, is that of a man conventional in his tastes but provided with the financial means to indulge them, and possessing a flamboyant temperament that sought every opportunity for displaying his position and power. In the light of his supposed ancestral connection with the Crusades, his love of chivalric ceremonial, and his traditional tastes in the arts, *La Fleur des histoires* is just the sort of work calculated to appeal to Buckingham.

HENRY VIII

The general preface to the Royal manuscript's collection of translations begins rather surprisingly with the following statement: 'To the honour of almyghty God and to accomplisshe your high commaundement as towching the passage of an army and hoste of pylgrymes by your highnes blessedly to be purposed and conducted ayenst infideles for the recouery of the Holy Lande' (fol 2r). The reference to 'your highnes,' the plans for leadership of a crusade expedition, and the bias towards the crusading efforts of English princes in the contents of the collection suggest that the work may have been intended for Henry VIII. If Pynson's dedication to the duke of Buckingham is accounted for by the duke's generally conservative tastes, and more particularly by the desire to broadcast his illustrious and chivalric ancestry, the manuscript's preface, rather surprisingly, points towards the supposedly anachronistic idea of the crusade as a motivating force for this translation of Hetoum's work. However, if we look more closely at the chivalric atmosphere of the early Henrician court, and in particular at the way in which the idea of a crusade against the Turks figured prominently in the diplomatic manoeuvrings of Henry and Wolsey in the years following the Lateran Council of 1515, it may not appear so unusual that between 1516 and 1520 Henry was likely to have wanted to appear interested in a projected crusade.

Traditionally the crusade figured low in the priorities of English rulers in the later Middle Ages. Edward I was the last English king to participate actively in a crusade to the Holy Land; later Lancastrian and Yorkist kings were generally too embroiled in wars with France or with dynastic disputes at home to involve themselves with the relatively remote Turkish problem. And in the days before a concerted English commercial penetration of the East, English interests were seldom directly threatened by Ottoman Turks or Moorish pirates. However, when presented with the fairly conventional responses of English kings at this time to the idea of the crusade, it should be remembered, as Robert Schwoebel points out, that 'behind the ruthless ... power politics of Lancastrian, York and Tudor, lurked a conscience impregnated with the ethical norms of Christian chivalry. However short of the ideal they may have fallen in performance, knighthood remained their one measure of princely aims and attainment.'[21] As European sovereigns English kings were automatically included in any plans for a new crusade. As good Christians they were also honour-bound to interest themselves in the idea of Holy War when it was suggested to them. Philippe de Mézières in 1395, just before the crusade of Nicopolis and at the request of the king of France, dedicated an allegorical *Epistre au roy d'Angleterre* urging Richard II to join in the forthcoming crusade.[22] Henry IV, while still the earl of Derby, had crusaded with the Teutonic Knights in Prussia. And Guillebert de Lannoy on returning in 1423 from his reconnaissance mission to the East went to London to present his written report personally to Henry V.

While the accession of Henry VIII in 1509 does little to change this pattern in any very substantial way, it does mark a significant shift in the style and conduct of English foreign policy and court life. The dynamic, young king was eager to make his mark in European diplomacy and to enhance the prestige and reputation of his court. Moreover, Henry had the financial means to indulge his natural inclinations for display at home and abroad, since he had inherited from his father both domestic stability and a full treasury. Thus the new reign opened, in marked contrast to the old, 'with an extraordinary burst of spectacular entertainments – disguisings, maskings, plays, dances, tilts, tourneys, and foot combats. Every significant event, every notable ambassadorial reception, every diplomatic victory, was marked by such shows … And, whether the merriment was out of doors in the lists or indoors on the ballroom floor, the King himself was always in the thick of it.'[23] Henry's image of himself as the perfect knight meant a dedication to the chivalric trappings of court life – jousts, maskings, interludes – which along with diplomacy were the two arenas in which the idea of the crusade still figured. Thus the sumptuously illustrated Great Westminster Tournament Roll (commemorating the most expensive tournament of Henry's reign, organized in 1511 to honour the birth of his first son) ends with a poem celebrating the king as the Tenth Worthy:

Our clypsyd son: now cleryd is from the darke
By harry our kyng: the flowr of natewrs marke
… felowe to the worthye nyne
The noble nyne which was the worthyest
To thy begynnyng was not comparabyll …
Why not thow the tenthe: as well as they the nyne
Sethe non of them more nobyll for the tyme.[24]

Although it cannot be said that the idea of the crusade dominates these court festivities, the crusade and the Turk were certainly traditional elements in fashionable chivalric fantasies of the period. For the most part, the Turk, like his Saracen and Tartar predecessors, figures as a colourful exotic element. Hall mentions a disguising of 1510 when the king and the earl of Essex appear dressed, 'after Turkey fasshion, in long robes of Bawdkin, powdered with gold, hattes on their heddes of Crimosyn Veluet, with greate rolles of Gold, girded with two swordes, called Cimiteries, hangyng by grete bawderikes of gold.'[25] Other nobles appear disguised as Russians, Prussians, and 'Moreskoes' (ie, Moors).[26] A more elaborate and significant appearance of the Turk occurs in one of the major court spectacles of the period, the allegorical pageant given at Greenwich in October 1518 to celebrate the signing of the Treaty of London. The treaty was essentially a peace negotiated between England and France, but the English-French treaty was expressed in general terms of universal peace between all the great powers of Europe, in order, it was claimed, to undertake the projected crusade against the Turks. And it was this element of universal peace that the pageant stressed.[27] The entrance of a group of Turks playing on drums began the action,[28] and an allegorical character named Reaport, riding a winged horse, explained the meaning of what followed. Various trees bearing the arms of the kings of France, England, Spain, and of the emperor and the pope, were arranged before a rock in order to symbolize the universal peace. In front of them lay a girl dressed as a queen with a dolphin in her lap to indicate the proposed marriage. After Reaport announced that the whole world rejoiced at this universal peace, one of the Turks came forward to dispute this claim. A combat ensued between Turk and Christian and, although the result is not recorded, it can be presumed that the latter were triumphant. Anglo is probably right in insisting that 'it was political allusion without any real malice. It did not betoken action against the enemy: whereas the plays of 1522 and 1527 [attacks on the king of France and the emperor respectively] were the prelude to war with France and with the emperor.'[29]

But the presence of the Turks in this pageant does reflect the special topicality of ideas of universal peace and the crusade during this period (roughly corresponding to the pontificate of Leo x, 1513–21), and their importance in the complicated political manoeuvring going on in Europe at this time. To understand this one must look more closely at the renewed threat to Europe from the Turks in the first quarter of the sixteenth century, the precarious position of the papacy, and in particular at the ways in which Henry and Wolsey made the need for a crusade serve their own diplomatic ends. During the reign of Sultan Bayezid II (1481–1512) Europe had experienced a temporary calm in its battles with the Turk, tempering somewhat the panic caused in Europe by the sack of Otranto and the siege of Rhodes in 1480.[30] But the assassination of Bayezid by his son Selim I in 1512 began a renewed Turkish offensive both in Europe and in the Middle East. Selim occupied Syria and Palestine in 1516, conquered Egypt itself in 1517, from 1515 threatened the Hospitaller stronghold of Rhodes (finally eliminating it in 1521),[31] and in 1521–2 laid siege to and captured the city of Belgrade. Throughout this period the incidence of piracy in the Mediterranean was greatly increased as a result of the enlarged Turkish navy and the hostility engendered in the Barbary pirates by the Spanish conquest of Granada.[32] It was left to Pope Leo x to organize and head European resistance to these enemies of the faith. But the pope could not ignore other more pressing dangers to the security of the papal states in Italy, and with them the security of the papacy itself. The papal states were threatened on one side by Venice (seeking papal territories in Emilia Romagna) and by France (with designs on the duchy of Milan), and on the other by Spanish control of the kingdom of Naples. Only by means of a fluid series of alliances could Leo hope to achieve the necessary checks and balances on the major powers that would assure the independence of the papacy. In such diplomatic manoeuvring the traditional role of the papacy as advocate of universal peace and the crusade matched perfectly the more mundane political needs of papal policy.[33]

For a variety of reasons, then, talk of a universal peace and a crusade was very much in the air at this time. In 1517 the Lateran Council summoned by the pope to consider the crusade endorsed two proposals: one made by Emperor Maximilian, the other by an old advocate of the crusade, Bernardin Caravajal, Cardinal S Crucis. Maximilian's grandiose three-year plan was to begin with an invasion of North Africa, led by him but financed by the other European powers, and to end with the complete subjugation, partition, and conversion of the Turkish empire. The cardinal's plan, while more altruistic, was equally fantastical.[34] Henry of course gave his tentative consent, conditional upon a universal peace being arranged. But he and Wolsey quickly proceeded to try to gain whatever diplomatic advantage they could from the situation. The pope had sent a special legate *a latere* to England to try to increase support for the crusade (or at least for the collection of special crusade taxes from the English church). But before Cardinal Campeggio was allowed into the country Wolsey demanded that he too be raised from papal legate *de jure* to the extraordinary position of permanent legate *a latere*, and that he be confirmed in his unofficial usurpation of the bishopric of Bath and Wells from the disgraced Cardinal Hadrian. While negotiations dragged on, Cardinal Campeggio waited in humiliation at Calais. When the pope finally capitulated, the cardinal was received with great splendour in London by Wolsey and the king. But his usefulness over, he was allowed to lapse into obscurity.[35]

The triumph of English diplomacy, however, came with the Treaty of London in 1518. The peace between England and France was symbolized by the betrothal of Princess Mary and the dauphin, but at a more practical level the treaty removed a major obstacle to peace between the two countries by ceding Tournai back to the French. As we have seen, these more self-serving aspects of the treaty were cloaked in terms of a general European peace supposedly aimed at a crusade against the Turks. For the very fact that the treaty purported to be universal and inclusive, and that it dedicated itself to an indisputably noble end, would make it very difficult for any other ruler who feared a French-English alliance to oppose the treaty publicly or to break its terms. By adopting one of the papacy's traditional diplomatic roles, that is, as architects of universal peace and leaders of the crusade, Henry and Wolsey had established themselves, at least temporarily, as diplomatic arbiters of Europe. In the words of Giustiniani, Henry was the '*lapis angularis* which joined the two detached walls of the temple.'[36]

In strictly practical terms, however, the treaty was not a conspicuous success, and by 1522 England was again at war with France. For the death of Emperor Maximilian in February 1519, and the election of Charles v as emperor later the same year, had irrevocably altered the balance of power in Europe. Charles's territories included Spain, Flanders, and Austria, and thus encircled those of Francis. No longer did the English need to search out a diplomatic role for themselves or fear strategic isolation, for now, as the vital third power that could tip the balance of power between Charles and Francis, they were assured a dominant role in European affairs. Within this fast-changing political situation, there was no longer much advantage to be gained by dwelling on the diplomatic fiction of a universal peace and a European alliance against the Turk. Nonetheless, the treaty and the events leading up to it demonstrate how the idea of Holy War and the Turkish threat brought the crusade, at least occasionally, into the everyday policy of Europe's rulers.

In addition to its periodic usefulness in politics and diplomacy, along with other increasingly anachronistic concepts like that of the common body of Christendom and universal peace, the idea of the crusade survived in contemporary thinking as a reminder of a simpler, nobler past. For the mind of the day was accustomed to thinking in static terms, however much society as a whole was in a state of fundamental social and political change. Indeed, as Arthur B. Ferguson points out in his discussion of the survival of chivalric ideals in the fifteenth century, the very changes occurring in society often encouraged people to hark back to and try to preserve a romanticized conception of past values:

The men and women of late medieval England were quite capable of, were indeed habitually given to, embalming general principles in traditional forms and thereby isolating them quite effectively from the contingencies of daily existence. In this way facts that aroused the anxiety of contemporary observers or in any way elicited from them a strong emotional response could be interpreted in the light of accepted values. And, by the same token, those tendencies which the historian finds most obviously working against the chivalric way of life could become actually instrumental in preserving the chivalric tradition, even perhaps in enhancing its significance in the eyes of all but the most hard-headed observers. What seems at first glance to be merely lip-service to chivalric idealism can thus be considered a quite honest response to the upsetting events of the fifteenth century.[37]

It should not be surprising, then, that in such an atmosphere of nostalgia for established values, there should remain a strong residual attraction at least to the idea of the crusade and the chivalric ideals that surrounded it. And this general interest in the chivalric associations surrounding the crusade was perhaps intensified by the sudden topicality of crusade projects both because of the renewal of Turkish militancy after 1512 and because of the temporary importance of the crusade in Henry's European diplomacy in the period 1515–22.

CONCLUSIONS

We have already seen how the late medieval and early modern taste for literature connected with the exotic East, especially for works of geography and travel, probably accounts in large part for the continued popularity of *La Fleur des histoires*.[38] No doubt for a published translation like Pynson's, the printer could presume that the known audience for *Mandeville's Travels* would also be interested in Hetoum's work. But Pynson's choice of the duke of Buckingham as patron and, in particular, the crusade-oriented dedication to the Royal manuscript's collection of translations would suggest that other, supposedly anachronistic, aspects of Hetoum's work were also thought noteworthy and relevant. Certainly both Henry and Buckingham were capable of reading *La Fleur des histoires* in French, indeed perhaps already possessed manuscript copies in their libraries. What the dedications of these translations indicate is their encouragement of, or at least anticipated support for, the wider dissemination of a work embodying the ideals of chivalry and the crusade (however ceremonially or opportunistically they might be put into practice).

NOTES

1 Described briefly in *Fifty-Five Books Printed Before 1525, An Exhibition from the Collection of Paul Mellon* ([New York] 1968) No 49, p 56

2 Vienna, Hofbibliothek MS 2620 (Kohler's D); Paris, BN MS franç 12201 (Kohler's E); Paris, BN MS nouv acq franç 1255 (Kohler's F); Rome, Vatican Library MS Reg 606. The Latin Provincial begins 'Incipit liber provinciarum. In civitate rommana sunt quinque ecclesiae que patriarchales dicunter et sunt hec ...' and is introduced by a French summary 'Cy commerce le livre de toutes les provinces et les cités de l'universel monde, et divise et nomme les noms de toutes les cités et quantes il en a en chascune province selon le povoir et savoir de l'église rommaine ...' Cf *RHC Arm* II lxxxvi–lxxxix, xcv.

3 In the list of the duke of Buckingham's titles (A1r), at whose command the work was produced, he is incorrectly called the 'erle of Gloucestre' instead of Hereford. P1 is unique in retaining a correction slip pasted over it with 'Hereforde' printed in the same typeface. However P2 and P3 (the only other copies that I have been able to examine) both show traces of once having had a similar correction slip pasted over 'Gloucestre.' P3 contains an additional correction slip pasted over the 'Glouc=|estre' found in the colophon at the end of the book (14v), and P2 shows possible traces of once possessing a similar correction.

4 Cf *Bibliotheca Heberiana* I (London 1834) 179 (which wrongly attributes authorship to Barclay); *Bibliotheca Grenvilliana* ed John T. Payne and Henry Foss I (London 1842) 306.

5 C.M. Briquet *Les Filigranes* ed Allan Stevenson (Amsterdam 1968) nos 8707, 10061

6 Described by Edward Hodnett *English Woodcuts 1486–1535* (Oxford 1973) No 1512

7 *Printers' and Publishers' Devices in England & Scotland, 1485–1640* (London 1913) No 44

8 *Wynkyn de Worde & His Contemporaries* (London 1925; rpt 1974) 153

9 He spent £1,500 for the entertainments at Penshurst and at least £3,000 on the visit to France, according to Carole Rawcliffe *The Staffords, Earls of Stafford and Dukes of Buckingham 1394–1521* (Cambridge 1978) 138–43.

10 Cf M.B. Parkes *English Cursive Bookhands 1250–1500* (Oxford 1969) xix–xxiii.

11 According to the *Catalogue of Western Manuscripts in the Old Royal and King's Collection* ed George F. Warner and Julius P. Gilson (London 1921) II 298–9, the sources of the first four books are: for Robert of Normandy, one of the prose paraphrases of Wace's *Roman de Rou*; for Godfrey of Bouillon, 'the ix[th] boke of the ix worthies in Frenche' (as the text itself says), and William of

Tyre's *History*; for Richard Coeur-de-Lion and Edward I, the chronicle of
Walter of Hemingsburgh.

12 *Catalogue Royal Collection* I xxvi
13 Rawcliffe *The Staffords* table II p 13
14 Ibid 37–9
15 *Helyas, Knight of the Swanne* trans R. Copland (London: Wynkyn de Worde
1512; *STC* 7571), A1v–2r; rpt in facsimile as *The History of Helyas, Knight of
the Swan* (New York 1901); rpt in a critical edition 'Wynkyn de Worde and his
1512 Edition of *Helyas, Knight of the Swanne*' ed Stanley Daniel Lombardo,
Diss Indiana 1976. Cf Anthony Wagner 'The Swan Badge and the Swan
Knight' *Archaeologia* 97 (1959) 127–38.
16 *The Great Chronicle of London* ed A.H. Thomas and I.D. Thornley (London
1938) 311, 313, reports that at the wedding of Prince Arthur and Katherine
of Aragon, Buckingham played an active role in the magnificent jousts held in
honour of the occasion, and for the wedding celebrations themselves 'ware
a goune ... valuyd at xvCli. or M & vCli.' For the meeting with the Emperor
Maximilian at Ardres in 1513 'The noble men of the kynge campe were
gorgeously aparelled ... but in especial ye duke of Buckingham, he was in
purple satten, his apparell and his barde full of Antelopes and swannes of
fyne gold bullion and full of spangyls and littel belles of gold meruelous
costly and pleasant to behold' (Edward Hall *The Union of the Two Noble and
Illustre Famelies of Lancastre and York* ed Henry Ellis [London 1809] 544). For the
cost and spectacle associated with the Field of the Cloth of Gold in 1520
and Buckingham's participation in it, see J.G. Russell *The Field of Cloth of
Gold* (London 1969) esp 49–51, 116, 174, 191.
17 Russell *Field of Cloth of Gold* 7. For a description and photographs of Thornbury Castle and Buckingham's plans for it, see H. Avray Tipping *English
Homes* I *Period II: Early Tudor, 1485–1558* (London 1924) 86–90, plates 90–104.
Cf also Rawcliffe, 137–8, for the financial side to Buckingham's ambitious
building programme. Some idea of the grand style in which the duke lived
can be obtained from the entries in his Household Book for the Christmas
celebrations held at Thornbury in 1508. See 'Extracts from the Household
Book of Edward, Duke of Buckingham, 1508–9' ed J. Gage *Archaeologia* 25
(1834) 311–41. For the Epiphany Day festival alone, there were 134 gentry,
188 yeomen or valets, and 197 garcons (ie serving-men, attendants) dining at
Thornbury (ibid 321).
18 Rawcliffe *The Staffords* 94
19 'In 1521 Robert Brook, "Scoler of Oxford and nowe admitted scolemaister to
the said Duke's Hinxmen and Wardis," obtained a yearly allowance so
that he could continue with his own academic career'; ibid 94–5.

20 Ibid 95
21 Robert Schwoebel *The Shadow of the Crescent: The Renaissance Image of the Turk (1453–1517)* (Nieuwkoop 1967) 138. At an individual level, Englishmen took a more active role in the defence of Europe against the Turk, especially those belonging to the English *langue* of the Hospitallers of St John. The order had many possessions in England and the grand priors in England 'played important roles in the affairs of the order at home and in the East.' For example, one grand prior, Sir John Kendal, 'served as representative of his order to Rome, Venice, France, and England, as papal envoy to various countries in the West, and as English ambassador to France and Austria' (Schwoebel 137). Moreover, 'By letters and reports from the continent and through foreign residents and travelers the doings of the Turks were regularly publicized. English chroniclers recorded the details of all the important battles with the Ottomans – the fall of Constantinople, and the sieges of Belgrade and Rhodes. English pilgrims and adventurers brought home first-hand reports of the East and the much feared enemy of the faith' (Schwoebel 134). Thus, John Kay had translated Guillaume Caoursin's popular eye-witness account of the siege of Rhodes within three years of the event. See note 26 below.
22 BL MS Royal 20.B.6; Philippe de Mezières *Letter to King Richard II* ed and trans G.W. Coopland (Liverpool 1975). See also Aziz S. Atiya *The Crusade in the Later Middle Ages* (London 1938) 150–2; and J.J.N. Palmer *England, France and Christendom, 1377–99* (London 1972).
23 Sydney Anglo *Spectacle, Pageantry and Early Tudor Policy* (Oxford 1969) 108
24 Anglo *The Great Tournament Roll of Westminster: A Collotype Reproduction of the Manuscript* (Oxford 1968) I plate XXIII (Membrane 36). See also Anglo's introduction in vol II, where he deals in detail with the chivalric background of the early Henrician court – especially the jousts and tournaments.
25 Hall *Union of the Two Noble and Illustre Famelies* 513
26 Moors were also a common feature of the City of London Midsummer Show pageants. The Midsummer Show of 1521 featured a king of the Moors 'royally presented on a stage, with wild fire playing about him, and a pavilion borne over his head' according to Sheila Williams 'The Lord Mayor's show in Tudor and Stuart Times' *The Guildhall Miscellany* 1 (1959) 5. Wild fire also figures in accounts of real battles with the Turk. Cf Gulielmus Caoursin *The Siege of Rhodes* trans John Kay (London c 1482; rpt in facsimile as No 236 in The English Experience Series [Amsterdam 1970]) 25–6, 31 and *Capystranus* (Wynkyn de Worde nd) sig B4v. In the same 1521 Midsummer Show there was also a Castle of War pageant that may be a topical reference to the siege of Rhodes or Belgrade. According to the description given by Spinelli, secretary

to the Venetian Ambassador, within the castle were 'armed men, who as they moved caused the draw-bridges to fall and rise, and on the walls were men standing with stones in their hands for its defence against a Turkish horseman in pursuit, armed with a very long tin sword tinged with blood, who terrified those within, shouting in English ["*wo be*"!]' (*Calendar of State Papers (Venetian)* ed Rawdon Brown III [London 1869] 244).

27 My description follows the most complete contemporary account, given in an anonymous letter reproduced in *Calendar of State Papers (Venetian)* ed Rawdon Brown II (London 1867) 1088. Hall's chronicle (595) mentions only the rock and allegorical trees, and gives no account of the disputation or battle with the Turks.

28 This was also the prelude to real battles with the Turk. Cf Caoursin *The Siege of Rhodes* [16].

29 *Spectacle, Pageantry and Early Tudor Policy* 135

30 See Dorothy Vaughan *Europe and the Turk: A Pattern of Alliances 1350–1700* (Liverpool 1954) 85–93; and Schwoebel 202–3.

31 For the series of appeals made by the grand masters of the Hospitallers to Wolsey and Henry VIII in the years 1515–22, see *Letters and Papers, Foreign and Domestic, of the Reign of Henry VIII* ed J.S. Brewer II (London 1864) 1319, 1320, 1756, 2457, 3607, 3695, 4252; and *Letters and Papers* III (London 1867) 1741, 2117, 2118, 2324, 2325. Cf also Alexander Barclay's lament for the plight of Rhodes in *The Ship of Fools* ed T.H. Jamieson II (Edinburgh 1874) 198.

32 See *Letters and Papers* II 1874, 4282, for accounts of Turkish pirates raiding towns in Italy. Even the pope himself was not safe, for a letter of 1516 (II 2017) claims that 'a fleet of Turks entered the Tiber, and had nearly made the Pope prisoner whilst hunting at Pali. If they had stayed a little longer, and not shown themselves by day, they would certainly have taken him.'

33 For Leo X and the crusade, see Kenneth M. Setton 'Pope Leo X and the Turkish Peril' *Proceedings of the American Philosophical Society* 113 (1969) 367–424, rpt as No IX in Setton *Europe and the Levant in the Middle Ages and the Renaissance* (London 1974).

34 For a brief summary of Maximilian's plan, see *Letters and Papers* II 3816. According to the cardinal's plan a double army of 60,000 men would proceed, one by the Danube and one by the Mediterranean, to Constantinople and thence to the Holy Land. The armies would be led by all twenty European rulers, the heads of the six military orders, and the two Greek pretenders (to facilitate the conversion and support of the native Christian population). Help was also expected from the Persian sophi and Prester John (*Letters and Papers* II 2362, 3815). Cf also the reference to similar English crusade plans in the General Preface to the Royal manuscript (fol 2). Hetoum's

proposals in Book IV for a new crusade would be of obvious relevance to this kind of endeavour.

35 The English were not alone in using the crusade for personal ends. Because the pope had agreed to remit part of the money gained from the sales of crusade indulgences to Francis I (for future crusade expenses he would incur as its leader), Francis is accused of gaining 'more money by pardons of the crusade than by all his exactions ... They will not use the money against the Saracens, but against England' (*Letters and Papers* II 3818). And in a letter of 1518, Wolsey writes to the deputy of Tournai that 'the French are raising men in Gelderland and elsewhere, on pretence of an expedition against the Infidels' (II 3907). Nor is the pope exempt from criticism. Erasmus writes to Colet in 1517 that 'Hypocrites reign in the courts of princes; the court of Rome is shameless, what can be more gross than these continued indulgences? And now a war against the Turks is made the pretext, when the real purpose is to drive the Spaniards from Naples; for Lorenzo, the Pope's nephew, who has married the daughter of the King of Navarre lays claim to Campania' (II 3992).

36 Sebastiano Giustiniani *Four Years at the Court of Henry VIII* trans Rawdon Brown (London 1854) II 177. Garrett Mattingly in *Renaissance Diplomacy* (London 1955) 167–8, reminds us of the positive aspects of the Treaty of London, and its advances on past efforts: 'The Treaty of London was ... in announced intention, completely inclusive and European wide ... Its language sought to avoid the reservations and ambiguities which had flawed previous treaties ... If it did little directly to advance the crusade, it left the way open for united action. It had no secret provisions ... The peace-loving humanists hailed the treaty as a masterpiece of constructive European statesmanship, the realization of an ancient dream by the most modern methods.'

37 *The Indian Summer of English Chivalry* (Oxford 1955) 27. Thus Henry was as capable of fine words and promises about the crusade as any other European ruler, offering in 1516 'to go in his own person and be captain of the sea' (*Letters and Papers* II 3874). But in practice his reactions were generally those of a monarch interested, above all, in European affairs as they impinged on England, and only too aware of the way in which others used the crusade to mask their own self-interest. See *Letters and Papers* II 712, 2642, 4047; and Giustiniani *Four Years at the Court of Henry VIII* I 12–13. Cf Mattingly *Renaissance Diplomacy* 167–8, for what he has to say about the gulf between what diplomats of the period said in their treaties and what their real aims were. Cf also Robert P. Adams *The Better Part of Valor: More, Erasmus, Colet, and Vives, on Humanism, War, and Peace, 1496–1535* (Seattle 1962)

esp 262–4, 285–91, 298–9, for the continued support given by humanists of the period to the idea of universal peace; and Franklin L. Baumer 'England, the Turk, and the Common Corps of Christendom' *American Historical Review* 50 (1944) 26–48.

38 See chapter 1, above.

3

Hetoum's Prose and the Tudor Translations

Hetoum's French Prose

Hetoum writes at the beginning of a period in French prose which falls between the simpler paratactic style of the chroniclers and the more elaborate hypotactic prose of the *style curial*. As Jens Rasmussen points out:

En France, des écrivains avaient composé en prose dès le xiiiᵉ siècle, tels les chroniqueurs Villehardouin et Joinville. Ils avaient usé d'un style simple et nu qui disait bien ce qu'il voulait parce que, dans leur rédaction, les événements avaient le pas sur la forme stylistique. L'ancien style de la chronique, caracterisé par un vocabulaire impersonnel et une phrase simple et peu variée, se retrouve encore dans de larges parties des romans du xvᵉ où il s'agit de présenter une suite continue d'événements. Cependant, au xvᵉ siècle, le gout n'était plus à la simplicité et il était naturel que ce fût un style de prose pleinement réalisé qui façonnât d'une manière décisive la prose narrative ... le style curial.¹

Although this style originated in the Latin of the papal curia and the medieval chanceries, it provided French prose writers (among others) with the sophisticated model that they were looking for. Characteristics of this style are frequency of introductory formulae, a desire to list events repeatedly in the same framework, a preference for periphrases like 'il leur donna congié' instead of simple verb forms, the indiscriminate use of terms of reference like 'dessusdit' or 'ledit,' epic lists and residual categories like 'et maints autres choses,' synonyms and doublets, and technical and law terms like 'Item,' and generally a desire to exhaust a subject by amplification and decoration. Perhaps the most striking element of the *style curial* is its love of asymmetrical sentences packed with as many subordinate, and especially relative, clauses as possible. Thus, according to Diane Bornstein, 'clauses progress in chains, one being embedded in another' so that 'it is often hard to tell where a sentence begins and ends.'[2]

As one might expect from the early date of its composition, the prose of *La Fleur des histoires* often has more in common with the simpler style of chroniclers like Villehardouin and Joinville than with the *style curial* described by Rasmussen. However, Hetoum's prose does at times manifest certain characteristics of the later style. Perhaps because of the polemical and hypothetical nature of Book IV, this elaboration shows up more frequently there. Formulaic introductions are fairly rudimentary in the first three books, but Hetoum rarely starts a chapter or statement in the middle of things. Instead, they are framed by a few endlessly repeated phrases – 'Après ce,' 'En cele temps,' 'il avint que,' etc – all of which have the effect of placing action or description in identical conditions. Occasionally in these earlier books the introduction is more elaborate (eg, 'Encores dirons aucune chose de la manere e de les coustumes des Tartars' III xlix).[3] But most of this kind of introduction is found in the arguments of Book IV: for example,

Raison requiert que chascun qui voet movoir guerre contre ses enemis doit considerer IIII choses ... Primierement ... la seconde ... la tierce ... la quarte ... (IV i),[4]

and

Puis que raisonablement avons mostré la juste occasion, laquele les Crestiens ont de movoir guerre contre les Sarazins, e soufisablement avons dit la puissance de la saint Eglise, avons devisé ensement de la condicion, e de l'estat du regne d'Egipte e de celui de Surie e du poeir du soldan e de sa gent, reste encore à dire du temps covenable à guerre comencier contre les enemis de la foi crestiene (IV xi).[5]

In addition to introductory phrases, Hetoum uses inverted parallelisms and repetitious words and phrases to create a description made up of identical chains: for example, 'En celui pays ... les homes de celui pays ...' or 'La gent ... la creance de ceste gent ... Cestes gens ...' As well, his repeated use of phrases like 'asses e bones,' 'meniers y a,' 'molt grant e riche' demonstrates a need to appear to be totally comprehensive and to exhaust his subject. This can be seen most clearly in his fondness for epic lists and residual phrases like 'par arbalestres, engins, pierres, par mines desouz terre e par feu qui ne se puet esteindre, e par aultre maneres' (iv iii) and 'en despenses e en totes autres choses à la guerre commencer' (iv i).[6]

While Hetoum does not overuse terms of reference or employ many technical terms, he does use repetition as a unifying device in Book iv. Chapter xi gives a Latin verse and its French translation ('Ore est temps covenable'), which is then used to begin Chapter xii ('Ore est temps acceptable e temps covenable'), Chapter xiii ('Ore est temps acceptable e temps covenable'), and Chapter xiv ('Encores est temps covenable').[7] He also very precisely enumerates the argument of Book iv, Chapter i: 'IIII choses. Primerement ... la seconde ... la tierce ... la quarte ... A la secunde raison ... De la tierce raison e de la quarte ...'[8]

La Fleur des histoires is full of parallel constructions and doublets, more as a habit of composition, it would appear, than as a means of emphasis and clarity. A random sampling would produce examples like the following: 'vindrent e assagerent,' 'reverence e honor,' 'ne por seignorie, ne por richesces,' 'à croire e à nomer le nom,' 'felon e cruel.' Perhaps because of the nature of his narrative Hetoum frequently uses simple active verbs. But he also makes great use of impersonal verbal formulae like 'il avint que,' 'convient que,' 'fu comencée la bataille,' as well as periphrases such as 'prist congié,' 'il ot petit de repos (misericorde de, etc),' 'fist fermances,' and 'grant domage firent.' He also has a tendency to use passive constructions in the non-descriptive sections of Book iv.

In Hetoum's prose there is a minimum of differentiation between syntactical units; subordinate and relative clauses, even phrases, are inserted almost *ad infinitum* in a loose chain-like structure. One finds this sort of spontaneous generation of relative clauses even in the earlier, simpler narrative:

Après que les Sarazins se furent reposez aucun temps, il penserent d'entrer au regne de Perse; dont il assemblerent grant ost e pristrent le roiaume de Mesopotame e celui de Caldée, qui estoit de la seignorie du roiaume de Perse, dont estoit roy Assobarich; lequel, doubtant la puissance des Sarazins, manda ses messaiges as rois e seignors ses voisins, qui estoient deçà le flum Phison, e requist leur aide, promettant grans dons à touz ceaus qui vendroient (ii iii).[9]

But more often in the first three books the syntactical organization is simply paratactic, made up of smaller units loosely related to and arising out of one another:

En roiaume de Tharse si ha III provinces, e les seignors de celes provinces, se font apeler rois, e ont une letre e un lengage par eaus, e celes gens sont apelez Jougour: e tous temps ont esté ydolatres, e encores le sont au jour d'ui touz, sauve la nacion de ceaus III rois qui vindrent aorer la nativité Nostre Seignor Jhesu Crist, par la demonstrance de l'estoille (I ii).[10]

However, the last two phrases and relative clause ('sauve ...') show a tendency to elaboration on an earlier, simpler structure. Again, it is Book IV, with its longer, more abstract, units of thought that most clearly shows the effect of a hypotactic syntactical organization. For example,

Ore est temps covenable, ouquel les corrages des feaus de Crist se doivent enbrascer au passaige de la Terre Sainte, à ce que des mains des ennemis soit delivré le saint sepulcre de Nostre Seignor, qui est comencement de nostre creance; ne n'avons, ne souvient esperance d'avoir en ces jors passés si covenable temps come ores, si come Deus, por sa pitei, nos demostre en maintes maneres. Car tout primerement ... (IV xi).[11]

Indeed the period before 'Car' is a sign more of modern editorial intervention than an intended full stop on Hetoum's part; for there is, in fact, a minimum of differentiation between the two syntactical units.

The Tudor Translations

SYNTAX

The French syntax appears to have presented a number of difficulties for P. The omission of French pronominal subjects for verbs can result in an erroneous subject (as at 34/26) or more frequently the mixing up of French subject and object. Thus Fr 'Et à tant soufist à parler des Tartars' becomes 'And as moch as is sufficyent the Tartas speketh' (64/38–9), and Fr 'adversités porroient avenir' becomes 'aduersytes it myght come to the ennemys' (76/29). P will also translate the pronominal subject and indirect object of an understood clause with a totally different and incorrect subject: for example, 'ne onques puis n'out Guiboga feauté des Crestiens de la Surie, *ne ceaus de lui*' as 'Ginboga had neuer trust nor loue with the christen men of Syrie, *nor his men*' (43/15–6). And he will even occasionally omit the subject and object of a verb. Thus Fr 'o grant diligence *le* recontait à ses enfans e à ses nevous, e *les* nous faisoit mettre' becomes 'In great dilygence rehersed to his sonnes and to his neuewes, and dyd vs put in writynge' (61/6–7).

Like R, P will sometimes incorrectly place a phrase or clause with a nearby sentence to which it does not belong.[12] A similar syntactical error, but one peculiar to P, is his habit of occasionally separating two linked phrases or noun-modifier units by the addition of a co-ordinate conjunction or verb. For example, Fr 'le roy prist congiei de Haloon, e retorna en Ermenie, *après III ans e demi*, sainz e haitiés' becomes 'the King toke leue of Halcon and retorned vnto Armeny *and taryed there, iii yeres and a halfe after*, in good helthe' (39/27–8) and Fr 'dont il avint que le soudan d'Egipte, qui avoit proposement d'atendre Casan *en* [var *et*] *le contrées de Hames*' becomes 'Than it fortuned that the Sowdan of Egypt, which did purposlye tary for Casan, *went into the countreys of Hames*' (52/19–21).[13]

In contrast, R seems to have had relatively few problems with the French syntax. Only once is he confused by the French habit of omitting the pronominal subject in third person verb forms, and that is by a particularly confusing instance of the French practice (one that P also translates incorrectly).[14] Twice R misunderstands the relationship of pronominal subjects and objects within the sentence.[15] On one occasion R inserts a negative not included in the French, perhaps as a result of the rather awkward French syntax.[16] And at one point R adds a parallel construction not in the French, which might be an attempt to clarify what he considered as a difficult French passage.[17] R's only recurrent syntactical error is in matching a phrase or clause with the wrong sentence. However, because of the asymmetrical sentences common to the French and the possibility of confusion caused by an unpunctuated copy, it is often difficult to tell at a glance whether a clause or phrase is part of the sentence before or after it.

VOCABULARY

P's great number of lexical mistakes would appear to be the result of carelessness or a habit of translating from context rather than according to the literal meaning of the French. In trying first of all to render the general sense of a French passage, P frequently fails to understand individual words in phrases. The process can be seen in the following examples: 'his goodes and his frendes' (36/26) for Fr 'sa bienvoillance e s'amisté,' 'cost' (63/30) for Fr 'ost,' and 'called Meser' (72/30) for Fr 'devant la cité de Meser.' A good example of the differing methods used by R and P can be seen in their translation of Fr 'ostours e autres oiseaus de proie.' R, anxious to give an exact equivalent of Fr 'ostours' while not really understanding its exact meaning, translates with a similar sounding English word that he knows, ie, 'ostriches' (fol 147v). P also seems not to have understood the French word, but he tries to make up for this with a simple generalization sure to cover the situation, ie, 'gret byrdes of diuers kynde' (11/2). P, then, appears to have been a much speedier translator, concerned more with rendering the general sense of a French passage than translating every detail exactly. If an English word seemed to fit, it was used, and P moved on, unwilling to waste time over details. On a number of occasions P gives a translation not literally correct but suitable in its context: for example, 'mystlyn' (9/27, 12/25) for Fr 'millet'; 'carpet' (27/9) for Fr 'feutre'; 'betwene two waters' (58/9) for Fr 'environnés de II pars d'un lac e d'un montaigne'; and 'foteball' (71/17) for Fr 'la Solle.'

As might be expected, P makes few direct borrowings from the French. Both P and R borrow 'thoman' (P 28/1, R fol 166v), 'seyserach' (P 63/3, R fol 203r), and 'cocalx' (P 72/20, R fol 214r) directly from the French (but all three French words were probably borrowings themselves). And they also translate Fr 'natures' and 'maisons' literally, probably because of their unfamiliar usage in the French. P does translate Fr 'nomé' with 'prefeke' (82/16), a borrowing not recorded in the OED but a word which may have been in his French exemplar. P's 'of length in length' (17/4–5) for Fr 'de lonc en lonc' is also not recorded in the OED. In addition P uses 'abordreth' (3/11), 'reclamed' (27/34), and possibly 'duke' (28/33), in senses that the OED does not record until later. P appears to have extended the normal meaning of 'hauntyng' (63/32) to suit a specific context (to translate Fr 'de chace'). None of P's vocabulary errors is obviously the result of a muddled exemplar.[19]

R makes proportionally far more lexical than syntactical errors. The majority of these vocabulary errors are single words or phrases that he did not understand (often for paleographic reasons) and consequently translated incorrectly.[20] There are a number of other examples where it is possible that a corrupt French exemplar, not R's ignorance of French, led him to mistranslate. As well, R occasionally gives a textbook correct translation that in its context proves incorrect: for example, 'were there to the royalme' (fol 195v) for Fr. 'lors estoient en royaume' and 'faders' (fol 200v) for Fr 'parens.' More often R borrows a word directly from the French of his exemplar: like P, 'thoman,' 'seyserach,' 'brigandie'; and in addition, 'millet' (fol 146r, fol 149r), 'dizaine' (fol 166v), 'somages' (fol 208r), 'rouchins' (fol 208r), 'the Solle' (fol 212v), and perhaps 'habitantes' (fol 225v). Or he forms a new word on a French model: 'dispurviaunces' (fol 207r) and 'brigandie' (fol 218v). R also uses 'sompter' (fol 208v) in a way not recorded in the OED, and employs the variant spelling 'draffte' (fol 145r) well before its first recorded use listed in the OED.

One final difference between R and P in the matter of vocabulary should be noted. R, overall, tends to prefer words borrowed or formed from French that look or sound like those in his exemplar. Thus R prefers to be as literal a translator as possible in his choice of English vocabulary. However, R does not introduce many new borrowings of his own. Instead, in his choice of vocabulary he would appear to be aiming simply at what he thought was a more authentic and elevated style (ie, more French). P, on the other hand, generally uses freer, more idiomatic constructions, and tends to use an English word not resembling the French one of his exemplar. He generally employs more words of English origin, and simpler words of French origin. In his choice of vocabulary P seems to be aiming more at ready comprehension than at an elevated or literally translated vocabulary, consequently providing greater explanation and giving less attention to copying the French exemplar in its every detail.[21]

OMISSIONS

P makes no major omissions. Of the omissions which do occur, none appears to be the result of eye-slip or editorial revision. Instead, the majority are simply individual words, phrases, and short clauses that P has omitted out of carelessness or a habit of freer translation. P (or his compositor) has also on occasion omitted an auxiliary verb, indeed sometimes the main verb itself.[22]

R makes approximately twenty more omissions than P. Roughly one-fifth of R's omissions are short co-ordinate clauses, generally beginning with the French conjunction 'e' and forming part of a list of simple clauses. Similarly, R also omits short subordinate (especially relative) clauses, although in fewer numbers. He occasionally leaves out single phrases and words. Certain omissions can definitely be attributed to eye-slip. And several of R's omissions (or those of his exemplar) are probably responsible for mistakes in translation.[23] A number of important or substantial omissions occur at the beginning and end of the French chapter divisions. These may also be due to eye-slip or R may have treated them as superfluous material included in the preceding or following chapters.[24]

EXPANSIONS

As might be expected, since P tends to be a freer translator than R, he makes far more expansions (approximately a third again as many). Many of P's expansions are simply of an ornamental nature. He often tends to choose a longer way of translating the French – a periphrastic verbal construction for a simple active verb in the French, or a subordinate clause for a French adjective. For example, Fr 'se despent monoie' becomes 'is money currant for comen and vniuersall dyspences' (8/11). P generally shows a fondness for doublets and other parallel constructions: for example, 'which in beauty and fayrnesse of draught resemble and are moche lyke vnto Latten letters' (7/9–10) for Fr 'qui de beautey resemblent à letres latines'; 'the peple eteth and fede for the moost part on' (9/26–7) for Fr 'mangent'; or 'well furnysshed and stored with people' (9/36) for Fr 'bien pueblée.'

The majority of P's expansions, however, would seem to have been added because P felt the need for greater clarity or emphasis. Perhaps P himself found the French confusing or felt that his readers might have difficulty in appreciating a frenchified vocabulary or syntax. Therefore he makes frequent use of doublets, clausal expansions, emphatic conjunctions and phrases, and parallel constructions, in order to make the sense quite clear, even at the risk of belabouring what might seem obvious. For example,

E dient les Catains que il sont ceus qui voient de II oils, e des Latins disent qu'il voient d'un oil, mès les autres nacions dient que sont aveugles. E por ce puet om entendre que il tienent les autres gens de gros entendement.

becomes

And, as the Cathayns say, these people be they which seyth with bothe eyen, bycause of their subtyll insyght in bodyly werkes. And they say the Lattyns seeth but of one eye, as theym reputynge lesse ingenious and lesse inuentyfe. But the other nacions say that these Cathayns are but blynde, as in reprouynge theyr subtylyte. By this may we vnderstande that these Cathayns repute other people of grosse wyt and vnderstandynge and themselfe onely ingenyous (7/21–8/2).

The English passage is considerably longer than the French. More important, by means of three additional subordinate clauses and two participial phrases, P has transformed the paratactic structure of the

French (with its dependence on a synthetic syntax) into clearer, more idiomatic English. P's additions not only make clear the sense of the French (at least as P mistakenly understood it) and its rhetorical climax, but also retain the parallelism of Fr 'E ... que ... e ... mès ... que ... E por ce ... que' by translating as 'And ... which ... And ... But ... that ... By this ... that.' Indeed P emphasizes this parallelism with his 'as theym reputyng ... as in reprouynge.' P's other additions are perhaps less remarkable, but they show a similar concern for the overall design of the prose argument and a desire that this design reflect, at least in its broad outlines, the intentions of the French original. Thus P adds 'where lettred men frequent' (9/33); 'there be founde namely all the balayses' (11/32–3); 'and called it by his owne name' (12/19) – to make explicit what is implicit in the French; and 'And because of that' (25/36–7) – to relate more clearly the growth of the Sultan's power not only to the coming of the Corasmins but also to his clever dispersal of them throughout his kingdom. Similarly, Fr 'n'a que une entrée par devers la mer oceane, ains est come un lac' becomes 'onely one entrey towarde the occean see; *all the remenaunt within is but lyke a lake or standynge water*' (11/6–7); Fr 'se troevent pierres precieuses e les bones espices' becomes 'be founde precyous stones, *also in them groeth right* good spices' (12/6–7); Fr 'Une isle qui est nomée Celan' becomes 'one yle *preeminent aboue the other* (which yle is named Celan)' (12/7–8); Fr 'se porroit l'om bien merveiller, qui [ie, the Tartars] ont conquis' becomes 'it is marueyle, *seynge that* they haue conquered' (27/16–17); Fr 'une chambre' becomes 'in a *close* chambre' (40/12); Fr 'e dona' becomes 'and gaue *gyftes*' (48/27); and Fr 'Casan qui petite cure avoit de la foi des Crestiens, e qui molt estoit covoitous d'avoir seignorie, otroia de ce que ceaus requeroient' becomes 'Casan, that set nat moche by the fayth of Christ, *was lightly torned*, for he was moche couytus to haue the lordship, *and was content* to do after thyr desyre' (51/16–18).

Despite R's habit of close translation and his tendency to omit and compress the French, he sometimes expands or adds to his original. These additions are seldom long, nor are they major reworkings of the French text. Instead, R will occasionally expand generalized adverbs or add introductory phrases to his translation: for example, 'in this derk prouince' (fol 151r) for Fr 'là,' or 'to departe fro the bataill or sege' (fol 204r) for Fr 'de partir.' Occasionally R includes apparently gratuitous repetition like 'into sundrie garisons and places of his landes' (fol 162v) for Fr 'par ses terres.' But often the use of this type of repetition has a functional value in emphasizing and clarifying what is said: for example, 'They drynke no wyne, howbeit they may drynke wyne' (fol 146r) for Fr 'vin n'ont point';

'to euery dizaine, which was x men' (fol 166v) for Fr 'à chaque dizaine'; 'I leve it to the wise capitayne which shall entreprise this werkes' (fol 220v) for Fr 'je lais à dire ores'; or the addition of 'that is to say, at the said tyme of compilyng of this booke' (fol 182v).

CONCLUSIONS

R follows what appears to have been a common view of the time, that the best English translation is that which tries to imitate the style of the French. Samuel K. Workman, speaking of fifteenth-century translators, points out that 'Though there apparently was no literary standard to compel them, the prevailing practice among these men was to adhere to the original as closely as their English would naturally permit ... At least eighty percent of the translated books were composed in this way.'[25] For R this imitation consisted in trying whenever possible to approximate the French syntax and vocabulary in his English. His generally wider knowledge of French allowed him to translate word for word or phrase for phrase. But whenever possible he also tried to give an English word that sounded like, or had the same root as, the French (even at the risk of using unidiomatic or erroneous English expressions). What is interesting is that R is seldom forced to resort to frequent borrowings from the French, as translators before him so often were. A close translator like R, with a marked preference for French vocabulary and construction, apparently now had an adequate stock of borrowed words that had become part of regular English usage.

While R clearly tries to transfer the French prose style into English by means of close translation, P's technique is quite different. P proceeds by larger units, aiming more at giving the general sense of the French in his translation. As we have seen, this leads him into more syntactical errors and a less close imitation of the French diction and syntax. P is more often at pains to make the meaning of the French comprehensible to the average English reader, and thus expands and reorganizes for sense when translating. P also tends to use more idiomatic English constructions, although his looser method of translation leads him more often than R into anacolutha and omitted subjects, verbs, etc. Sometimes these errors were caused by the peculiarities of Hetoum's French, but more often they are the result of P's looser style of translation leading him to write in his own native style. Here he is particularly interesting. For what P seems to have considered good prose, that is, what he chooses to add to or emphasize in Hetoum, is the *style curial*. P enjoys writing in an asymmetrical, hypotactic style, using the profusion of doublets, subordinate construction, and other padding typical of the *style curial*. He does this, not only for emphasis and explanation, but also, it would appear, as an inherent habit of thought. If P is occasionally difficult for the modern reader to follow, so is his French model and so is the *style curial* generally. But for the most part his prose is readily comprehensible and he can handle long trains of thought. In this P would appear to be illustrating that 'sign of maturity in composition, the ability to plan and control structure by broad units,' which, according to Workman, 'is one of the principal differences between early sixteenth century [English] writers and those of a hundred years before.'[26] If P is more willing to depart from the French immediately before him, it is very often in order to make his prose resemble more closely a style of writing itself borrowed by means of earlier translations from the French.

NOTES

1 'In France, writers had been composing in prose since the thirteenth century, among them chroniclers like Villehardouin and Joinville. They had used a simple, unadorned style, which said exactly what the writers wanted it to say, because in their chronicles events were more important than stylistic elaboration. This earlier chronicle style, with its impersonal vocabulary and simple unvaried sentence form, is still found at many points in the romances of the fifteenth century when presenting a continuous sequence of events. However fifteenth-century taste no longer valued simplicity, and it was natural that narrative prose should adopt an existing, fully elaborated prose style as its definitive model ... this was the curial style.' Jens Rasmussen, *La Prose narrative française du XVe siècle: Etude esthètique et stylistique* (Copenhagen 1958) 32. Cf Samuel K. Workman *Fifteenth Century Translation as an Influence on English Prose* (Princeton 1940; rpt New York 1972) 65.
2 Diane Bornstein 'French Influence on Fifteenth-Century English Prose as Exemplified by the Translation of Christine de Pisan's *Livre du corps de policie' Medieval Studies* 39 (1977) 371
3 Cf P 63/16 (R fol 203v).
4 Cf P 65/3–10 (R fol 206v).
5 Omitted by some Fr mss and probably absent in the exemplars used by P and R
6 Cf P 68/11–2 (R fol 209v), P 65/6–8 (R fol 206v).
7 Cf P 73/35–7 (R fol 215v), P 74/21 (R fol 216v), P 74/34 (R fol 216v), P 75/15 (R fol 217r).

8 Cf P 65/4,5,8,9,21, 66/1 (R fol 206r–v).

9 Cf P 20/30–8 (R fol 157r).

10 Cf P 8/29–35 (R fol 145v).

11 Cf P 73/38–74/7 (R fol 215v–216r).

12 Cf P 10/20–3, 17/2–5, 56/29–30, 67/3–4.

13 Cf also P 25/19–20, 42/28–9, 43/24–5.

14 'And the Cathaines say that thyse be they that seen with ii eyn, and the Latynes see but with oon eye. The *other nacions say* that thise ben auugelles' (R fol 145r–v) for Fr 'E dient les Catains que il sont ceus qui voient de II oils, e des Latins disent qu'il voient d'un oil, mès *les autres nacions dient* que sont aveugles.' Cf P 7/21–6.

15 'Whan the kyng is crowned, a lorde beryth *to that kyng rubyes* in his hand' (R fol 148v) for Fr 'quant le seignor doit estre coronés *au roi*, il porte cele rubie en ses braz'; and 'the chieuetains afore said assembled the people of the Tartars, and made theim to do obeysaunce and reuerence vnto Cangius, *and that thei shulde make hym their natural lorde*' (R fol 165v) for Fr 'le vii chevetaines desus nomées assemblerent le pueple des Tartars, e firent faire obedience e reverence à Cangius, *e eaus firent ce meismes, come à leur naturel seignor.*'

16 'He knew *not* the way were he went, and so rode after' (R fol 187r) for Fr 'La voie sout don il aloit e chevaucha après lui.'

17 'Shuld be to the Soldan a thing perillous and damageous: *perillous,* for treason of his people; *damageous and annoyous,* for by the enuasions of Cristen men thei myght be so troubled that thei shuld haue no power to auaunce theimself; *also damageous,* for he shulde consume and waste all his treasoure' (R fol 221v) for Fr 'seroit au soudan ennuieuse et dommageuse e perillouse [*var* perilleuse chose, ennuyeuse et dommaigeuse] pour la trahison de sa gent ennuieuse. Car par les envassemens des Crestiens poroit estre si troblés que ilz n'aroit repos si non damagiouse, car il consumeroit et gasteroit tout son tresor.'

18 Cf P 7/14 (R fol 144v), P 46/6 (R fol 185r), P 60/7 (R fol 200r).

19 However, some are probably the result of paleographic confusion (eg, 'anthetinoyson,' P 16/1, for Fr 'en chetivoison'; 'Kyng of Anyne,' P 41/3, 47/15–6, 55/28, for Fr 'roiaume'; and 'they be vp,' P 64/33, for Fr 'mentent') or compositorial error (eg, 'the habitauntes,' P 72/28, for Fr 'habitans').

20 Eg, 'a grounde' (R fol 187r) for Fr 'un tertre,' 'priorie' (R fol 191v) for Fr 'praeries,' 'strong people' (R fol 209r) for Fr 'gens forestiers,' 'arriuage' (R fol 225v) for Fr 'la rive'

21 A general survey of the two translations shows R choosing this kind of French-rooted vocabulary four times as often as P. Some examples of this tendency:

Fr	R	P
despences	dispence (fol 206v)	all the cost and furnyssh (65/7)
navie	nauys (fol 213v)	shippes (72/16)
conduis	conducttes (fol 214r)	dykes (72/23)
travail	trauaile (fol 217r)	payne (75/9)
semblant	semblant (fol 227v)	maner (84/37)
porveance	purviaunce (fol 228r)	commaundment (85/13)
abatirent	abated (fol 214v)	brake downe (73/10–1)
sourdre	sourde (fol 227r)	come (84/20)
aornez	anourned (fol 200v)	full (60/34)

22 For example, 'slayne' (P 43/14) for Fr 'furent mors,' 'obedyent' (P 76/23) for Fr 'sont obeissans'; and Fr 'demoere' omitted before 'his lyfe' (P 77/3), Fr 'seroit' omitted before 'great aduersytes' (P 77/21), Fr 'les feroient' omitted before 'shulde come' (P 84/4–5)

23 Eg, the omission of 'rubie' from Fr 'le roi de cele isle ha la plus grant rubie e la meillor [var le plus riche et le plus grant] que soit en tout le monde' produces 'the kyng of that land is the gretest kyng and the mooste riche kyng of all the worlde' (R fol 148v).

24 Cf R fols 180v (P 43/16–8), 182r (P 36/5–6), 189r (P 50/29–32), 190r (P 51/5–9).

25 *Fifteenth Century Translation* 163

26 Ibid 161

4

Editorial Procedure

Compositorial abbreviations have been accepted and expanded without notice. Word-division, punctuation, capitalization, and paragraphing follow modern usage. Obvious compositorial errors and omissions (eg, transposed single letters or end-line omissions) have been silently emended, with the original readings noted in the list of textual variants printed after the text. Editorial emendations necessary to clarify the sense of the English translation are put within square brackets, and the original English and French readings noted amongst the list of textual variants. A second set of notes on English/French variants elucidates obscurities in Pynson's translation or records significant omissions from the original French. Whenever possible, English translations in this second set of notes are taken from the Royal manuscript (indicated by an 'R' in parenthesis); otherwise they are my own.

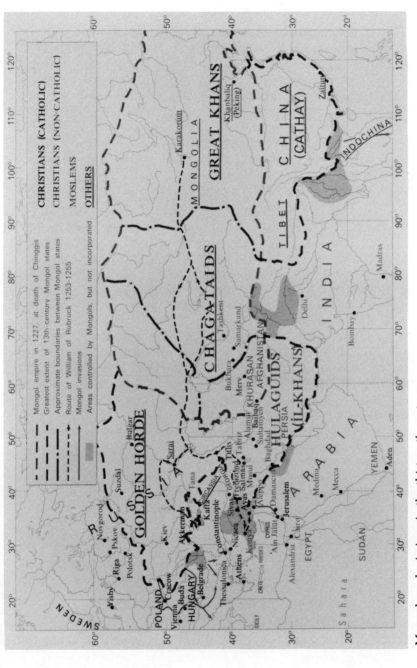

CHRISTIANS (CATHOLIC)

CHRISTIANS (NON-CATHOLIC)

MOSLEMS

OTHERS

Mongol empire in 1227, at death of Chinggis

Greatest extent of 13th-century Mongol states

Approximate boundaries between Mongol states

Route of William of Rubruck 1253-1255

Mongol invasions

Areas controlled by Mongols, but not incorporated

GOLDEN HORDE

CHAGA-TAIDS

GREAT KHANS

HULAGUIDS (IL-KHANS)

MONGOLIA

TIBET

CHINA (CATHAY)

INDIA

INDOCHINA

ARABIA

AFGHANISTAN

PERSIA

KHURASAN

POLAND

HUNGARY

SWEDEN

EGYPT

SUDAN

YEMEN

Sahara

Karakorum

Khanbaliq (Peking)

Zaitun

Madras

Bombay

Delhi

Samarkand

Tashkent

Bukhara

Merv

Alamut

Baihaq

Sultaniyeh

Tabriz

Baghdad

Tiflis

Trebizond

Mosul

Damascus

Aleppo

Abu Salmas

Ayas

Jerusalem

'Ain Jalut

Cairo

Alexandria

Medina

Mecca

Aden

Konya

Nicaea

CYPRUS

CRETE

Athens

Thessalonica

Constantinople

Sivas

Kars

Ani

Georgia

Circassia

Kaffa

Tana

Akkerman

Kiev

Sarai

Bulgar

Suzdal

Novgorod

Pskov

Polotsk

Riga

Visby

Belgrade

Budai

Crakow

Vienna

RHODES

SICILY

Mongols and missions in the thirteenth century

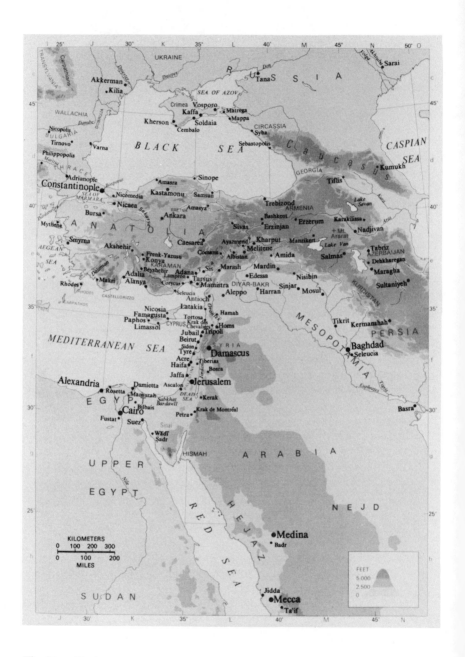

The Near East

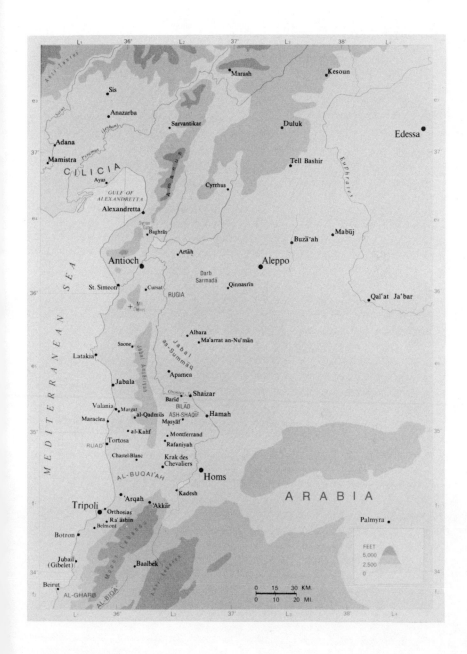

Northern Syria

Palestine

The colophon of Richard Pynson's translation of *A Lytell Cronycle* C 1520.
By permission of the Newberry Library, Chicago

A LYTELL CRONYCLE

Here begynneth a lytell Cronycle, translated and imprinted at the cost and charge of Rycharde Pynson, by the commaundement of the ryght high and mighty prince, Edwarde Duke of 5 Buckingham, therle of Hereforde, Staffarde, and of Northamton.

[A1v] This present boke is dyuided in foure partes. The first parte speketh of the lande of Asie, the which is the thyrde part of the worlde; and in the same first part is diuised and treated how many
10 realmes be in the same part of Asie, how the realme marcheth and abordreth to the other, and fynally what maner of people inhabyt the same realmes. The seconde part of this boke speketh of themperours and kynges which hath ben in the lande of Asie sythe the incarnation of Our Lorde Ihesu Christe, and of their actes and dedes in their tymes;
15 moreouer, how they conquered their lordshippes, how longe tyme ech one of them was lorde and gouernour. And we shall folowe the discripcyon hereof as it is founde in histories of dyuers nacyons of the orient or eest part of the worlde wrytten in dyuers letters and langages. The thyrde part treateth of the hystories of the Tartaryans:
20 how their name began and how they conquered those landes which thei holde nowe in possessyon, into how many partes their lordshyp is dyuided, and who is lorde and ruler of that part of ther lande which is moost nere vnto the Holy Lande. The fourth parte of this boke speketh of the passage into the Holy Lande beyonde the see: how
25 thei whiche shall make suche passage ought to demeane and behaue themselfe from the begynnyng tyll ende to conquere the said Holy Lande. Which processe is written after the ordring of the symple knowlege and vnderstanding of the compyler of the boke.

Here haue we deuysed a table briffely conteyning all the tytles of the
30 sayd boke, wherby ye may lightly fynde by the folio the thyng that ye wolde rede.

4 A Lytell Cronycle

[BOOK ONE]

[BOOK TWO]

[BOOK THREE]

5 A Table

[BOOK FOUR]

6 A Lytell Cronycle

[BOOK ONE]

[The realm of Cathay]

[A3r] The realm of Cathay is counted and holden for the moost noble
and rich realm of the worlde. This realme marcheth on the cost of
the occean see; so many yles be there about in the see that men may
5 nat well knowe the nombre of them. The people which inhabet this
realme of Cathay be called Cathayns, and amonge theym be founde
many fayre and comely men and women after theyr nacion, but all
haue theyr eyen very smale and lytell heer on their berdes. This
people in theyr wrytynge haue letters which in beauty and fayr-
10 nesse of draught resemble and are moche lyke vnto Latten letters,
and they speke a language which is moche dyuers from other
languages of the worlde. The beleue of this people is moche dyuers:
for some beleuyth in the sonne, some in the mone, some in the
sterres, some in naturs of thinges, some in the fyre, some in the
15 water, some in the trees, and some beleue in oxen bycause they
labour the grounde wherupon this people haue theyr lyuely susten-
aunce; and some people of this realme haue no lawe nor beleue at
all, but lyue as brute beestes vnresonable. These same people, whiche
are this symple in theyr beleue and in thynges spyritual, ar more
20 subtyll than all other people in corporall or bodely werkes and
busynes. And, as the Cathayns say, these people be they which
seyth with bothe eyen, bycause of their subtyll insyght in bodyly
werkes. And they say the Lattyns seeth but of one eye, as theym
reputynge lesse ingenious and lesse inuentyfe. But the other nacions
25 say that these Cathayns are but blynde, as in reprouynge theyr
subtylyte. By this may we vnderstande that these Cathayns repute

other people of grosse wyt and vnderstandynge and themselfe
onely ingenyous. And for very treuth, out of this realm of Cathay are
brought many strange and meruelous thynges of subtyll labour
and art ingenyous, wherby this peple well seme to be the moste
5 subtell and inuentife of the worlde in arte and laboure of handes.
The men of this countrey ar no stronge warryours nor valyant in
armes, but they be moche subtyll and ingenyous; by mean wherof,
often tymes they haue disconfyted and ouercome their ennymes by
their engyns, and they haue dyuers sortes and maners of armours
10 and engyns of warre whiche other nacions haue not. In the same
lande is money currant for comen and vniuersall dyspences; which
money is made of papir in form quadrate or fouresquared, sygned or
imprynted with diuers sygnettes of the lorde of the same lande.
And the same coygne is of valour, more or lesse, after as it is signed
15 with diuers impressyons. With this same money [A3v] there they
by and sell all thynges concerninge theyr exchaunges. And whan
this same money is impered or worne by oldnesse or otherwyse, he
which hath the same in possession shall render it vp in the court of
the lorde of that lande, and for the same shal receyue new of equall
20 valoure. In this same lande the oyle of olyffe is in grete scarcyte and
holden at very dere pryce, and whan the kynges and lordes may
fynde of the same they cause it to be kept as a grete dere thynge and
for medycine. Vnto this lande of Cathay marcheth or bordreth
none other lande, saue onely the realme of Tharsay on the occident
25 or west part, where it adioyneth nerest; on all other partes this
realme of Cathay is inuyroned or compased aboute other with desert
or with occean see.

Of the realme of Tharsey

In this realme of Tarsey be thre prouynces or countreys, and the
30 lordes of the same do themselfe to be called kinges; they all haue
one lyke letter and language semblable. The people of these coun-
trees be named Iobgontans, and all tymes they haue ben idolatrers,
and so they contynue to this present day, saue the nacion or kynred
of those thre kynges which came to worshyp Our Lorde Ihesu
35 Chryst at his natiuyte by demonstracyon of the sterre. And the linage
of the same thre kinges be yet vnto this day great lordes about the
lande of Tartary, which ferme and stedfastly beleue in the fayth of

Christ. The people of this lande of Tharsay trauayle nor labour not
in feat of armes, but they be of subtyll vnderstandynge and moche
ingenious to lerne artes and sciences. All the moost part of this
people eteth no flesshe, nor drynketh no wyne, nor kylleth nothynge
5 which bereth lyfe. They haue good cytees and ryche, with very
great temples wherin they holde their ydols, whom thei haue in great
reuerence. In this same lande groweth plenty of corne and of other
sedys ynough; but wyne haue they none, but counte it great synne to
drynke wyne. This same realme of Tharsay marcheth towarde to
10 orient or est vpon the realm of Cathay before sayd; and towarde the
occedent or west it marcheth to a realm named Turquestan; toward
the north it marcheth on a desert; towarde the south it marcheth on a
prouynce which is called the lande of Sune, which is betwen the
lande of Cathay and the realme of Inde – in this same lande be founde
15 the fyne dyamantes.

Of the lande of Turquestan

The realme of Turquestan marchith on the est parte to the realme of
Tharsey; on the west parte to the realme of [A3r] Persy; towarde
the north it bordreth on the realme of Corasme; and on the southe
20 part it extendeth towarde one heed of the wyldernes of Inde. In
this realme be fewe good cytees, but in it be many grete playns and
large feldes of plentyfull and good pasture. Wherfore this people
be al for the moost part pastours or heerdmen, and thei be loged in
tentes and other such houses which they may lightlye cary from
25 place to place. The heed cyte of this realme is named Hoctecar. In
this lande groweth ryght lytell whete or barly; the peple eteth and
fede for the moost part on mystlyn and rysse; wyne haue they none,
but they drynke alys and other maner of drinkes. The people of the
same lande be named Turkes, and all they for the moost parte
30 beleue in the fals doctryne of the law of Machumit, and some be
among them which haue nother lawe, fayth, nor beleue. They haue
no letters proper vnto theyr langage, but vse the leters of Arrabyans
by their cytes and townes where lettred men frequent.

Of the realme of Corasme

35 The realme of Corasme is wel garnisshed with cytis and townes, and
the lande well furnysshed and stored with people. There groweth

corne sufficyent, but wyne haue they lytell or none. This same realme
of Corasme marcheth towarde the est towarde a parte of the desert
contaynynge largely a hundreth dayes iournay in length; towarde
the west it extendeth vnto the see called in Latten, Mare Chaspium
5 (Englysshed, the see of Caspy); towarde the north it marcheth on the
realme of Commanye; towarde the southe it marcheth on the realme
of Turquestan. The heed cyte of this realme is named Corasme; the
people of the lande be called Corasmyns. All be panyms, and haue
nother lawe nor letters proper vnto theymselfe, but beleue as Grekes
10 and ar vnder obedience of the patriarke of Antyoch. In theyr churches
their syngynge and seruyce is moche dyuers: they celebrate and
consecrate as Grekes, but theyr language is not Greke.

Of the realme of Comanye

The realme of Comany is on of the gretyst realmes of the worlde. This
15 lande is yll inhabited for great distemperaunce of the ayre of the
same lande. For some partes of the same be so colde that nother man
nor best may lyue in the same for excessyue coldnes, and some
other partes and countreys be in the same lande which be so hote in
somer that no man may endure there for grete hete and for flyes
20 which there abounde. This lande of Comani is all playn; but no tree
there groweth wherof men may make tymber, nor no busshe there
groeth, saue in some certayn [A4v] places where the inhabytauns
haue planted some trees for to make gardens and orchyards. A
great part of the people dwelleth in tentes, and theyr chefe fuell for
25 fyre is beestes donge dryed. This lande of Comany on the est part
marcheth on the realme of Corasme, and in parte of the same syde on
a great desert; towarde the west it marcheth to the Grete See, and
to the see called the see of Reme; towarde the northe it marcheth to
the realme of Roussy; and on the southe part it extendeth vnto the
30 grettest flodde which men knowe in the worlde, which is called the
flode of Etyll. This flode freseth euery yere, and somtyme dureth
frosen all the hole yere in suche maner that men, women, and beestes
passe ouer the same as vpon stedfaste lande. On bordes or bankes
of the same flode groweth some smale trees. But on the other part of
35 this flode, towarde the west and towarde the southe, dwell dyuers
nacyons of pepyll which count not themselfe of the realme of Comanie
and be not obedient to the Kynge of Comanye; this nacions inhabet

about the mountain of Cocas, which mountayn is very great and hye. On this same mountayn be bred many gret byrdes of diuers kynde, and all be white of coloure. This mounntayn of Cocas is betwene ii sees, that is to say, the Gret See which is on the west parte of the
5 same, and the see of Caspys which is on the est part of the same. This see of Caspys hath but onely one entry towarde the occean see; all the reminaunt within is but lyke a lake or standynge water; but for gretnes of the same it is called a see or mere, for it is the grettest lake and largest of the worlde. This lake or mere of Caspys extendeth
10 forthe itselfe from the mountayn of Cocas vnto the heed or begyninge of the realm of Persy, and it departeth in sonder all the countray of Asye; and that same parte which is on the est parte of this lake is called Asya the Lesse or Lower Asya, but that part which is on the west syde is called Asya the Greter. The water of this mere is nat salt
15 but fresshe and swete, and in the same is great aboundance of diuers fysshe. Also in this same lande of Comanie are founde wylde oxen. And in the foresayd mere of Caspys be diuers yles in which byrdes of sondry kynde make theyr nestes, and namely fawkons and marlyons of suche shape and quantyte that none lyke may be founde
20 anywhere els saue in the same yles. The chefe cyte of the realme of Comanye is named Sartay, which was in aunsyant tyme a ryght good and ryche cyte, but at this tyme it is wel nere all wasted and dystroyed by the Tartaryans.

Of the realme of Inde

25 The realm of Inde is a verye longe lande, and bordreth alonge vpon the occean see [A5r] (which see is called in those countreis the see of Inde). This realm of Inde begineth at the boundes of the lande of Persy, and so extendeth forth to a prouince or lande named Balazam – in these countreis be founde precyous stones which be called balayses.
30 Towarde the north parte by the long and great desert of Inde, where Kynge Alexandre founde so great dyuersite of serpentes and of beestes as his hystorie recounteth, there be founde namely all the balayses. In the same lande of Inde, Saynt Thomas the Apostle preched the fayth of Christ and conuerted many prouinces and
35 countreis of the same to the Christen fayth. Neuerthelesse, for that the same countreis and peple be ferre distant from other landes where the fayth of Christ is worshipped, right fewe be in the same

lande which maynten the fayth of Christ; for there is but one cytie alone where Christen men inhabit, and all the other ar become ydolaters. Towarde the south part of this realme of Inde is thoccean see; and there about be many yles wherin Indyans or men of Inde
5 inhabet, which be all blacke, and all go naked bycause of great heate, and all these worshippe ydols. In these yles be founde precyous stones; also in them groeth right good spices. There is also one yle preeminent aboue the other (which yle is named Celan) wherin be founde the best rubyes and saffirs of the worlde. The kyng of the
10 same yle hath the moost riche ruby and grettest which is in the worlde, and whan the kynge of the same yle is crowned, he bereth the said rubye in his hande for excellence and royaltie. This kyngdome of Inde is also in maner of an yle; for on the one part it is enuyroned or set aboute with the occean see, by which partie the
15 entryng into the same land is nat easy, saue onely on the syde of the lande of Persey. Wherfore suche as wyll entre into this land of Inde resorteth fyrst of all vnto a cytie named Hermeis, the which cyte the famous phylosopher Hermeys made by his grete arte (as it is written) and called it by his owne name. From this cytie of Hermeys
20 thei passe by a streit passage of the see vnto a cytie which is called Courbaeth. In this cytie and in the countrey about ar found the strange byrdes called popyngays, and as great plenty of the same byrdes is in that countrey as of sparois in these parties. In the same lande fyndeth marchauntes all maner of marchaundises. Lytell whete and barley
25 groweth in this lande, but the peple of the same eteth rysse, mystlyne, mylke, butter, dates, and other maner of fruytes wherof thei haue great plenty.

Of the realme of Persey

The realme of Persey is diuyded in ii parties; howbeit it is all but
30 one realme, for one lorde hath alway had gouernaunce [A5v] of the same. The first part of this realme of Persy is extended by the west part vnto a fludde named Physon, which is one of the foure fluddes floynge forth of Paredise Terrestre; towarde the north it extendeth vnto the see of Caspis; towarde the south it stretcheth forth itselfe
35 vnto the see of Inde. This lande of Persy is also in maner all playne. And in the same be ii great and riche cyties; of whom the one is named Borraca, and the other, Semorgraunt. The people of this

countrey be called Persyens, and thei haue a langage proper which
they speke. They lyue moost on marchaundyses and tyllyng of the
grounde; armour nor warre they meddyll nat gladly, at this tyme
vnconstrayned. In auncyent tyme they worshipped ydols, but namely
5 thei honoured the fyre for theyr god; but sith tyme that the wicked
and false sect of Mahomet spredynge abrode came into those parties,
the Persyens haue all ben Sarasyns and beleue in the false lawe of
Mahumet. The other part of Persey begynneth at the fludde of
Physon, and extendeth on the weest syde vnto the realme of Mede
10 and of Armeny the Great; towarde the south it marcheth at one
prouince of the realme of Inde, and in some part at the occean see,
and other part at the lande of Mede. In the same party of Persey be
also two great cyties: the one is named Nezabor; the other, Spahan.
And the maner and custome of the people of this part of Persey is
15 semblable to them of the other part afore named.

Of the realme of Mede

The realme of Mede is very longe towarde the eest, but it is nat large.
Towarde the eest it beginneth at the realme of Persy, and at the
realme of Inde the Lesser in part of the same; and it extendeth forth
20 by the weest part vnto the realme of Calde; towarde the north it
begynneth at the realme of Armeny; and extendeth forth by the south
vnto the Aquissan (which is on the occean see), and there be
founde the grettest and fayrest perlys. In the realm of Mede be great
mountayns and lytell playn grounde. In the realme of Mede be ii
25 maner of people: the one is called Sarasyns, and the other, Cordyns.
And in this countrey ben ii gret cyties: the one is called Sarras, and
the other, Querem. And there they kepe the lawe of Mahumet and
vse of Arabyke letters. Afote they be good archers.

Of the realme of Armeny

30 In the realme of Armeny ben iiii realmes, of the which one lorde
holdeth all the lordship. The length of the lande of Armeny begynneth
at the realme of Persy, and extendeth forth by occident to the realme
of Turkey. The brede of Armeny towarde occident begynneth at the
great cytie [A6r] which is called Port de Ferre, that is in Englysshe the

Yren Gate – the which Kinge Alexander commaunded shulde be
shytte for bycause of dyuers nations of people that resorted into
the Depe Asye, the which he wolde nat that they shulde passe in the
Great Asye without his commaundement. The sayd cytie is in the
5 narow of Caspis See, and recheth to the great mountayn of Cocas.
The brede of the realme of Armeny from the sayd cytie extendeth
forth to the realme of Mede. In the realm of Armeny be dyuers gret
cyties and riche, amonge the which Towres is the moost named in the
lande of Armeny. In Armeny be great mountayns and brode playnes,
10 great waters and fluddes – salte and swete, with great plenty of
fysshe. The peple that inhabit in the lande of Armeny be named by
diuerse names after the maner of the countrei that thei be inhabited;
and there they be good men of warre both afote and a horsbacke,
and as for harnes and vestment, they folowe the maner of the Tartas
15 bycause that they haue ben long vnder their lorde. There letters
be dyuers; and some be named Armonoses, and the other, Alcen.
In Armeny is a great mountayn, the which is the grettest, and that
mountayn is named Ararach; and ther was set the arcke of Noe after
the Deluge. But yet there can no man clyme vpon that mountayn for
20 the great noyse and murmure that is there, bothe wynter and somer;
but in the very toppe of it appereth a great blacke thinge, which they
say that is the arcke of Noe.

Of the realme of Georgie

The realme of Georgie towarde thorient hath a gret mountayn, which
25 is named Abbers and is inhabited with many diuers nations of peple,
and for that cause it is named the countrey Alayne. And from thens
extendeth the realm of Georgy by thoccydent towarde septentrion to
the prouince of the realme of Turky. The length of the realme of
Georgie extendeth all vpon the see towarde the south, and finys-
30 shed with the Great Armeni. This realm of Georgi is deuydyd in two
realmes: the one is named Georgie, and the other, Abcas. The realm
of Georgy is vnder the iurisdiction and subiection of themperour
of Asye; the realm of Abcas is mighty of peple and of strong castels
and was neuer subget to themperour of Asie nor to the Tartas. In
35 the realme of Georgi appered a gret meruayle, which I darre nat tell
nor reherse yf I hadde nat sene it. But for bycause I was there and
se, I dare say that in Georgi is a prouynce which is called Haynsen,

the which is well of iii dayes iourney of length or there about; and
as long as this sayd prouynce lasteth, in euery place is so great ob-
scurite that no man is so hardi to come into the sayd lande, for they
can nat cum out agayn. And the dwellers within the same lande sayde
5 that [A6v] often tymes there cometh noyse of men, cockes crowyng,
and horses neynge; and by a fludde that cometh out of that place
come tokens appering that there is resorting of peple. Verily they
fynde in thistores of Armeny redyng, and Georgi, that there was a
cruell emperour in Persy named Sauorelx. This emperour wor-
10 shypped the ydols, and cruelly persecuted the Cristen men. Vpon a
day he commaunded that all they that dwelled in Asye shulde
come to do sacrifice to the ydols, and that they that wold nat come
shulde be put to deth. Among the which it happened that some
true Cristen men receyued the martyrdom or thei wolde sacrifice the
15 ydols, some sacrified for fere of deth and for fere of losyng of thir
temporall goodes, and the other fledde away into the mountayns. In
that tyme inhabyted dyuers good Cristen men in a countrey which
is called Morgan; which Cristen men forsoke their goodes and flede
away towarde Grece. And whan thei were in that contrey aboue
20 sayd, the sayd cruell Emperour met with them, and commaunded that
all the sayd Cristen men shulde be cut all to peces. And than the
sayd Cristen men made a gret cry to Our Lorde God, and sone after
came this great darknes that blinded themperour and all his men;
and so the Cristen men scaped, and the sayd Emperour with his men
25 taryd in the sayd darknes. And there thei shall abyde, as they
beleue, to the worldes ende.

Of the realme of Caldee

The realme of Caldees towarde thorient begynneth at the mountayns
of Mede and extendeth to the great Ninyue, the olde cytie which is
30 nygh to the fludde of Tygres. This Ninyue is the cytie of the which
the Holy Scripture speketh and in the which was Ionas the Profet
sende to prech the commaundement of God; this cytie is nowe all
wasted, but for cause that it is yet well apparaunt it is sene that it is
one of the moste grettest cyties of all the worlde. The brede of the
35 realme of Calde towarde septentrion begynneth at a cytie that is
called Maraga, and extendeth to the south to thoccean see. The
grettest cyte in the realme of Calde is called Babylone. In this lande

Nagabudonosor brought anthetinoyson the Chyldren of Israell whan
he toke Iherusalem. In the realme of Calde be great playnes and
fewe mountayns and not moch ronning waters. The people that is
inhabyted in Calde be called Nestoryns, and vsed of Arabe letters,
5 and kepe the false lawe of Mahomet.

The realme of Mesopotamy

The realme of Mesopotamy toward orient beginneth at the gret cytie
Mosell, that is nigh to the flude of Tigres, and extendeth by thoccydent to the cyte of Rohais, which is set vpon the flud named
10 Eufrates. This cytie of Rohays was Kyng Agers, to whom Our Lord
sende the vernicle that is now at Rome. And [B1r] nygh to this cytye
is the lande of Baram, in the which dwelled Abraham and his
kynred in the olde tyme, whan Our Lorde commaunded hym that he
sholde leue this lande and passe the flode of Eufrates and come to
15 the Lande of Promysson that is the Holy Lande, as is contayned in
the Bible. This is called Grioise and the land of Mesopotamy for
cause that it is betwene the two great flodes Tygris and Eufrates. The
brede of the realme begynneth at a mountayn which is called San-
son in Armenie, and extendeth by mydday to the desert of Arabe the
20 Leste. In this lande of Mesopotamy be great playnes aboundant
and delectable, and great mountayns with great plenty of fruytes and
of goodes – one of the mountaynes is called Symare, and the other,
Lysson. In the sayd realme is nat moche ronnynge water, but the
peple of this countrey drynketh well water out of cesterns. In this
25 realm of Mesopotamy inhabet Christen men; some be Siryens, some
Armyns, and the other, Sarasyns. The Syrians and the Sarasyns of
the sayd countrey medyll with no dede of armes, but they be shepar-
des and labourers of the grounde for the moste part; except some
that dwelled in a countrey that is called Meredyn, the which be good
30 archers, and they ben called Cordyns.

The realme of Turky

The realme of Turkey is moche riche: and there be mynes of syluer,
brasse, and other good ynough; and also there is plenty of whete,
wynes, and fruytes; and also there is moche catell and good horses.

This lande endeth by the Gret Armeny towarde the orient, and
with the realme of Georgy towarde the occydent; and extendeth to
the cyte of Satalie (which is vpon the see of Grece) towarde septentrion; and hath no endes with any other lande, and extendeth of
5 length in length vpon the see syde; and towarde midday endeth
part with the Seconde Armeny and with Sylice, and part extendeth to
the see of Grece and to the syght of the yle of Cipres. And the sayd
realme of Turkey is called Grece of all the peple of the Orient for
cause that in the olde tyme themperour of Grece kept that lande as
10 his owne, and ruled all the lande by officers that he sende thyder
euery yere. And after that the Turkes toke the sayd lordship of
Turky, they ordayned a lorde amonge them, the which they called
theyr sowdan; and from that tyme the Turkes inhabyted in the
sayd lande, and than it was named Turky. And there be many good
15 cities: the fyrst prouince is called Helcone, that is the noblest cyte
of Elconye; the ii is named Capadoce, that is the cyte of the great
Cesar of Grece; the thryde prouince is called Saury, and there is
the cyte of Salern; the iiii is called Briquie, and there is the cyte of
Lichoe of Grece; the v is called Quisiton, and there is the cyte of
20 Effeson; the vi is called [B1v] Depictrony, and there is the cyte of
Niquie; the vii is called Pascagonie, and there is the cite of Germana-
polis; the viii is called Genesti, and there is the cyte of Trapesonde.
And this onely prouynce is made a realme within fewe yeres. For
whan the Turkes toke the lordship of Turky they could nat take
25 the cite of Trapesonde, nor no place longyng therto, bycause there
were so many strong castels, and so it remayned to themperour of
Constantinoble. And the sayd Emperour had a custome to send a
bayly that was called duke to gouerne the sayd lande. And it
fortuned so that one of the dukes rebelled agaynst themperour and
30 toke the lordship of Trapesonde for hymselfe, and made hymselfe
to be called emperour. All they that dwell in the sayd land be Grekes.
We put Trapesonde in the nombre of the prouinces and nat in the
nombre of the realmes, after as we fynde in the histores of the Orient.
In the realme of Turky inhabet iiii maner of people; that is to say,
35 Grekes, Armyns, Iacobins, and Turkes (which ben Sarasyns, and
they haue taken the lordship of the sayd lande of the Grekes). Thei
that be dwellers in the cites ocupied marchandise and labouryng the
ground; and the other, sheperdes that dwelled in the feldes in
tentes, winter and somer, and fed their beestes – and also they be
40 good men of armes afote and a horsbacke.

The realme of Syrie

The realme of Syrye towarde the est begynneth at the flode of Eufrates,
and extendeth by occident to the cyte of Gasere, which is toward the
see of Grece to the heed of the desert of Egypt. The brede of the realme
5 of Syrie towarde septentrion begynneth at the cyte of Baruth, and
extendeth to the Cricke of Mount Royall. Towarde the eest it endeth
at the realme of Mesopotamy; towarde septentrion with the Seconde
Armenye and part with the realme of Turky; towarde mydday, endeth
at the see of Grece and at the desert of Araby. The realme of Siry is
10 depar[t]ed in iiii prouinces that in the olde tyme were realmes, and
in eueri one of them was a king. The first prouince is called Sein; the
ii, Palestin, and in that is the cyte of Heirusalem; the iii is called
Antioquie, and there be ii gret cytes Halap and Antioch; the iiii is
called Silyce, and there is the cytie of Tarsot in the which was
15 borne the Apostle Saynt Paule. The sayd Silyce is now called Armeny; for, syth that the enemis of the Cristen fayth had taken this
lande from the Grekes handes, the Armins traueyled so moche that
thei recoverd the realme of Silyce, and now the Kyng of Armeny
holdeth it by the grace of God. In the realm of Siri inhabet diuers
20 peple: Grekes, Armins, Iacobyns, Nestorins, Sarasins, and two
other nations that is Syrisins and Maroins. The Cristen men holdeth
the maner of Greioyse, for in the olde tyme they were obedient to
the Church of Rome; they speke language Arabyke; the seruyce and
the office of the [B2r] Church is made in letters Greioises. The
25 Maronyns holde the maner of Iacobyns, and haue a langage and
letters Arabyke; and this peple inhabyted about the Mount Lyban
and towardes the partes of Iherusalem, and they be good men of
armes. Of the Siriens be men inow, but of the Maroyns be but
fewe, and amonge them there be valyant men. The realme of Siry is xx
30 dayes iourney of length and fyue in bredthe, and in some places
lesse, after as the desert of Arabyk and the see cometh more or lesse.

[BOOK TWO]

Sythe that we haue spoken of the xiiii pryncipall
realmes that be in Asye, we shall speke after of the em-
perours of Asye – the which hath holden the lordship
of Asye after the byrthe of Our Lorde Ihesu Chryst – after
5 the rehersynge of the hystores of the Oryent.

How the Kynge of Persy was fyrst Emperour of Asye

As Saynt Luke sayth in his Gospell, the Emperour of Rome, Cesar
Augustus, helde the lordshippes of all the worlde in that tyme that
Oure Lorde Ihesu Chryst was borne. After that came a Kynge of
10 Persye which was called Cosserossath; he rose ayenst the Emperour of
Rome, and made hymselfe to be called the emperour of Asye. This
Emperour toke the lordeshippe of Persy, of Mede, of Armeny, and of
Calde; and his power encerased so moch that he droue themperour
of Rome and his men from all the foresayd landes, and the Persyens
15 reygned in Asye the space of CCC yeres. And after, the Sarasyns
toke the sayde lordship from them, as hereafter shal be declared.

Whan the Sarasyns entred into Syri

In the yere of the Incarnacion of Our Lorde vi C and xxxii yeres the
euyll sede of Mahomet cam into the realme of Syri. And fyrst they
20 toke from the Grekes handes the noble citie of Damas, and after they

ocupyed all the realme of Sirie; after, they came and beseged the cytye
of Antyoche. Whan themperour Eracles men were come to a playne
that is named Pofferit, the Sarasyns came and met theym. And there
began a great batayle that lasted longe, but at the ende the Sarasyns
5 had the victory; and so many men were slayne in the same batayle that
the bones yet be sene in the felde. Of the whiche thynge the Grekes
that kept the citie of Antioch were so afrayed, insomoche that they
delyuerd the lande into the Sarasyns handes by appoyntmentes. Than
the enemys of the holy faythe ocupyed Cylice, Capadoce, Lyconie,
10 and [B2v] other ryche landes. Wherof they rose in so great pride that
they apparellyd galeys and shippes, and went to Constantynople.
And fyrste they aryued in Cipres, and there they toke a cytie that
was called Constance (and there was the graue of Saynt Barnabe the
Apostle); and whan they had taken all the ryches of the sayd cytie,
15 they brake the walles downe to the foundacion, and neuer syth the
sayd citie was inhabyted. And than they departed, and came to the
yle of Rhodes, and toke it with other dyuers yles of the Rhomayns
landes, and brought prysoners without nombre. And after they went
to Constantinople, and layd therto sege bothe by see and by land. In
20 great fere were the cytizens, insomoche that they cryed Our Lorde
mercy; wherof it fortuned God that is mercyfull sende a great tempest
of wynde and rayne in that somer, that all the galeis of the Sarasyns
were broken and the enemis almoost all drowned. And than the
Sarasyns retorned without doinge any other thynge.

25 How that the Sarasyns entred into the realme of Mesopotamy

Whan the Christen men of Constantynople se that they were delyuerd by the grace of God, they made a solempne day for to
worshyp God for the honour of theyr saluation; which day is kept
30 euery yere to this day with great worship. After that the Sarasyns
were refresshed, a certen tyme after thei thought to gather a great
nomber of people to take the realme of Mesopotamy and Calde that
were of the lordship of the realme of Persy. The Kynge of Persy, that
was called Asobariothe, feringe the great myght of the Sarasyns,
35 sende his messangers to the kyng and to the lordes, his neyghbours,
that were at the syde of the flode of Phison, and required them of
helpe and socoure, promysinge great gyftes to all theym that sholde
come. And vpon that, thei came togyther to the realme of Turky

aboute foure thousande men of armes that were called Turkmens, and thei moued for to com and helpe the Kinge of Persy agaynst the Sarasyns, and so they passed ouer the flode of Physon. But for cause it is the maner of that peple to cary wyues and chyldern with
5 theym wheresoeuer they go, they coude nat take great iourneis. The Sarasyns that were in the realme of Calde, that had taken the sayd realme, thought that, yf the hoost of the Turkmens sholde come together with the hoost of Persy, they sholde not lightly acom- plyssh there owne men of the realme of Persy; and toke counsayle
10 to sende to the Kyng of Persy. And the Kyng of Persy, that coude nat chuse, put hym ayenst them; and therby a cytye that is called Maraga began a great batayle which lasted longe, in the which was of bothe partes many men slayn; [B3r] and at the later ende the Kinge was slayne in the batayle, and so dyed. This was in the yere of Our
15 Lorde God VI C and xxxiii.

How the Sarasyns chose theyr sowdan

After that the Sarasyns had taken the lordshyp of Persye and dyuers realmes in Asye, they chose there amonge them a lorde, the which they called the sowdan – that is to say, kynge, in Latten tonge. The
20 foresayd Sarasyns toke the lordshyppe of the lande of the Great Asye, except the realme of Abcas that is in Georgy and a countray in the realme of Armeny that is called Glausegarfordis. These two countreys holden agaynst the Sarazyns so well that they coude neuer haue the lordship of it, and there the Crysten men fledde away for
25 fere of theyr enemys.
Of the Turkmens that came for to helpe the Kyng of Persy we shall say somethynge shortely, bycause that their hystory shall be of more clere vnderstandyng. The aboue sayd Turkemens came to a lande that is called Corasten, and there they herde tydinges of the
30 vndoynge of the Persyens and of the Kynges deth; wherfore they wolde go no farther, but they thought to holde this sayde lande of Corasten for themselfe, and thought that they shold kepe it well ayenst the sayd Sarasyns. Wherof it hapened that the Sarasyns brought a great hoost togyder and came agaynst them. The Turk-
35 mens, feryng the batayle, dyde send theyr messengers to the Cal- yfe of Baldach, proferynge them to his commaundement; the which thinge pleased moche the sayd Calyfe and to the Sarsyns. And so they receyued the Turkmens to a trust and chased theym out of the

sayde lande of Corasten, and put them out to dwell in another
lande where they sholde nat fere their rebellion, and ordayned that
they sholde pay euery yere a tribute to the lordeshyp. And in this
maner abode the Turkemens vnder the lordshyp of the Sarasyns longe
5 tyme, to the tyme that the Sarasyns toke the lordshyp of Persy, Mede,
and of Calde; and there they turned all to the false lawe of Mahomet.
And after, it fortuned that the Calyfe of Baldach commaunded to
come before hym all the moost old and wysest men of the Turkmens,
and desyred them that they sholde beleue in Mahometes lawe and
10 that they sholde teche the other Turkmens to beleue so, and promysed them to do them great grace and honour yf they wolde do his
commaundment. The Turkmens, that had no lawe, were lightly con-
sentynge to the Calyfes wyll; wherof it came that the Turkemens,
that were lxiiii nacions, were made all Sarasyns, except two kynredes
15 that were deceyu[er]ed of the others. And than thei began to loue
the Turkmens and to do them honoure and grace. And so longe
dwelled ther the Turkmens [b3v] that they multiplyed of goodes
and people, and there humbly and wysely kept themselfe. And the
Sarasyns kept the lordshyppe of Asye IIII C and xviii yeres, and
20 after they loste the sayde lordshyp as we shall deuyse hereafter.

A cuniuracyon amonge the Sarasyns

In that tyme it happed that a great debate fell amonge the Sarasyns,
which lasted in contynuaunce xxx yeres, that the sowdans and the
lordes of the landes wolde nat obey to the Sowdan of Baldache but
25 they rose agaynst hym, and so the Sarsyns power began to mynisshe.
In that tyme was in Constantynople a valiant emperour which was
called Diogines, the which began valiantly to enter into the landes
that the Sarasyns had taken from Cristen men in themperour Erac-
los tyme, and to recouer the noble cytyes of Antyoch, Sylice, and
30 Mesopotamy. The other landes the Sarasins kept tyll the tyme that
the Turkmens toke it from them, as it shal be deuysed hereafter.

The fyrst reygnynge of the Turkes in Asye

In the yere of the Incarnacion of Our Lorde M li began fyrste the
Turkmens to haue the lordshyp in Asye; in suche maner that,
35 whan the Turkmens were multiplyed of men and goodes and se the
great trouble that was amonge the Sarasins, they thought to haue
rysen agayne. Wherfore they cam togyder and chose amonge them a

kynge, that was Salyoth; and afore that they had neuer lorde of
theyr kinred. Whan they had that done, they began so valyantly
vpon the Sarasyns, that in shorte space they had and occupyed
the lordship of Asye. But to the Calyfe of Baldoche they dyde hym no
5 grefe, but they yelded hym great honour; wherof it cam that the
Calyfe, more for fere than for loue, ordayned Saliothe lorde of the
Turkmens. But not longe after, themperour Salioth dyed, and after
hym was his sonne made lorde, which was called Doloryssa. This
man moued the warre agaynst themperour of Constantynople, and
10 toke dyuers landes and castels a Grece. And after, he send to the
realm of Mesopotamy one of his cosyns which was called Artoth;
vnto the which, he gaue men ynow, and gaue hym the realme of
Mesopotamy and al the other landes that he myght gete ayenst the
Grekes. Than the great Artothe went with a great nombre of men and
15 layde sege to the cytie of Rohays, and toke all the lande of Mesopotamy; he toke his owne sege in the cytye of Meredyn, and there
made hymselfe sowdan.
   In that tyme dyed Dolorissa, Kynge of Persy, and his sonne which
was called Alpasselem kept the lordship after hym. This Alpassel-
20 em had a neuewe that was called Solyman, which longe tyme had
serued his father; this Solyman [B4r] was moche valyaunt in armes.
Wherfore the forsayd kyng of Persy, Alpasselem, gaue a great nomber of men of warre to his neuewe Solyman and send hym to
Capadoce, and graunted hym to holde and kepe all that he coulde
25 take vpon the Grekes. And vpon that wente Solyman and entred
in the realme of Turky, and there toke cytes, realmes, and castels.
And almoost all that lande put them vnder his lordship; wherfore
he dyd chaung his name, and was called Solymansa. And of these
men hystores maketh mencion of Godfray de Bullayns passage,
30 whan he fought with the pylgrimes, and dyde them moche harme or
they coulde passe the landes of Turky.

How the Grekes were dryuen out of Asye

After that dyed Alpasselem, the Turkes emperour, and than was his
sonne made emperour, which was called Melacacerath; the which
35 send a commaundment to Artoth, the Sowdan of Mesopotamy, and to
Solimansa, the Sowdan of Turky, that thei sholde go and lay sege to
the cyte of Antyoche. Wherfore they brought togither a great hoost,

and laid sege to Antyoche, the which the Grekes kept; and not long
after thei toke it, and so were the Grekes dryuen oute of all the
landes of Asye by the myght of the enemys of the Crysten fayth. And
than after, Melacacerath, themperour of the Turkes, dyed, and laft
5 two chyldern; the fyrst was called Balryarothe, whiche kept the lordshyp after hym, but his brother that was more valyant in armes
ocupyed a great part of the landes of Persy. And at that tyme that
Godfray de Bullen passed, the sayd Balryaroth was Emperour of
Asye, and Solymansa was Sowdan of Turky; and dyde many enter-
10 prises to the pylgrems or they coulde passe the landes of Turkey.

How the Crysten men layde sege to Antyoche

Whan the Emperour of Persy vnderstod that the Crysten men had
layd sege to the cyte of Antyoche, he brought togyder a great
people of the realme of Turkey and sende for them for to socour the
15 cyte. Or the Turkes coulde come, the myght of the enemys were so
great that they layde sege rounde about the cyte. Wherfore the Cristen men that had layde sege before were themselfe beseged, and at
the later end our pilgrimes fought ayenst this great nomber of enemys
so well that by the grace of God the other were all disconfyted,
20 and Corberam the chefe captayn slayne. They that scaped out of the
batayle went agayn into Persy, and there the founde that theyr
emperour Balryarothe was deed; than his broder wold haue take the
lordship, but his enmis dyde rone vpon [B4v] hym, and kylde hym.
Great trouble was amonge the Sarasyns, insomoch that neuer sithe
25 they coulde nat agre to make no emperour nor generall lorde, but
they began to make ware the one ayenst the other. Wherfore the Greces
and the Armenys of the Great Armenye entred vpon them and droue
theym oute of all the landes of Persye, bothe theyr wyues and chyldern;
and so they went into Turky, and there they kept the lordship in
30 great prosperyte tyll the comyng of the Tartas, the which ocupyed
the lande and lordship of Turky, as it shal be declared hereafter.

How the Corasmyns conquered the realme of Persy

In the realme of Corasmyns was a maner of pepyll that dwelled in the
mountayns and in the feldys fedynge theyr beestes, the which were
35 bolde men of armes. These men vnderstode that the realm of Persy was

without a lorde; wherfore they thought for to conquer it lightly. And
than thei cam togyder, and dyde chose a lorde amonge them, which
was called Ialadyn; and whan they had so done, they went to the
noble cytye of Torys without any contradictyon of any man. And
5 there they dwelled, and made theyr lorde Ialaadyn Emperour of
Asye, for they thought to occupy other realmes of Asye as they had
taken the realm of Persy. This Corasmyns rested there certayn
dayes, and there they were al full of goodes and ryches of Persy;
wherof they toke so great pryde that they entred into the realm of
10 Turkye, and thought to haue ocupyed it and enioyed it. But the
Sowdan of Turky, that was called Ialaadyn, gethared his hoost
and fought agaynst the Corasmyns, and ouercam them and droue
theym out of Turky; and Ialaadyn theyr emperour was slayn in
batayle. And they that scaped went into the realme of Mesopotamy;
15 and than came togyther into the playne of Royhas, and there they
toke counsayl betwene them to entre into the realme of Syry, which
was at that tyme gouerned by a lady. And then the Corasmyns
cam, and brought togyther agayne the hoost, and entred into Siry.
And this noble lady brought her men togyder in the cyte of Halap,
20 and nygh to the flode of Eufrates cam to mete the Corasmyns, and
fought there. Great was the batayle, but at the later ende the Corasmyns were ouercome, and fled awaye towarde the desert of Arabe.
And after, they passed ouer the flod of Eufrates, nygh to a castell
that was called Racabe, and entred into the realme of Syry, and cam
25 to the prouince of Palastyne that is in the realme of Hyerusalem; and
dyde great damage to the Cristen men, as it apereth in the historis of
the passage of Godfray de Bullayn. And at the last this Corasmins
began to murmure, and wolde not [B5r] obey to theyr lorde. And than
they departed, so that some went to the Sowdan of Hames and to
30 other sowdans, which were v in Syry. Whan that the Corasmins
duke, that was called Beretall, se that his men were wasted, [he]
send his messangere to the Sowdan of Babilon and profered hym his
seruice. Wherof the Sowdan was ryght glad, and receyued hym
with a good wyll, and dyde great honour to the Duke and to them
35 that came with hym; and departed the Corasmyns by all his landes
bycause that he wolde nat haue theym all togyther. And because of
that the Sowdans power of Babylon rose moche for the commyng
of the Corasmyns, that before was ryght smale. And in conclusyon
and in short tyme the natyon of the Corasmyns cam to nought.
40 And then after, the Tartas began to haue the lordshippe.

[BOOK THREE]

What countray the Tartas inhabited fyrste

The lande and countrey there as the Tartas dwelled fyrst is betwene
the grete mountayne of Beligian; of this mountayn speketh the
hystores of Alexander, there as he maketh mencyon of the wylde men
5 that he founde. In that countrey dwelled fyrst the Tartas as beestysshe men, that had no faythe nor lawe but went from place to place
as beestes fedynge; and of other natyons they were kept subgettes
– to the which they were seruauntes to. Dyuers natyons of Tartas
that were named Malgothz came togyther and ordayned captayns
10 and gouernours amonge theym, and so they multyplied so moche
that they were departed in vii nations; and to this day these nations
be taken more noble then the other. The fyrst of this nation is called
Tartar; the seconde, Tangothe; the thryde, Curach; the iiii, Iason;
the v, Sonithe; the syxte, Mangly; and the vii, Tebethe. And as it
15 happened that these vii nations dwelled in the subgection of theyr
neyghbours as is before sayd, it fortuned a poore olde man that
was called Cangius sawe in dremynge a visyon; the whiche to hym
semyng was a knyght in armour vpon a white horse, that called hym
by his name and sayde vnto hym: 'Cangius, the wyll of thy immortall
20 God is suche that he oweth to be shortli gouernor made vpon the vii
natyons of the Tartas that ben called Malgothz, and that by hym
they shal be delyuerd oute of the saruage that thei had longe ben in,
and shall haue worship vpon theyr neighbours.' Cangius rose vp
merily, herynge the worde of Christ, and rehersed the vision that he
25 se to all the gentilmen. But they wolde nat beleue, but skorned
hym. Wherfore it fortuned the night folowynge the captayns of the

vii nations se the white horse in vision as Cangius had rehersed,
which commaunded by the immortall God [B5v] that they sholde obey
all to Cangius, and that they sholde kepe all his commaundementes.
Wherfore the vii captayns aboue said brought the people togyther,
5 and dyde make obesaunce and reuerence to Cangius; and they themselfe dyde so, as to theyr naturall lorde.

How Cangius was elect emperour of the Tartas

After that, the Tartas ordayned a seat in the myddes of them all, and
putte there vpon the grounde a blacke carpet, and made Cangius
10 to syt therupon; and the vii captayns of the vii natyons reysed hym
vp with the sayd carpet and set hym vpon the seate, and named
hym Can, and with knelinge dyde hym all honour and reuerence as
to theyr owne lorde. Of the solempnyte that the Tartas dyde to
theyr lorde in that tyme sholde no man maruayle of it, for peraduen-
15 ture they coulde do no better, or they had no fayrer clothe to set
hym on; but for that they wolde nat change theyr first vsage, it is
marueyle, seynge that they haue conquered so many landes and
realmes, and yet they kepe theyr fyrst maner for thei wyll chuse their
lorde. And twyse haue I ben at thelectyon of the Tartas emperour.
20 They assemble togyther in a great felde, and he that sholde be theyr
lorde they caused hym to sytte vpon a blacke carpet, and put a
ryche seate in the myddes of them all. And than after cam the noble-
men and the chefe of his kynred, and lyft hym vp on hye and set
hym vpon the seate, and after dyde hym all honour and reuerence as
25 to theyr natural lorde. And for al the lordship or riches that they
haue conquered, they wolde neuer chaunge theyr fyrst gyse.
    And after that Cangius Can was made emperour by the commen
wyll and consent of all the Tartas, first of all, or Cangius Can
wolde do any other thinge, he wolde knowe if they all wolde be
30 obedient vnto hym. And than he commaunded iii commaundementes. The fyrst commaundement was that they sholde all beleue and
worshyp one God immortal, by the which he was made emperour.
And forthe withall the Tartas began to beleue and worship God, and
reclamed the name of God in all theyr warkes and dedes. The
35 seconde commaundement was that they sholde viewe and nombre all
them that were able to bere harnes. And ordayned that vpon euery
x sholde be a captayn, and ouer C a captayn, and ouer x M was a

captayn, and they called the company of the x thousande, thoman.
After that, he commaunded to the captayns of the vii natyons and
lynages of the Tartas that they sholde yelde vp all theyr armes and
lordships, and that they sholde holde and pay vnto hym as he sholde
5 ordayn them. The iii commaundement that Cangius Can made was
thought moche cruell to them all [B6r] for he commaunded to the foresayd vii great captains that euery one sholde brynge his eldest sonne
before hym; and whan they had so done, he commaunded them that
euery captayn sholde stryke of his sonnes heed, the which com-
10 maundment they thought was moche felon. And not for because that
they shold fere the people but bycause that they knew well that
Cangius Can was made emperour by commaundement of the immortall God, and so euery one of the vii captayns strake of his sonnes
heed. And than whan Cangius Can knewe the goodwyll of his people
15 and se that they wolde obey hym vnto the dethe, than he commaunded
that they sholde be apperylled in knyghtes armour with hym.

How Cangius Can was saued by a byrde

Whan Cangius Can had ordayned well and wyselye his batayle, he
entred into the landes of them that had longe tyme kept the Tartas
20 subgettes and fought with theym, and ouercame them all and put
theyr landes in his subiectyon. After that, Cangius Can went forthe,
conquerynge landes and countreis and all thinges as he wolde.
Vpon a day it happened that Cangius Can rode with a smale company, and met with a great nombre of his enemys which set sharpley
25 vpon hym. Cangius Can defended him valyantly, but at the last his
hors was slayne vnder hym. And whan Cangius men se that theyr
lorde was in the prese, incontynent they lost their corages and
began to fle away; and theyr enemys chased after them, and toke no
hede to Cangius Can, themperour, that was afote. Whan Cangius
30 Can se that, he hyd hym in a lytell busshe that was nere. The enemis
that had the victory began to serche for theym that were fled. And
as they wolde haue serched the said busshe wherin Cangius Can was
hyd, a byrde that is called a duke cam and sat vpon the sayd
busshe. And whan they that sought for Cangius Can se the byrde
35 syttynge vpon the sayd busshe there as Cangius Can was, they
supposed nobody to be there; and departed, sayenge, if anybody
were there, the byrde wolde nat syt there. And so they went away

without any more serchinge, thinkyng that nobody sholde be in the sayd busshe.

How and wherfore the Tartas were fethers

Whan that nyght cam, Cangius Can wente out of the busshe. And
5 dyde so moche that he cam to his men, and counted to them all his auenture, and how the byrde lyght vpon the busshe there as he was hyd, and for that cause his enemys serched nat for hym. And [B6v] than the Tartas rendred grace to God; and from thensforthe they had the sayd byrde which was called duke in great reuerence, for who
10 that myght haue a feder of the sayd byrde, gladly wolde were it vpon his heed. Of this history I haue made mencyon to thende that ye sholde knowe wherof the Tartas were the feders vpon their heedes. Cangius Can rendred grace to God that he was so delyuerd in that maner.
15 After that, he assembled his hoost togyder and fought with his enemys, and discomfyt theym and put theym all in his subiection. And Cangius Can conquered all the landes that were from thens to the mountayn of Belgyan, and helde them – so moche, that he se another vision, as it shal be deuysed hereafter. Whan Cangius Can
20 had conquered the lordships of all those countreis that were a this syde the mountayne of Belgyan, vpon a nyght it happened that he se in vysion the white knyght agayne. The which sayd vnto hym: 'Cangius Can, the wyll of the immortall God is that thou passe the mountayn of Belgyan. And thou shalt conquere the realmes and
25 countreis of dyuers nations, and shalt reygne and be lorde ouer them. And to thende that thou shalt know that this that I say is the wyll of the immortall God, ryse vp and goo to the mount of Belgian with all thy men. And whan thou shalt come there where the see is ioyning to the sayd mountayn, thou shalt discende with all thy
30 men, and shalt knele ix tymes agaynst the orient, and shalt pray to the immortall God that he wyll shewe the the way. And he shall shew the the way, and so thou mayst passe with al thy people.'
Whan Cangius Can was waked out of his slepe, he beleued well in the vision; and forthwith commaunded his men that thei sholde
35 get them to horse, for he wolde passe the mountayn of Belgian. Than they rode forthe tyll they came to the see, and there they coulde nat passe ouer bycause there was no passage greate nor smale. And

incontynent Cangius Can descended from his horse; and commaunded to all his army that they sholde lyght and knele downe ix
tymes towarde the orient, and that they sholde pray to almighty
God immortall that he wolde shewe them the way to passe. And all
5 that nyght Cangius Can and his men abode in prayers, and on the
morowe Cangius Can se that the see was gone from the mountayn ix
fote and they had a fayre large way. Whan Cangius Can and his
people se that thing, they marueyled moche of it. Wherfore they
yelded grace to God, and passed all towarde the partes of the
10 Orient, as it is rehersed in the Tartas histores.

How Cangius Can fell sycke

After that Cangius Can had passed the mountayne [c1r] of Belgian,
he founde moche water marese and the lande desert; so moche,
that or he and his people coude come in a good lande, they suffred
15 great penure. After that, they founde gode landes and plentyfull
of all thinges; wherfore they dwelled in the countrey many dayes,
and reposed them. And as it plesed God a gret sykenesse toke
Cangius Can, and than he commaunded to come before hym xii
sonnes that he had, and commaunded them that they sholde euer be
20 all of one wyll and acorde, and gaue theym suche example. He commaunded that euery one of them sholde bringe an arowe. And whan
the xii sonnes were com togyder, he commaunded to his fyrst sonne
that he sholde take all the arowes, and that he sholde breke them
with his handes. And so his first sonne toke the sayd arowes, but he
25 coude nat breke them with his handes. And than he toke theym to
his seconde sonne, but he coude nat breke them. And than Cangius
commaunded that the arowes sholde be departed. And commaunded
to the leest of his sonnes that he sholde take euery one of the arowes
by theymselfe, and that he sholde breke them; and than the chylde
30 brake all the xii arowes. And than Cangius Can torned hym towarde
his chyldern, and sayd to them, 'Wherfore coulde you nat breke
the arowes as I commaunded you?' And they sayde, 'Bycause that
they were all togyder.' And than he sayde, 'Wherfore hath this
lytell chylde broken them?' And they answered that, 'Bycause that
35 he brake them euery one by themselfe.' Than sayd Cangius Can,
'It shall come so by you. For as longe as ye shal be all of one wyll and
one accorde, your lordshyps shall euer last; and whan ye shal be

departed one from another, soone after, your lordshipes shall torne
to nought, and shall nat contynue.' Dyuers more commaundementes and examples gaue Caungius Can to his chyldren and to his men,
which the Tartas kepe yet in great reuerence.

5 How Cangius Can themperour dyed

Whan Cangius Can had that done, seyng that he coulde nat lyue
long, he made one of his sonnes, the best and wysest, lorde and
emperour after hym, and comaunded that they all sholde obey vnto
hym and serue hym as theyr naturall lorde; and this sayd sonne
10 was called Hactoca. After that, the good Emperour, and fyrst of the
Tartas, dyed and passed out of this worlde, and his sonne Hoctoca
helde the lordships after hym. And before that we make an ende of
thistory of Cangius Can, we shal say how the Tartas haue the
nombre of ix in gret reuerence and honour. In worship of the ix
15 knelynges, and of the ix fote that the see went backe from the coost
and made way of ix fote (where they passed all the mountayn of [c1v]
Belgyan by the commaundement of God), the Tartas haue the nombre of ix in great reuerence; wherfore he that wyll present anythinge
to his lorde, and wolde that his present sholde be receyued gra-
20 ciously, he must present the nombre of ix. And so is the vsage of the
Tartas vnto this day.

How Hoctoca Can made ware in Asie

Hoctoca Can that was Emperoure of the Tartas after the deth of his
father Cangius Can – which was valyant, good, and wyse, and
25 also his people loued hym well and were to hym faythfull and true
euermore, Hoctoca Can thought to conquere all the lande of Asie.
And before that he departed from the lande there as he was, he
wolde knowe the power of all the kynges that were in Asie, and
wolde knowe which was the moost pusaunt – purposynge to fyght
30 fyrst with hym. For he thought that he sholde lightly ouercome the
other if he might conquer the moost mighty. Than Hoctoca Can
sende a wise and a valiant captayn which was named Gebesabada,
and sende with hym x thousande fightynge men, and commaunded them that they sholde entre into the landes of Asie and to viewe

the state and condicyon of the sayd land; and if thei founde any
mighty lorde whom thei were nat able to resyst, they sholde shortly
retorne backe agayn. As Hoctoca Can commaunded, it was acom-
plysshed; for the sayd captayn, with his x thousande Tartas, entred
5 sodenlye into the landes of Asie, and there he toke cyties and
landes or the inhabitauntes were ware or before that thei coude make
them redy to batayle or defende them. They kylde all the men of
armes, but they dyde no harme to the people. They toke horse,
harnes, vitayle, and all suche thynges that they neded, and went
10 so farre in the lande that they came to the mountayn of Cocas. For
this mountayn of Cocas, one can nat passe the depe of Asie into
Great Asie but by the lycence of the peple of a cyte that the Kynge
Alexander closed vpon a narowe see that toucheth the mountayne
of Cocas. This sayd cytye was taken by these x thousande Tartas in
15 suche maner that the inhabytantes of the sayd cyte had no space
nor tyme to defend themselfe. And than they toke this cyte and all
that was therin, and put all the men and women to the swerde;
and after that, they brake downe all the walles of the cyte bycause
that whan they sholde come agayn they shold fynde nothing
20 agaynst them. This cytie was in the olde tyme called Alexander, but
nowe it is called Porte de Ferre. The renowne of the Tartas was
sprede ouer all the countreis and landes; wherof it fortuned that the
Kynge of Georgi, which was caled Ynaims, brought his hoost togyder and [c2r] came agaynst the Tartas, and fought with them in a
25 playne that is called Morgam. The batayle lasted longe, but at
thende the Georgyens were constrayned to fle away as discomfyt.
The Tartas passed so ferre that they came to a cyte of Turkey that is
called Arseon, and than they vnderstode that the Sowdan of Turkey
was nere, and how he had asembled his host togyder; therfore the
30 Tartas durst go no farther. Seynge that they were nat able to en-
counter agaynst the Sowdan of Turkey, they went backe agayne by
another way to theyr lorde, the which they founde in a cyte that is
called Amelect, and tolde hym all that they had done and founde
in the lande of Asie.

35 Whan the Tartas lerned fyrst letters

Whan Hoctoca Can vnderstode the maner and condicyon of the lande

of Asie, he thought that there was no prynce that was able to
withstande hym; and than he called thre sonnes that he had, and
gaue them gret ryches with a great nombre of men of armes, and
commaunded them to entre into the lande of Asie conquering all the
5 realmes and landes. And commaunded to his sonn Iochi that he
sholde go towarde the parties of occident vnto the flode of Physon,
and to his seconde sone that was called Bacho he commaunded
that he sholde kepe his way towarde septentrion, and to the leest,
that was called Chasada, commaunded that he sholde ryde towarde
10 the south; in this maner he departed his thre chyldren and sende
them for to conquere these landes and prouynces. After that, Hoctoca Can sprede his hoost abrode by the countreis so moche that the
forefronte of his hoost rought to the realme of Cathay and the
other front to the realme of Trase. In those partes the Tartas lerned
15 leters, for before that tyme thei had no letters. And therfore the
dwellers of the sayde countrey were all ydolatours, the Tartas began
to honour the ydols; but many of them confessed the immortall
God gretter than the other.

After that, themperour Hoctoca Can gaue to his eldest sonne, that
20 was called Bacho, xxx thousande Tartas that were called Tanachy,
that is to say conquerers, and commaunded that they sholde go that
way that the x thousande Tartas kept, and that they sholde tary
in no lande tyll they sholde come into the realm of Turkey. And
moreouer he commaunded that thei sholde proue if thei were able to
25 fyght agaynst the Sowdan of Turkey; and if that they dyde se that the
Sowdans power were to great, they sholde nat fyght with hym,
but they sholde do so moche to one of his chyldren which sholde be
next them that he wolde gyue them helpe and men of warre. And
than after they met, began the batayle of Bacho with xxx thousande
30 Tartas. [They] went so moche by theyr iourneis that they [c2v]
came to the realme of Turkey, and there he vnderstode that the Sowdan that had dryued away the X M Tartas was deed. After hym
one of his sonnes that was called Giriacadyn was made lorde. This
Sodan was in great fere for the Tartas commynge, and than he
35 gathered and waged all maner of men that he coude haue, as Barbarins
and Latyns – that had two captayns: of the which one was called
Iohnn de la Limynate, which was of the yle of Cipre, and the
other was called Bonyface de Moulins, and he was of the cyte of
Venyse.

Of the batayle that was betwene the Sowdan of Turkey and the Tartas

Whan the Sowdan of Turky had gathered his hoost of all the parties, he came and fought with the Tartas in a place that is called Asadache.
5 The batell was grete and many men slain of bothe parties, but at the later ende the Tartas had the victory, and entred into the landes of Turky, and conquered the sayd landes in the yere of Our Lorde God M CC xliii.
And than, nat longe tyme after, Hoctoca Can, themperour of the
10 Tartas, dyed; and after hym one of his sonnes was made lorde, which was called Guyot Can. This Guyot Can lyued nat long after hym. One of his cosyns was made lorde which was called Mango Can, the which was moche valyant and wyse, and conquered many landes and lordships. But at the ende, as a man that hath a great
15 hert, he entred vpon the see. And as he layde sege to an yle the which he wolde haue taken by the see syde, the men of that lande, that were subtyll, sende for men that coude swym vnder the water; which men entred vnder the vessel in the which Mango Can was in, and there they taryed so longe vnder the water that they brake
20 the vessell in dyuers places, so moche that the water entred into the sayd vessell. Of the which thing Mango Can toke no hede tyll the sayd vessell was well nygh full and began to synke vnder the water; and so was Mango Can themperour of the Tartas drowned. His men went home agayn, and made his brother lorde that was
25 called Cobila Can; the which kept the lordship of the Tartas xlii yeres, and made them Christen men. And closed a cyte which is called Ioing, that is gretter than Rhome; and in this cytie dwelled Cobila Can, which was the v emperour of the Tartas, tyll the last ende of his dayes. We shall leue to speke of Mango Can, and shall retorne to
30 speke of Hoctoca Cans chyldren, of Halcon, of his heyres, and of his warkes.

How Iochy conquered the realme of Turquestan and Persy

Iochy, the first sonne of Hoctoca Can, rode towarde occydent with all

his men that his father had gyue hym, [c3r] and conquered the
realme of Turquestan and of Persy the Lest. And than he went to the
flodde of Physon; and there he founde the countreis full of all
goodes, and dwelled in the sayde countrey in rest and peace, and
5 multiplied in gret richesse. And vnto this day the heyres of the
foresayd Iochy holde the lordeship of the sayd lande. And there be
two lordes that holde the lordshippe of the sayd lande: the one is
called Chapar, and the other, Thochay; and they be brethern and
lyue in rest and peace.

10 How Bacho and a great parte of his men were drowned in the ryuer of Austrich

Bacho, the seconde sonn of Hoctoca Can, with the men that his
father had gyuen vnto hym, rode towarde the partyes of septentrion,
and dyde so moche that he cam to the realm of Comany. The Kyng
15 of Comany, thinkynge well for to defende his lande, gathered
his hoost and fought agaynst the Tartas, but at thende the Comayns
were disconfyt. And they droue the Comains vnto the realme
of Hongrye, and yet vnto this day be many Comayns dwellyng in
Hongry. After that Bacho had dryuen the Comayns oute of the
20 realme of Comany, he entred into the realme of Roussy and toke it,
and he conquered the realme of Gezere and the realme of Bulgary.
And after, he rode to the realme of Hongry; and there he founde
some Comayns, and toke them. After that, the Tartas passed toward Almayn, and dyde so moch that they came to the ryuer syde
25 that ran by Almain by the Duchy of Austrych. The Tartas thought to
passe by a bridge that was there, but the Duke of Austrych caused
the brydge to be garnysshed so that the Tartas coude nat passe ouer.
And whan Bacho se that he coude nat passe ouer the brydge, he
rydde into the water with his horse and dyde begynne to swym; and
30 than he commaunded to his men that they sholde passe ouer swymming.
Wherin he put hymselfe and his men in great danger; for before that
they coude passe ouer, theyr horses was so wery that they coude
swymme no lengar, and so Bacho and a great parte of his men were
drowned in the foresayd ryuer of Austrych or they coude pas ouer
35 or come to the other syde. Whan the other Tartas that were nat
entred into the water se theyr lorde Bacho and theyr other company

drowned, full sory and heuy they daparted and went backe to the
realme of Roussi and of Comany. And neuer after the Tartas entred into Almayn. The heyres of the sayd Bacho holde the lordshippe
of the realme of Corasme, the realme of Comany, and the realm of
5 Roussy; and he that is nowe lorde was Hoctoca [c3v] Cans thyrde
sonne, which was called Chacaday.

How Iochy receyued his broder Chacaday

Chacaday, the thyrde sonn of Hoctoca Can, with his men that his
father had gyuen vnto him, rode towarde the southe tyll he came
10 to the parties of Inde the Leest. And there he founde moche voyde
lande and no men dwellynge therin, and so he coude nat passe,
but he lost his men and many of his beestes. After that, he went
towarde the occydent, and dyde so moche that he came to his
brother Iochy and rehersed to hym all his fortune. Iochy receyued his
15 brother and his company full humbly, and gaue vnto them part of
his landes that he had conquered; and incontinent were the two
brothers togyder, and there men, in good peace and rest. And he
that is nowe lorde is called Baretath.

How and whan the Kynge of Armeny laft his owne
20 countrey and came to the Kynge of the Tartas. And how
he required vii peticyons of hym.

In the yere of Our Lorde God a thousande two honderde and thre
and fyfti, Hayton, the King of Armeny of good remembraunce,
seyng that the Tartas hadde conquered all the countreys and realmes
25 to the realm of Turkey, he toke counsayle for to go to the Kyng of
the Tartas and to take with hym his goodes and his frendes. The King
of Armeny, by the counsell of his barownes, send before for his
brother, Sir Symme Batat, constable of the realme of Armeny; and than
the constable went to the realme of the Tartas and to the lorde Mango
30 Can, and brought hym many riche presentes, and was courtesly receyued. And whan he had accomplysshed well all his besynesses

for the whiche his brother the Kynge of Armeny had sende hym for,
veryli he taryed foure yeres or that he came agayn into Armeny.
And whan he had tolde to his brother the Kynge what he had done
and founde, by and by the Kynge apparylled hym and his men of
5 armes, and wente pryuely, he and his men, by Turky, for that that he
wolde nat be knowen. And he mette with a captayn of the Tartas,
the whiche had ouercome the Sowdan of Turkey. The Kynge of
Armeny gaue him knowlege and tolde to hym how that he was
goynge to themperour of the Tartas, and than the sayd captayne
10 gaue hym company to bryng hym to the Port de Ferre. And after
that, the King founde other company that brought hym to the cytye
of Maleth. And there was Mango Can themperour of the Tartas; the
which was [c4r] ryght gladde of the Kynge of Armenes commyng,
and receyued hym honorably and gaue hym great gyftes and great
15 graces.

After that the Kynge of Armeny had taryede certayn dayes, he
made his requestes, and required of themperour seuen thinges.
The first thing that the Kynge required of themperour was that he
and his men sholde becom Cristen men, and that they sholde be
20 baptised. The seconde, that he requyred that perpetuall peace and
loue sholde be betwene the Tartas and the Christen men. The
thyrde, he required that in all the landes that the Tartas had conquered and sholde conquere, the churches of the Christen men –
as preestes, clerkes, and all the relygious persons – sholde be
25 fre and delyuerd of all seruages. The iiii that the Kynge required
of Mango was to gyue helpe and counsell to delyuer the Holy Lande
oute of the Sarasyns handes, and to put it agayn into the Christen
mens handes. The fift, he required that he wolde gyue commaundement to the Tartas that were in Turkey, that they sholde helpe to
30 distroy the cytie of Baldach and the Calyf (that is chefe and techer
of the fals lawe of Mahomet). The sixt, he requyred a priuilege
and commaundment that he myght haue helpe of the Tartas that
were nygh to the realm of Armeny whan he sholde requyre them.
The vii request was that all the landes that the Sarasyns had taken
35 that were of the realme of Armeny, that after was come into the
Tartas handes, sholde be restored frely vnto hym; and also all the
landes that he myght conquere agaynst the Sarasyns that he myght
holde them without any contradiction of the Tartas in rest and
peace.

How themperour Mango Can and his barownes agreed to the vii peticions of the King of Armeni

Whan Mango Can vnderstode the requestes of the King of Armeny, before his barownes and all his court [he] answered and sayd:

5 'Bycause that the Kyng of Armeny is come from ferre countreis into our empyre of his owne frewyll, it is metely that we shall fulfyll all his requestes. To you, Kyng of Armeny, we shall say, as we be emperour, we shal be baptysed first, and shal beleue in the faith of Christ, and shall do christen all them of our house, and shall kepe all

10 the fayth that the Christen men holde to this day. And to the other we shall gyue them counsell that they shall do lykewise, for the fayth wyll haue nobody by force. The seconde request, we answere and wyll that perpetuall peas and loue shal be amonge the Christen men and the Tartas, but we wyll that ye shal be pledge that the Christen

15 men shall holde good peace and trewe loue towarde vs as we shall do towarde them. And [c4v] we wyll that all the churches of the Christen men, prestes, clerkes, and all other persons – of what degre or condicyon so euer they be, seculer or relygiouse persons – shall be free and delyuerd of all seruages, and also they shal be defended

20 from all maner of hurt both of body and goodes. And vpon the dede of the Holy Lande, we say that we shall go personally with a right gode wyll for the honour of Our Lorde Ihesu Christ. But for bycause that we haue moch to do in those parties, we shall commaunde to our broder Halcon that he shall go with you for to fulfyll this

25 warke, and shall delyuer the Holy Lande fro the Sarasyns power, and shall restore it to the Christen men; and we shall sende our commaundement to Bacho and to the other Tartas that be in Turky, and to the other that be in that countreys, that they shall obey to our brother Halcon. And he shall go to take the cyte of Baldach, and

30 shall distroy the Calyfe as our mortall ennemy. Of the priuilege that the Kyng of Armenye requyringe to haue helpe of the Tartas, we wyll that the priuilege shall be diuysed all after his owne mynde and pleasure; all we commaunde and confirme. And all the landes that the King of Armeny requyred that sholde be restored vnto hym, we

35 graunt it with a right good wyll, and commaunde to oure brother Halcon that he yeld to hym all the landes that were of his lordshyppe; and moreouer we gyue vnto [hym] all the landes that he may conquere agaynst the Sarasyns, and of our specyall grace we gyue hym all the castels that be nere to his lande.'

How Mango Can was christened at the request and desyre of the Kynge of Armeny, and dyuers other of his people. And how the Kynge of Armeny and Halcon wente to the Assasyns countreis

5 Whan Mango Can had fynisshed all the peticions and requestes of
the Kynge of Armeny, soone after, he caused a bysshoppe to christen
hym – which bysshoppe was chaunceler to the sayd Kyng of Armeny; and after, he caused all his housholde seruauntes to be
chrystened, and many other, both men and women. Than after, he
10 ordayned men of warre that sholde go with his brother.
    And than Halcon and the King of Armeni, with a great compani of
men of armes, rodde tyll they came to the flodde of Physon; and
dyde so well, that or syx monethes were at an ende, Halcone occupyed the realme of Persy. And toke all the landes and countreys
15 there as the Assasyns dwelled – that be men without any fayth or
belefe, saue that thei haue [that] a lorde, the which is called the Olde
[c5r] Mountayn, dyde teche them to beleue; and they be so moch
obedient to their lorde that they put themselfe to deth at his commaundement. In the sayd lande of Assasyns was a stronge castell
20 well fornysshed with all maner of thinges, that was called Tigado.
Halcon commaunded to one of his captayns of the Tartas that he
sholde lay sege to the sayd castell, and that he sholde nat depart
away tyll he had taken the sayd castell; and than the Tartas taryed
to besege the sayd castell without any departing xxvii yeres, and at
25 thende the Assasins yelded the castell for defaut of clothyng and
for no other thyng. Whan Halcon vnderstode the taking of the sayd
castell, the King toke leue of Halcon and retorned vnto Armeny
and taryed there, iii yeres and a halfe after, in good helthe thanked
be God.
30   After that Halcon had ordayned the garde of the realme of Persy,
he went into a delycate countrey that was named Soloch, and
there he taryed all the sommer in gret rest. Whan the wether was
colde again, Halcon went and beseged the cyte of Baldach, and the
Calyf that was maister and techer of Mahometz lawe. And whan he
35 had gathared his hoost he caused the cite of Baldach to be assayled
vpon all parties, and dyde so moche that they toke it by force; and as
many men and women as they founde, thei put them to the swerde.
The Calyf was brought alyue before Halcon. So moch richesse they

founde in the cytie of Baldache that it was wonder to beholde it.
And than Halcon commaunded that the Calyf, with all his treasoure,
sholde be brought afore hym. And than he sayd to the Calyfe, 'Knowest
thou nat, that all this tresoure was thyn?' And he answered, 'Ye.'
5 Than sayd Halcon vnto hym, 'Wherfore dyde you make no good
ordinance and prouysion for to defende your landes from oure
power?' And than the Calyf answered hym, he thought that the olde
women had ben sufficyent to defende the lande. Than sayd Halcon to the Calyf of Baldach, 'Bycause that thou art maister and techer
10 of Mahometz lawe, we shall make the fede of these preciouse tresour
and richesses that thou hast loued so moche in thi lyfe.' And than
Halcon commaunded that the Calyf sholde be put in a close chambre,
and that some of his tresour sholde be layd before hym, and that he
sholde eate of it yf he wolde. And in the same maner the wretched
15 Calyfe endede his lyfe, and neuer sythe was calyfe in Baldache.

Whan Halcon had taken the citie of Baldach and the Calyf and all
the countreis about, he departed the lordships, and put in eche of
them baylies and gouernours as it plesed hymselfe. And he dyd
moche honour to the Christen men, and put the Sarasyns in great
20 seruage euer after. A woman that was called Descotacon, which
was a good Christen woman and was of the lynage [c5v] of the thre
kynges that came to worship the natiuitie of Our Lorde Ihesu
Christ, this sayd woman made to be buylded agayn all the churches
of the Christen men; and caused all the temples of the Sarasyns to
25 be put downe, and put them in so great seruag and subiectyon that
they durst nat come abrode.

Why Halcon sende for the Kynge of Armeny for to come to hym

Whan Halcon had refresshed hym the space of an yere, and his men,
30 in the cite of Rohais, he sende for the Kyng of Armeni that he
sholde come to hym, for he was disposed to go and delyuer the Holy
Lande and to restore it agayne into the Christen mens handes.
The Kyng of gode remembraunce was full glad of the sayd commaundement, and gathered a gret hoost of valyant men afote and a
35 horsbacke. For in that tyme the realme of Armeny was in prosperyte,
so that he made xii thousande horsmen and xii thousande afote; and
that haue I sene in my dayes. Whan the Kynge of Armeny was come,

he helde a parlyment and counsell to Halcon vpon the dede of the
Holy Lande. Than sayd the Kyng to Halcon: 'Sir, the Sowdan of
Halap holdeth the lordship of the Kyng of Anyne and of Syrie, and
syth that ye entende to go to the Holy Lande, me thinke it for the
5 best to lay sege first to the cyte of Halap, which is the moost strongest
cyte in the realm of Syrie. For if we may take the cyte of Halap, all
the other may be lightly taken.' Halcon was well pleased with the
Kynge of Armenis counsell, and than he layd sege to the cyte of
Halap, which had full strong walles. But the Tartas toke the cytye by
10 mynes that they had made vnder the grounde. And by other craft
and ingins that they dyde make, they toke the cytie by force in nyne
dayes, but there was within the cytie a castell that was so stronge
that it defended them that were within aleuen dayes after that they
had take the cytie. Great haboundaunce of riches and other sub-
15 staunce found the Tartas whan they were entred within the cytie of
Halape. And so Halap was taken, and after that, all the realme of
Syrie, in the yere of Our Lorde God a thousande two hondred and
threskore.
   Whan the Soudan of Halap, that was at that tyme in the cytie of
20 Damas, vnderstode that the cytie of Halap was taken by the Tartas,
and that they had taken his wyfe and his chyldren, he knewe nat
what to do but yeld hymselfe to the mercy of Halcon, thynkinge by
that mean that Halcon sholde render to hym his wyfe and his chyldren
and parte of his lande. Than Halcon dyde send the Sowdan, his
25 wyfe, and his chyldren to the realme of Persy bycause that he might
be the more surer of hym. [c6r] After that, Halcone departed great
richesse amonge his men. And to the Kyng he gaue a great nombre of
goodes, and also he gaue hym of his landes and castels that he had
conquered, and specially dyuers that were nygh to the realme of
30 Armenie; and after the Kinge furnysshed the castels with his men.
Than, after that, Halcon dyd send for the Prince of Antioch, which
was the Kyng of Armenes sonne, and dyde hym great grace and
honour, and dyde gyue hym all the landes and lordships that he had
taken from the Sarasyns.
35   After that Halcon had ordayned all that was nedefull about the
cytie of Halap, Damasse, and the other landes the which they
had conquered and taken from the Sarasyns, as he had thought to
entred into the realme of Hierusalem for to delyuer the Holy Lande
vnto the Christen men agayne, there came a messangere to hym,
40 and brought hym worde that his brother was deed and passed oute

of this worlde and how the barownes sought for to haue made hym emperour.

How that Halcon departed oute of the realme of Syrie

Whanne Halcon had herde this tidynges, he was ful sorye for his
5 brothers dethe. And by the counsayle of his men he went away, and left one of his barownes that was called Garboga with x thousande Tartas for to kepe the realme of Syrie; and commaunded that all the landes that had ben in the Christen mens handes sholde be restored agayne. After that, he went toward the orient, and left one of his
10 sonnes at Thores, which was called Agaba. And from thens departed Halcon and wente to the realme of Persy, and whan that he was com thyder, tydinges was brought vnto hym how Cobyla his cosyn was made emperour.

Whan Halcon vnderstode those newes, he wolde go no farther,
15 but retorned agayn to Thores, there as he had left his sonne, his housholde, and his seruantes. As Halcone taryed at Thores there cam newe tydinges vnto hym that Barta, whiche at that tyme helde the lordship that Bacho helde (whiche was drowned in the flodde of Austrich), as he was cominge to haue entred into Halcons landes.
20 And whan Halcon herde that, he gathered his hoost togither and cam agaynst his ennemys, and betwene Halcons men and Bartas men was a great batayle vpon a frosen ryuer or an yse. And for the great heuynesse of the men and beestes, the yse brake, and there was drowned aboue xxx thousande of the Tartas; and than the bothe
25 parties retorned backe agayne without doyng any more, and made great lamentatyon for the dethe of theyr frendes. [c6v]

How Ginboga and the men of Saiect fyll at varyaunce

Ginboga, the which Helcon had left with hym x thousande Tartas in the realme of Syri and went to the Palestines parte, which kept the
30 lande in peace, and worshiped and loued moche the Christen men (for he was of the thre kynges kynred which cam to Bethlehem to honoure the byrth of Christ); Ginboga trauayled moche to recouer the Holy Lande. And than the deuyll put great trouble betwene hym and the Christen men that were of the partes of Saiect. For in the

lande of Belfort, that was of the lordshyp of Saiect, was diuers
townes in the which the Sarasyns dwelled and payd a tribute to the
Tartas; wherof it came that the men of Saiect and of Belfort came
togyder to make a course, and robed the sayd townes frome the sayd
5 Sarasyns; some were slayne, and some were brought prysoners.
One of Ginbogas neuiewes was in that countrey, and went after the
Christen men with a smale company a horsbacke. And as he began
to blame them of that that thei had done and wolde take the prey that
they brought, some of the Christen men ranne vpon hym, and so
10 kylde hym. Whan Ginboga vnderstode that the Christen men of
Saiect had slayn his neuiewe, he rode with his men and came to
Sarepte; and as many Christen men as he founde, put them to the
swerde. But the peple of Sarepte wente away in the yle, and but fewe
slayne. Ginboga dyde putte fyre in the cyte and brake the walles,
15 and neuer sythe, Ginboga had neuer trust nor loue with the Christen
men of Syrie, nor his men. After that, the Tartas were dryuen oute
of the realme of Syrie by the power of the Sowdan of Egipt, as it shal
be declared hereafter.

How the Sowdan of Egipt droue the Tartas out of Syri

20 In that tyme that Barca began warre agaynst Helcone, as we haue
sayd before, the Sowdan of Egipt gathered his armye and came
into the Palestins countreys, in a place that is called Haymelot. And
there he fought with the Tartas; but they coude nat abyde the
Sowdans power, and so they fled backe with theyr captayns. It was
25 sayd that Gynboga was slayne in the batayle. The Tartas that scaped
from the said batayle went into Armenie. At that tyme the realme of
Syrie torned to the Sowdans power, but some cytes that were by
the see that the Christen men kept. Whan Helcon vnderstode that
the Sowdan of Egipt was entred into the realme of Syrie and that
30 he had betyn his men and kylde them, he gathered his hoost, and
sende to the Kynge of Armenie, to the Kynge of Georgy, and to
the other Christen men [D1r] of the parties of Syrie, that they sholde
be redy to go with hym agaynst the Sowdan of Egipt. And whan
Halcon had all his army redy for to go to the realme of Syri, a sharpe
35 sykenesse toke hym that helde hym xv dayes, of which he dyed;
and so his deth lette the goynge into the Holy Lande.
After hym his sonne Albaca helde the lordeshippe of Halcon. This

Albaga wolde that Ambyla, his vncle, sholde confirme hym his
lordship; which thinge he dyde with a good wyll, bycause that he
knewe well that Albaga was the best and the wysest sonne that
Halcon had. And so he was called Albaga Can, and began his raygne
5 in the yere of Our Lorde God a thousande CC lxiiii.

How Albaga wolde nat become Christen, which fortuned hym yll

Albaga, that was moch valyant and kept wysely his lordeshyp, and
was moche fortunat in all maner of thinges – saue that he wolde
10 nat become Christen as his father Halcon was, and so he was an
ydolatrer. And another thing was that he made warre vpon his
neyghbours, whiche caused hym that he coude nat ouercome the
Sodan of Egipt; and bycause of that the Sowdan of Egiptes power
encreased moche. Yet the Sowdan of Egipt dyd another subtyll
15 poynt; for he sende his messangers to Tartas that were in the realme
of Comany and of Roussy and made couenable peace and loue
with them, and ordayned, if Albaga wolde come into the lande of
Egipt, that they sholde inuade his landes and that they sholde
warre vpon hym. And for this composicyon, the Sowdan had great
20 ioy to haue the Christen mens landes of Syri; and for that cause the
Christen men loste the cyte of Antyoch and many other, as it is
wryten in the cronicle boke of the Holy Lande.

    Bendonedar, which was Sowdan of Egipt, was moche mighty and
puysaunt. He sende his hoost into Armeny, but the Kynge was
25 gone to the Tartas. Than his two sonnes gathared the hoost of Armeny, which was at that tyme of great power, and came agaynste
their ennemys and fought with them. The batayle was great, but at
the ende the Christen men were ouercome; and of the two sonnes,
the one was taken prisonere, and the other slayn in batayle. And
30 than the Sarasyns entrede in the lande and wasted all the playn of
Armeny. The Christen mens power was moch minysshed bycause of
that, and the puysaunce of the Sarasyns power was moche enhaunced. Whan the Kyng of Armeny vnderstode this tidynges of his
sonnes and of the lande, he was moch sorowfull, and thought in
35 his mynde how that he myght do harme to his ennemys. Thanne
went he to Albaga and to the other Tartas, desiryng and prayeng
them [D1v] that they wolde come to helpe the Christen men. The
Kyng trauayled moch, but Albaga wold nat go for bycause that he

had warre with his neyghbours. The Kyng, seyng that he coude nat
haue helpe so shortly of the Tartas, sende his messangers to the
Sowdan of Egipt; and confirmed peace with hym, to thyntent that he
myght haue his sonne out of prison. And the Sowdan made poynt-
5 ment with the Kyng that he shuld rendre vnto hym one of his felowes
which was called Sangolagar, that the Tartas kept, and that he
sholde yelde to hym agayn the castell of the lande of Halap that he
helde; and he shulde gyue to hym his sonne agayn. The Kyng
dyde so moch that the Tartas gaue hym Sangolagar, the Sowdans
10 felowe abouesayd, and the Kynge yelded to the sayd felowe the
castell of Trepessache and two other castels that he brake downe at
the Sowdans request. And in this maner the King of Armenis sonne,
Baron Lynon, was delyuerd out of the prison of the Sarasyns. After
that, the Kyng Hayton of good remembraunce, which had donn grete
15 good to the Christendom in his lyfe, gaue his realme and lordship to
his sonn Lynon aboue named; and left the pryde of this worlde and
toke the order of relygion, and chaunged his name after the gise of
the Armins and was called Macayres. And than the Kyng Hayton
dyed monke, in the yere of Oure Lorde God a thousande two
20 honderde lxx.

How Albaga toke the traitour Pernana and put hym to deth

The sonn of Kyng Hayton, Baron Lynon, was wise and valyant, and
gouerned his realme and his lordship wisely. He was well beloued
25 of his people, and the Tartas dyde to hym great honour. This sayd
Kyng Lynon toke moche labour for to greue the Sarasyns by the
Tartas, and diuers tymes sende his messengers to Albaga that he
sholde come for to helpe to recouer the Holy Lande and to confounde the power of Egipt. At that tyme the Sowdan of Egipt entred
30 with his power into the realme of Turky. He kylde and droue out
all the Tartas that were there, and toke many landes and countreys
by a traitour that Albaga had made chefe captain of Turky, that was
called Parnana (whiche torned and was obeydient to the Sowdan
of Egipt, and toke moch labour for to dryue the Tartas out of Turky).
35 Whan Albaga vnderstode this tydinges, he gathered his hoost and
rodde hastely – for of xl dayes iornay he made but xv – and came
to Turky. Whan the Sowdan knewe of the Tartas comming, he durst

nat abyde, but fledde away hastely. And Albaga sende his men for-
warde; and before that the Sowdan myght come and retorne into
the realme of Egipt, the Tartas ouertoke the last parte of the Sarasyns
hoost in a place is called Lepas Blanc. And [D2r] entred into the
5 Sarasins hoste and toke II M horsmen and gate great richesse, and
moreouer they toke V M houses of Cordyns that were in the sayd
parties. And than Albaga had counsell that he shuld nat entre into
the lande of Egypt, for the great hete that was there and for theyr
horses that had so moch laboured. And than Albaga retorned to
10 Turkey and toke the landes and the cites, and dyd so moche that he
toke Parnana. And sone after, as the maner of the Tartas was,
Pernana was put to dethe. And than Albaga commaunded that, in all
maner of his mete that he shulde ete, shulde haue some of the
flessh of Parnana; and so Albaga dyd ete of the flesshe, and gaue
15 some to his men. And that was the vengeaunce that Albaga toke of
the traitour Parnana.

How Albaga profered the realme of Turky to the King of Armeny

Whan Albaga had taken all the landes and had ordred the realme of
20 Turky to his plesure, he dyde call before hym the Kynge of Armeny, and profred hym to haue and holde the realme of Turky at his
pleasure bycause that the Kyng of Armeni and his kynred had
euer ben true to the Tartas. The Kynge of Armeny, as a wise man,
thanked moch Albaga of so great a gift; and excused hym, sayeng
25 that he was nat sufficient to gouern two realmes, for the Sowdan of
Egypt toke moch labour for to do hurt to the realm of Armeni. And
than the Kyng of Armeny counselled to Albaga that he shulde nat
gyue the lordship of the realm of Turkey to a Sarasyn. This counsell plesed moch to Albaga, and so he wolde that no Sarasyn shulde
30 haue no lande nor holde in Turkey.

After that, the Kyng of Armeni praied to Albaga that he wold go,
or sende his brother, to delyuer the Holy Lande out of the Sarasyns
handes and to gyue it to the Christen men agayn. Albaga promised
hym that he shulde do it with a good wyll. And commaunded to
35 the Kyng of Armeny that he shulde sende to the Pope and to the
other kynges and lordes of the Christen men of the Occident, that
they shulde come, or send their men, to the helpe of the Holy Lande

for to kepe the landes and the cytes that thei shuld conquere. Than
the King of Armeny departed and retorned into his landes, and sende
his messangers to the Pope and to the kynges of the Occident. And
whan he had ordayned that that was nedefull to the realme of Turkey,
5 he came to the realm of Corasten, there as he had left his housholde.
  Bendonedar was poysoned as he retorned to Egypt, and coude nat
retorne on lyue to the cyte of Damas. Of Bendonaders deth were
the Christen men glad, and the Sarasyns moche sory; for he was a
valyant man of armes. After Bendonader was one made sowdan that
10 was called Melecset, but he taried nat longe for he was put from
the lordshippe; [D2v] and one that was called Esly was made sowdan.

Of the batayle betwene Mangadamor and the Sowdan

Whan the tyme and the season came that Albaga myght ryde for to
entre into the lande of Egypt, firste he sende Mangadamor with
15 XXX M Tartas; and badde that they shuld occupy the Kyng Anyne
of Syri, and he wolde ryde after. And yf the Sowdan shulde come
agaynst them, that they shulde valyantly fyght with hym; and if the
Sowdan durst nat come in the batayle, he commaunded that they
shulde occupy the landes and the cyties, and that they shuld deliuer
20 them into the Christen mens handes to kepe. Mangadamor rode
with xxx thousande Tartas that Albaga his brother had gyuen hym,
and the King of Armeny put him in his company with a grete
nombre of horsmen. Whan Mangadamor and the Kyng of Armeny
entred into the realme of Syri, they went wastyng the Sarasyns
25 landes to the cyte of Hames (that is called la Chalemelle) which is in
the myddes of the realme of Syri. Before this cyte is a fayre playne,
and there was the Sowdan with all his power. The Sarasyns on one
parte, the Tartas and the Christen men of another parte, began to
fyght. The Kyng of Armeny, that conducted the right part of the
30 hoost, sette them in aray, and sette vpon the lyft part of the Sarasyns
host and discomfyt them, and droue them be-ende the cytie of Hames
thre leges and more. And the constable of the Tartas, that was
called Halmach Bech, set vpon the right part of the Sarasyns hoost
and ouercame them, and than euery of them went to a cytie that is
35 called Thara. Mangadamor, that taryed in the felde, se come a company of Bednyns, and putte hym in great fere, as a man that had
neuer sene batayle; and withoute reason departed from the felde

with the victori, and lefte the Kyng of Armeny and the constable that
were gone after theyr ennemys. Whan the Sowdan se that the
Tartas were departed from the felde, he went vpon an hyll with iiii
thousande horsmen. Whan the Kyng of Armeny retorned fro the
5 disconfiture and founde nat Mangadamor, he was moche abasshed;
whiche way he was gone, he rode after. Ameleth the constable
taryed ii dayes for his lorde Mangadamor, and also he was moche
abasshed of the way that he went. And whan he knewe that he
was gone, he rode after with his men tyl he came to the ryuer of
10 Eufrates, and coude nat ouertake Mangadamor. And so, by the
faute of the sayd Magadamor, they left the felde and the batayle
whan they had the victory. The Tartas went agayne into theyr
countreis, but the Kyng of Armeny suffred gret trauayle and moche
losse of his people. [D3r] Through faute of vitayle the men and
15 beestes were so wery that they coude nat go, and than they departed
asonder and went by dyuers wayes, there as the Sarasins were
and dwelled in the sayd countreis; which toke and slewe many of the
Christen men. And so the moost part of the King of Armenis hoste
was lost, and almoost all the gentylmen were slayn. This mysfortune
20 happened in the yere of Our Lorde God M CC lxxxii.

How Albaga and his brother was poysoned by theyr famulyer seruauntes

Whan Albaga vnderstode this tidynges, he sende and commaunded
that his barownes shulde come in all the hast vnto hym; and so
25 Albaga gathered a great hoost to thyntent to entre into the realme of
Egypt. But it happened that a Sarasyn came into the realme of
Persy; the which dyde so moch and gaue gyftes to Albagas famyliar
seruauntes that they gaue to Albaga, and to his brother, poyson,
and so they lyued but viii dayes after. And so Albaga Can dyed in the
30 yere of Our Lorde God a thousande two honderde foureskore and
two.
    After the dethe of Albaga Can the barownes came togyder and
ordayned one of Albaga Cans brothers that was called Tangader.
This Tangader was greter than any of the other brethern. Whan he
35 was a chylde his name was Nychole, but after that he was made
lorde he toke the Sarasyns company, and dyde call hymselfe Mahomet
Can. He putte all his wyt to conuert the Tartas to the false lawe

of Mahomet. Whan many of the Tartas were conuerted to the Sarasyns
lawe, this Mahomet, that was the deuyls sonne, dyde breke downe
all the Christen mens churches, and commaunded that they shulde
nat worshippe the lawe of Chryst nor the name of Chryst; and put
5 away all the Christen men prestes and relygious men, and dyd prech
Mahometes lawe through all his landes. And he sende his messangers to the Sowdan of Egypt and made promyse of peace and
loue; and promysed to the Sowdan that he shulde cause all the
Christen men that were in his lande to tornn and to be Sarasyns, or
10 els he shuld put them all to dethe. Of this the Sarasyns were all
gladde, and the Christen men were sory and of great disconfort.
Insomoche, that they wyst nat what they shulde do but put theymselfe into the mercy of Oure Lorde God, for they se come vpon theym
great persecucions. The sayd Mahomet sende to the Kynge of
15 Armeny, to the Kynge of Georgy, and to the other Christen men of
the Orient, that they shulde come to hym. The good Christen men
were in great thought and great fere all the whyle that the [D3v]
Christen men were in so moche trybulation vnder the lordshippe
of this euyll Mahomet. But God, that is with them that belyue in hym,
20 sende to the Christen men a great confort. For a brother of the
sayd Mahomet, and one of his neuewes that was called Morgon, rose
agaynst hym for his euyll warkes; and gaue knowlege to themperour
Cobyla Can how he distroyed and preched to the Tartas that they
sholde torne to the Sarasyns lawe. Whan Cobyla Can vnderstode
25 that, he sende a commaundement to Mahomet that he sholde leue his
euyl warkes, or els he shulde ryse agaynst hym. Of this mater
Mahomet was sore dyspleased, and dyd so moche that he toke his
brother and kylde hym. And than after, he went for to take Argon,
but Argon putte hym in a strong castell that was in a mountayne.
30 Mahomet dyde lay sege to the sayd castell, and at the ende Argon
yelde hymselfe, sauynge his owne lyfe and his seruauntes.

How the false Mahomet was slayne by his neuiew Argon

Whan Mahomet had his neuiewe vnder his power, he delyuerd hym
35 to one of his constables for to kepe. And after, ordained that his
men shulde come softly after hym, and he hymselfe wolde go towarde
Thoris, there as he had lefte his wyfe; and commaunded to the

constable that he shulde secretly kyll his neuiewe Argon, and that he
shulde bryng hym his heed to Thoris. A great myghty man founde
hym, the which Argons father had norysshed and done moche good
to hym. This sayd man had gret pyte vpon Argon; and than vpon a
5 nyght came and slewe the constable and all them that were of his
company, and delyuerd Argon from dethe and out of pryson. And
made Argon lorde ouer them all, and to hym they were obeydient
and redy to do hym seruyce. Whan this was done Argon rydde
hastely, and dyde so moche that he ouertoke Mahomet Can or that he
10 came to Thoris, and incontynently he cutte hym all in peces. And
after this maner the cursed dogge Mahomet fynisshed his lyfe the
seconde yere of his reygne.

In the yere of Our Lorde God a thowsande two honderde lxxxv,
after that Mahomet was deed, Argon was made lorde of the Tartas.
15 And the Great Emperour confermed hym in his lordship, and wolde
that he shulde be called Argon Can; and bycause of that, Argon
was moch more worshipped than any of his auncytours. This Argon
was fayre and plesaunt of visage, and a strong man of body; and
kept his lordshyppe wysely. He gouerned well his lordshippe, and
20 he loued well and honoured moch the Christen men; and the churches
[D4r] of the Christen men that Mahomet brake downe, Argon caused
them to be newe made agayn. And than came to hym the Kyng of
Armeny, the Kyng of Georgy, and the other Christen men of the
Orient, and prayed Argon that he wolde take payne to delyuer the
25 Holy Lande. Wherupon Argon toke aduysment, entendyng to make
peace fyrst with his neyghbours, to thyntent that he myght go the
more surer agaynst the Sowdans power. And as it happened that
Argon was in that good purpose, in the fourth yere of his raygne,
as it pleased God, he dyed. And one of his brethern that was called
30 Kalgato was made lorde after hym. This sayd Kalgato was the vnprofitablyst lorde that euer reygned in that countrey sith Cangius Can was
made lorde, as it shal be rehersed hereafter.

How Kalgato was drowned by his owne people

In the yere of Our Lorde God M CC lxxxix, after the deth of Argon
35 Can, his brother Kalgato helde the lordship. This sayde Kalgato
beleued nat well nor he was nothyng worth in armes, but demeaned
hymselfe lyke a foule beest in etyng of denteth metes and drinkynge

of swete wynes to fyll his belly. Non other thyng dyd he in vi
yeres whyle he kept his lordshippe. For the great peuisshnesse that
was in hym, his owne people began to hate hym and to disprayse
hym, and so at the ende his owne peple drowned hym.

5   After the deth of this Kalgato one of his cosyns was made lorde
which was called Baydo. This sayd Baido was a gode Christen man
and dyd moch good to the Christen men, but he lyued nat longe in
this worlde. After the deth of Kalgato, Baydo had the lordship of
his brother. This man, as a good Christen man, caused the churches
10 of the Christen men to be buylded vp agayn, and commaunded
that none shulde prech the lawe of Mahomet in his lande. Of that the
Sarasyns, that were multyplied, were sore greued. And than the
Sarasyns and the Tartas sende pryuely to Consan messanges, which
was Argons sonne, and promysed hym that they wolde make hym
15 lord, and that they shulde gyue hym Baydos lordship if he wolde
forsake the Christen fayth. Casan, that set nat moche by the fayth
of Christ, was lightly torned; for he was moche couytus to haue the
lordship, and was content to do after theyr desyre. Wherupon
Consan rose. Than Baydo gathered his hoost, and cam agaynst
20 Consan, and knewe nat the treason of his people.

How Casan was deceyued by the traytour Chapchap

Whan Baydo thought to come agaynst Consan, all they that kept
Mahometz law departed and went toward [D4v] Casan. Whan
Baydo se that his men had betrayed hym, he torned backe agayn, but
25 Casan send after and toke him. And so, as Baydo fledde away, he
was kylde. And than Casan toke the lordshippe.

   After Baydos deth, Casan kept the lordship. He shewed hymselfe
moche proude to the Christen men, and that dyde he for the pleasure of them that had put him in the lordship abouesayd. But syth
30 that he was fermed in his lordshyp, he began to loue moch the
Christen men and hatede the Sarasyns, and he dyde moch profet to
the Christen lande. Fyrste he put to dethe all them that gaue hym
counsell to do hurt to the Christen men. After that, Casan commaunded that all his men shulde be redy within a yere of all maner of
35 thynges that they had nede to; for he wold entre into the lande of
Egypt and put out the Sowdan. And sende to the Kyng of Armeny,
to the Kyng of Georgy, and to the Christen men of the parties of
the Orient, that they shulde be redy to come with hym.

Whan the season was come, Casan rode with all his power, and came into the cytie of Baldache. Whan Casan came into the Sowdans landes, he brought his men togyder. The Sowdan of Egypt, that was called Malecuaser, gathered all his power before the cytie of Hames, 5 that is in the myddes of the realme of Syrie. Casan vnderstode that the Sowdan was commyng for to fyght agaynst hym. And for cause of that he wolde nat tary for to take castell nor towne, but he went streight to the place there as the Sowdan was, and lodged by the hoost within a dayes iourney in a medowe wherin was great plenty 10 of grasse. Than Casan commaunded that thei shulde gyue rest to all their beestes that were laboured in commyng hastelye so ferre way. In the company of Casan was a Sarasyn that was called Chapchap, whiche had ben baylie of Damas, and was fledde away for fere of the Soudan. Casan had don many honours and graces to the 15 said Chapchap and trusted hym well. And than it happened that the sayd Chapchap sende by his letters to the Sowdan of Egypt all the secrettes and counsell of the Tartas; and sende to the Sowdan that he shulde come hastely agaynst Casan to the batayle, and as his men and his beestes were wery. Than it fortuned that the Sowdan of 20 Egypt, which did purposlye tary for Casan, went into the countreys of Hames by the counsell of the sayd Chapchap the traytoure, and came hastely with all his power to begynne vpon Casan and to make hym afrayed. The kepers of Casans hoost gaue knowlege of the Sowdans commyng, and than Casan commaunded to all his barownes 25 that they shulde ryde all in ordre in theyr batayles against the Sowdan and his men. And Casan rode euer with as many of his men that were by him, and [D5r] came agaynst the Sowdan which came hastely with a great nombre of the beest men of his hoost.

Whan Casan se that he coude nat vndertake the [ba]tayle, and that 30 his men that were abrode coude nat come to hym so soone, he taryed there. And commaunded to all them that were with hym that they shulde lyght afote, and that they shulde put theyr horses about them, and with bowes and arowes they shulde bete theyr ennemys downe that were commyng and ronnyng as fast as theyr 35 horses coude bere them. Than the Tartas descended afote, and put theyr horses betwene them, and helde their bowes and theyr arowes redy in thiyr handes, abydinge tyll theyr ennemys were come nere to them. Than the Tartas shot theyr arowes all togyder, and made them that came ronnynge fyrst to fall vpon the grounde, and the 40 other that came after, fyll vpon them, and so the one fyll vpon

another. And they shot styll and well, for they were good shoters, so
that fewe of the Sarasins skaped but that they were slayne or hurt.
Whan the Sowdan se that, he went backe agayne; and than Casan
commaunded incontinently to his men that they sholde lepe vpon
5 theyr horses, and that they shulde valiantly set vpon their ennemys.
Casan was the fyrst that went to fyght agaynst the Sowdan, and
ran into the prese with suche small company that he had with hym
tyll all the barownes came to the batayle. Than began the batayle
that lasted from the sonnrising tyll none. At thende the Sowdans
10 hoost coud nat endure afore Casan, for with his owne handes he
dyd gret meruelles, and the Sowdan with his people fledde away.
Casan and his men chased them tyll it was darke nyght, and they
slewe as many of theyr ennemys as they coude take; than there was
so many Sarasyns slayne that the grounde was all couered with
15 them. The sayd night Casan taryed in a place that is called Caner, full
gladde of the victory that God had giuen hym. This batayle was in
the yere of Our Lord God a thousande thre hondred and one, the
Wednisday before Christmasse.

How the cytie of Hames was conquered

20 After that, Casan comaunded to the Kynge of Armeni, and to one of
his barownes that was called Molay, that with forty thousande
Tartas they sholde go after the Sowdan vnto the desert of Egipt, that
was well twelfe dayes iourney from the place there as the batayle
was. And commaunded that they shulde tary his commyng in the
25 countrey of Cassore. The Kynge of Armeny and Molay, with XL M
Tartas, departed and went after the Sowdan; and as many Sarasyns
as they coude take, they kyld them. The thyrde day after, Casan
commaunded that the Kynge of Armeni [D5v] shuld come backe
again, for he wolde lay sege to the cyte of Hames; and commaunded
30 that Molay shulde go after the Sowdan. But the Sowdan ran away
nyght and day vpon ronnynge horses, in the company of Bednyns
that were his gyde, and in this maner myserably the Sowdan entred into Babylon without any company. The Sarasyns fledde away
into dyuers wodes, there as they thought to skape better; and a
35 great part of the Sarasins kept the way towarde Triple, the which
were taken and kylde by the Christen men that dwelled at the
mount of Lyban. The Kynge of Armeny retorned to Casan, and

founde that the cyte of Hames was yelded to Casan. And all the
riches that the Sowdan and his men had was brought before Casan,
and they marueyled greatly all that the Sowdan and his men had
brought with them so gret riches, there as they thought to feyght.
5 Whan Casan had brought togyder all the tresure and riches that were
goten, he departed all to his men.

And I, Frere Hayton, hath ben present to all the great besinesse
that the Tartas had to do with the Sarasyns, from Halcons tyme
hyderto, but I herde neuer speke that no lorde of the Tartas dyde so
10 great a ded in two dayes as Casan dyde. For the fyrst day of the
batayle, Casan, with a smale company of men, proued hymselfe
agaynst the Sowdan and a great nombre of his men, and of his person
dyde so well that he was named aboue all other in batayle. And of
his person shal be spoken among the Tartas euermore. The seconde
15 day the fredome of Casan was great; for all the riches that he had
goten, that was without nombre, he departed it to his men in such
manere that he kept for hymselfe but one swerde and a purse of
ledder full of writinges and dedes of the lande of Egypt, and all the
remnant he gaue frely. And marueyll it was that so lytell a body
20 myght haue so great vertu; for among a M men coud nat be so sklender
a man, nor so euyl made, nor a fouler man. He surmounted all other
in prowesse and vertue. And for bycause that Casan is of our
tyme, we must speke of hym lenger than of the other; for this sowdan
that was ouercome by Casan is yet lyuenge. And moreouer, all
25 them that tary the passage of the Holy Lande may take there many
good examples.

How they of Damas yelded themselfe to Casan

After that Casan had rested certain dayes and ordred his besinesses,
he rode to the cyte of Damas. Whan they of Damas vnderstode the
30 commynge of Casan they were afrayed; for if Casan sholde take them
by force, he shulde take all without any mercy. And than they
sende theyr messangers to Casan with great giftes, and sende to hym
the keys of the towne of Damas. Than it happened that Casan receyued
the gyftes, and comaunded to [D6r] the messangers that they shulde
35 retorn to Damas, and that thei shuld make vitayle redy for his
hoost, and that they shulde nat fere his commyng; for he wolde do no
hurt to the cite of Damas, but wold kepe it as his chambre. The

messangers departed full gladde for the good answere that Casan gaue
them. And than Casan rod after, and lodged nere the riuer of Damas.
And commaunded that no man shulde hurt nor oppres the cyte.
They of Damas sende to Casan great gyftes and habondaunce of
5 vitayle for him and his hoost. And so Casan soiorned many dayes
in Damas with his hoost (besydde the XL M Tartas that were with
Molay, the which were at Acasere tarieng for Casans comyng).
As Casan and his people taryed and reposed them at Damas, there
came a messanger that brought tidynges that Baydo was entred
10 into the realme of Persy and that he had donn moch harme in the
lande, and they thought he sholde do more hurt than he had
done. Wherfore Casan commaunded to Catholasa that he sholde tary
for to kepe the realme of Syri, and commaunded to Molay and to
the other Tartas that were with hym in Casere that thei sholde obey
15 to Catholasa, the which Casan had laft in his place. And than after
he ordayned baylies and gouerners in euery cyte, and made Cachap
baylie of Damasse – Casan vnderstode nat that Cachap was a
traytour. After all that, Casan called the Kynge of Armeny, and
shewed hym how he wolde retornn to Persy. Casan sayd: 'We haue
20 delyuerd you the lande of Syrie to kepe for the Christen men. If
they come, we leue our commaundement to Catholasa that he shall
delyuer the Holy Lande to the Christen men, and that he shuld
gyue counsell and helpe to make the landes agayn.'
When Casan had done that he went towarde Mesopotamy. And
25 whan he was at the flode of Eufrates, he commaunded to Catholasa
that he sholde leue Molay with XX M men to kepe the land, and that
he sholde come in all the hast to hym with the remnant of the hoost
of the Kyng Anyne of Mesopotamy. And so Catholasa departed and
dyde as Casan commaunded hym, and Molay taried for to kepe the
30 lande of Syri. By the counsell of the traitour Capchap, Molay went
into the parties of Hierusalem into a place that is called Gant, wher
was gode pasture for their horses. Whan the sommer was com, Capchap sende his messangers to the Sowdan and promysed to delyuer
hym Damas and all the other landes that the Tartas kept of the realme
35 of Syri. And the Sowdan promised to Capchap that he sholde gyue
hym the lordship of Damas and a gret part of his tresure and his
syster to be his wyfe. Than Capchap rose, and made to rysse all
the countres; for he knewe well that the Tartas coude nat come vpon
them bycause of the great hete of the sommer. Whanne Molay se
40 that Dames and the other countreis were vp, he durste nat abyde in

the realme of Syrie with so fewe men, [D6v] but went towarde
Mesopotamy; and there he founde Casan, and rehersed to hym what
Capchap the traytour had done. Whan Casan vnderstode those
tydinges, he was greatly displeased, but he coude no remedy for the
5 great hete that was there.

　　Whan the sommer was paste and the wynter began, Casan gathared
a great hoost vpon the flode syde of Eufrates. And sende firste for
Catholasa with xxx thousande Tartas; and commaunded that they
sholde go towarde the cyte of Antioche, and that he sholde sende for
10 the Kynge of Armeny and for the Christen men that were at that
tyme in realme of Cipres. And so they came by the see to the cyte of
Corcose; and there was the Lorde Sut, brother to the Kyng of
Cipres, which conducted the lordes and knyghtes, and there was the
Maisters of the Temple and of the Hospitall. And as they were
15 apparelled to do Our Lorde God seruice, tydinges came that a sore
sykenesse had taken Casan; wherfore Catholasa was fayn to retorne
to Casan with his men, and the Kyng retourned to his countrei, and
the Christen men that were com to the yle of Carcon went to Ciprez.
And for this cause the warre of the Holy Lande was laft. This mater
20 was in the yere of Our Lorde a thousande thre honderde and one.

Whan the Kynge of Armeny and Catholasa toke the cyte of Hames

In the yere of Our Lorde God M CCC and iii Casan gathared his
hoost agayn vpon the flodde of Eufrates, to thentent that he myght
25 enter into the realme of Siri and to distroy the Sowdan of Egipt and to
recouer the Holy Lande and delyuer it to the Christen men agayne.
Whan the Sarasyns vnderstode the commynge of Casan and that they
were nat able to fyght agaynst his power, they wasted and brende
all the lande and countrey by the which thei sholde passe. With theyr
30 beestes and catell and all that they coude fynde, they brought to a
stronge place, and all the remenant they sette on fyre for cause that
theyr horses sholde fynde na meat. Whan Casan vnderstode this
that the Sarasyns had done, thinkynge that the horses sholde fynde
no mete to lyue on, he toke counsell to tary the same winter at
35 the flode of Eufrates; and whan the grasse sholde begyn to springe,
they wolde take theyr waye. But they had more thought for their
horses mete than they dyd for themselfe, as men but of smale fedynge.

Casan was vpon the flode syde with his hoost, and sende for the
Kyng of Armeni. Casans hoost was so grete that it lasted iii dayes
iourney of length from the castell that is called Racale to another
that is called la Bire; these two castels were longing to the Sarasyns,
5 but they yelded them to Casan. And as Casan was tarieng at the
flode of Eufrates for the seson and wether for to delyuer the Holy
Lande out of [E1r] the Sarasyns power, he herde tidynges that
Baydo was come agayn into his lande, and how he hadde done moche
harme there and dryuen his men away that he left ther for to kepe the
10 lande. Vpon that, Casan had counsell that he shulde retorne into his
countrey, and in the next yere he might well entre into the realme
of Syrie. Casan was sore displeased that the mater of the Holy Lande
taryed so long.

Than he commaunded to Catholosa that he shulde entre into the
15 realme of Syrie with xl thousande Tartas, and that he shulde take
the cyte of Damas, and that he shulde put to the swerde as many as
he shulde take. And commaunded to the King of Armeny that he
shulde go with his men with Catholosa with xl thousande Tartas on
horsbacke, and that they shulde entre into the realme of Syrie and,
20 as they shulde go, to wast all the countrey. They had thought to
haue founde the Sodan in that countrey as they had done in tymes
past, but they found hym nat. But they herde say that he was at
Gazette and that he wold nat departe out of that countrey. Wherfore
Catholosa and the Kinge of Armeny dyd assayle and set vpon the
25 cyte of Hames; so well that within fewe dayes they toke it by force
and put all the men and women to the swerde without any mercy.
Thei founde there great ryches and great plenty of beestes and
vitayles.

And after that, they went before the cytie of Dames to thintent to
30 set vpon it. But the burges of the cyte desyred them that they
shuld gyue them terme for thre dayes, and after that they shulde
yelde them to mercy. The terme was graunted to them. But ronners
made a course from the Tartas hoost well a dayes iourney be-ende
Damas, and toke a certayne nombre of Sarasyns, whiche they sende
35 to Catholosa their captayn; and by those Sarasyns Catholosa knewe
that within ii dayes iourney from thens were xii thousande Sarasyns
on horsbacke taryeng for the Sowdans commyng. Whan Catholosa
vnderstode this tidynges, he rode hastely; and dyde so moche that he
came to the place there as the xii thousande Sarasins were, to
40 euynsong tyme, thinkyng to ouertake them or the Sowdan shuld

come. But a lytell whyle before, the Sowdan was come with his
power. Whan Catholosa and the King of Armeny se that the Sowdan
was come, they toke counsell what they shulde do. And bycause it
was almoost nyght, they had counsell to rest them; and vpon the next
5 day they shulde set wysely vpon the Sowdan. But Catholosa, that
dispraysed the Sowdan, wolde nat tary so long; but commaunded
that his men shulde take corage, and that valyantly they shulde set
vpon theyr ennemys.

The Sarasyns, that were lodged in a strong place betwene ii waters,
10 wolde nat depart to fyght, for they knewe well that the Tartas coude
nat come to them without great losse. And bycause of that, the
[E1v] Sarasyns wolde nat departe from thens. The Tartas rode hastely
to set vpon their ennemys, but thei found a lytel water that they
coude nat passe in dyuers places; that troubled them moch or they
15 coude passe the sayd water. Whan Catholosa, the Kyng of Armeny,
and the moost part of theyr men was passed, they set valiantly vpon
theyr enemys. Thei kylde all them that they met in theyr way, and
chased them tyll the nyght. The Sowdan wolde nat come from his
place, nor come to the batayle. That night Catholosa lodged by a
20 mountayn with his men, except X M that coude nat passe the water
by daylyght. Than the next day Catholosa ordayned his men for to
fyght, but the Sowdan wold nat come out of that place nor come to
the batayle. The Tartas toke moch labour for to haue the Sarasyns
out of that place, but they coude nat in no wyse. The batayle lasted
25 tyll none. But for faute of water the Tartas were wery and went
backe for to fynde water; and went in order one after another tyll
they cam to the playne of Damas, and there they founde pasture
and water inough. And Catholosa ordayned to rest his men and his
horses a certayne whyle there, bycause that they shulde be the
30 fressher for to retorne and fyght agaynst the Sowdan.

Whan the Tartas hoost was lodged in that playne and thought to
be in rest, the men of Damas lette ronne the water of the fludde by
cundittes and dyches so moche that, or viii of the clocke in the mornynge, the playne was all couered with water, and the wayes.
35 Wherfore the Tartas were fayne to ryse hastely. And also the nyght
was darke; the diches and the wayes were al full of water; wherfore the hoost was in great confusyon. Horse, beestes, and harnes
were lost, and many men drowned to great losse. Than the day
come, and so they were delyuerde by the grace of God out of that
40 daunger. But the bowes and the arowes, wherof the Tartas occupyed

the moost in batayle, were so weyt that they coude nat helpe them
therwith. In this maner the Tartas hoost were sore troubled, that yf
the Sarasyns had come sodaynly vpon them, they might haue ouercome them. The Tartas began to go backe agayne softly, bycause of
5 theyr horses lost, and came in viii dayes iourney to the fludde of
Eufrates. They were fayne to passe ouer vpon theyr horses the
beste that they coude do. The flud was gret and depe; so moche that
many Georgyns and Tartas were lost there. And so the Tartas
went backe agayne to theyr confusyon, nat for the power of their
10 ennemys but by euyll counsell; for Catholosa myght auoyded all
that myscheffe if he wolde haue beleued good counsell.

How the Kynge of Armeny went to Casan

I, Frere Hayton, that maketh mencion of this history, was [E2r]
present. And if I haue spoken to long of this mater, I pray you
15 pardon me; for I haue done it to the entent to put of the daungers in
lyke mater. For the warkes that be done by counsell ought for to
haue good ende.
　　After that the Kyng of Armeny had passed the fludde of Eufrates,
nat without great labour and losse of his men, he toke counsell to
20 go se Casan or he shulde go into Armeny. Than the King toke his
way and went streyght to the cyte of Ninyue, there as Casan
dwelled at that tyme. Casan receyued the King honorably, and had
pyte of the grete losse that he had of his men. And for bycause that
the King of Armeny and his men had serued truely in all theyr
25 besynesses, Casan dyde a speciall grace to the Kyng. For he gaue
hym a M Tartas that were good horsmen, and commaunded that
thei shulde dwell there for to kepe the lande of Armeny, to the Kynge
of Turkes cost, tyll that he shulde be able to gyue wages to a M
other knightes to his wyll. After that, the Kynge toke his leue at
30 Casan, and went into his countrey. And Casan sayde to hym, 'Se
that ye kepe your lande well tyll that I shall come personably for to
recouer the Holy Lande.'

How the Sowdan made trewse with the Kyng of Armeny

The Kyng of Armeny retorned into his countrey, but syth his com-
35 mynge there he had but lytell rest. For the Sowdan sende in the

same yere, almoost euery moneth, a great nombre of men a warre, that ran almoost all the lande of Armeny and wasted all the playn; wherfore the realme of Armeny was worse than euer it was before. But God almighty, that is with them that serue hym, had mercy of
5   the peple and Christen men of Armeny. Wherof it happened that in the moneth of Iuly, VII M Sarasyns of the best of the Sowdan of Egiptz house entred into the realme of Armeni and ronned all the playn, wastyng and robbing to the cyte of Tersot (in the which Saynt Paule was borne). This ennemys dyde moche hurt. And as they
10 were goynge backe agayne, the Kyng of Armeny gathered his hoost and met with them, and nygh the cyte of Layas was the batayle. And by the grace of Oure Lorde God theyr ennemys were ouercome in suche maner that, of the VII M Sarasyns, skaped nat iii hondred but they were slayn or taken. And that was vpon a Sonday, the xviii
15 day of Iuly. And after that batayle they durst no more com in the realme of Armeny, but the Sodan sende and made truese with the King of Armeni. And I, Frere Hayton, maker of this warke, was present to this thinges. And longe tyme afore that I was purposed to take the order of relygion, but I coude nat, for the great besinesse
20 that the Kyng of Armeny had at that tyme; I coude nat, for myne honour, forsake my lordes and my frendes in all nedis. But sith God of his grace hath gyuen [E2v] vs the victory agaynst our en- nemys, and also gyuen grace to leue the realme of Armeny in suffycient good state, shortly after, I thought for to make an ende of
25 my vowe. And than I toke leue of the Kyng and of my kynred and frendes, and in that tyme that Our Lorde gaue vs the victory agaynst the ennemys of our fayth I toke my way and cam into Cipres. And there, into Our Lady Delepiscopie chirch of the order of Premontrey, I toke the abyte of relygion – and longe I had ben knyght in this
30 worlde – to thyntent for to serue God the remenaunt of my lyfe. And this was in the yere of Our Lorde God M CCC v. Grace and mercy to God, for the realme of Armeny is reformed in better state than it was, by the yonge kinge, my lorde Lynon (in the olde tyme, baron), the which is full of vertue and grace. And also we trust that in this
35 yonge Kyng of Armenys dayes, the realm of Armeni shal be in his gode first state with the helpe of Our Lord Ihesu Christ.

The auctour

Yet I, that hath made this boke, se all that is in the thyrde parte of this

boke I knowe it in iii maners. For, from the begynnyng of Cangius
Can, that was the first emperour of the Tartas, tyll Mango Can, that
was the forth emperour, I se all as the Tartas historis rehersed.
And from Mango Can tyl Halcon dyed, I speke as I haue herde and
5 lerned of my lorde myn vncle, the Kyng Hayton, the Kyng of
Armeny, which hath ben present. In great dilygence [he] rehersed
[it] to his sonnes and to his neuewes, and dyd vs put [it] in writynge
for a remembraunce. And, from the beginnyng of Albaga, Halcons
sonn, tyll the thyrde part of this boke, there as the Tartas hystorie
10 finysshed, I speke as he that was present in person; and of that I
haue sene, I may reherse truely. We haue sayd of the Tartas dedis
and hystoris, yet we shal speke of theyr power.

Of the thre kynges that dyd honour to the Great Emperour

The Great Emperour of the Tartas that kept the lordshype is called
15 Tamor Cann; which was the vi emperour, and helde his sege in the
realme of Catay in a cyte that is called Iunig (the which his father
founded). The myght of this emperour is great, for hymselfe alone
might do more than all the Tartas princes. Themperours men be taken
for more noble, more riches, and more garnisshed of all thinges
20 than others; for in the realme of Catay is a great haboundaunce of
riches. And after, the iii kynges of Tartas that haue a great power
and do all reuerence [E3r] to the Great Emperour and obedient by his
iugement: the first of these kynges is called Capar; the seconde,
Totay; and the thyrde, Tarbanda.
25   Tarpar helde the lordship of Turkesten, and is more nygh of themperours landes than the others. This Kynge may bringe with hym
in batayle IIII C thousande men of warre an horsbacke. This men be
valyant and hardy; thei haue gode harnis and gode horses. Somtymes
themperour maketh warre against Chapchap; and wolde take his
30 landes from him, but he defended hym valyantly. The lordshippe
of Capar was all vnder one lorde, howbeit that his brother Totay
helde a great part of his lande.
     Totay, the Kynge of the Tartas, helde the Kyng of Cumanys lord-
ship, and his sege in a cytie that is called Sarra. This prynce may
35 bring to the batayle VII C thousande men an horsbacke, as the
sayeng is, but they be nat so valyant in batayle and in dede of armes
as Capars men be, howbeit that they haue better harnes and better

horses. Somtyme they make warre agaynst Carbanda; somtyme they make warre agaynst the Kynge of Hungarie; somtyme they haue ware amonge them; but nowe Totay kepeth the lordship in rest and peas.

5 How they of Lices haue knowlege by birdes whan any of theyr ennemys be commyng towarde them

Carbanda helde his power in the Great Asie, and kept his sege in the cite of Toris. He may bring to the batayle about iii C thousande men of armes an horsbacke, but they be men of dyuerse nations, rych
10 and well furnisshed of all maner suche thinges as thei haue nede. Capar and Totay make warre oftentymes agaynst Carbanda, but he defended his lande wisely. Carbanda medled nat with no warre agaynst no man but the Turke of Egypt, to the which all his aunces-tours haue had warre with the aboue sayd princes. Tapar and
15 Totay wolde fayne putte Carbanda out of his lordship yf thei coude, but thei haue no might, howbeit that they be more mighty of men and of landes.

This is the reson how Carbanda defended his landes from the myght of his neybours. For Asie is deuyded in ii partes, the one parte is
20 called the Depe Asie, the other is called the Maior Asie (and in that part Carbanda dwelled). There is no more but thre wayes by the which they mey entre out of Asie the Profonde and Asie the Great: the one way is by the which thei go from the realme of Turquesten to the realm of Persy; the other way is by the ende that goeth nigh to
25 the cyte that Alexander founded, that is called Port de Ferre; the other way is towarde the see of Maior, and passe by the realm of Dabcas. By the first way Capars men can nat entre in [E3v] Car-bandas landes without great danger and payne, for cause that they coude nat fynde pasture for theyr horses tyll manv dayes iourneys
30 ende. For this countrey is dry and barre, and so, or thei coude come to the good landes, theyr horses shulde dye for lacke of meate; and with a small company of ennemys they that shulde passe myght lese theyr lyues. By the other way at the ende, Totays men myght entre into Carbandas landes vi monethes in the yere in the wynter tyme.
35 But Albaga dyde make, a dayes iourney of length, lysses, dykes, and thynges in a place that is called Cyba; and now there be men of warre for to kepe the passages. Totays men haue many tymes

proued for to passe priuily, but they coude nat, for they must passe
by a playne that is called Mongan. In this playne be euer in wynter
a maner of wylde foule that they call seyserach; these byrdes be as
great as fesantes, and with feyre feders. And whan any men come
5 into this playn, these byrdes fle away, and passe the lyces towarde
the playn of Mongan. And by the token of these byrdes commyng, the kepars of the sayd lices knowe the commyng of theyr
ennemys, and than they puruey for them for the kepynge of the
sayde passage. By the other way, towarde the Maior See, they durst
10 nat entre; for they shuld be fayn to entre and passe by the realme
of Dabcas, which is garnysshed with men and stronge landes. And
so they can nat passe, and by this maner Carbanda and his auncetours haue defended theyr landes from the great myght of theyr
ennemys and neyghbours.

15 The maner and gyse that the Tartar vse amonge them

Yet shall we say somethynge of the Tartas maner and custome. The
Tartas be moche dyuers of maner and custome; it is nat possible to
reherse the dyuersite of them. The Tartas beleue in God, and name
God onely, and they saye that God is immortall; and none other
20 reuerence thei do to God, nother by praier, fasting, aflictions, nor
none other good dedes. The Tartas thynke no synne to haue kylde
a man; if the byt was in the horse mouth, they thinke to haue synned
deedly. The Tartas thinke that the deed of lechery is no synne;
they haue dyuerse wyues. And by theyr guyse and custome, after
25 the dethe of theyr father, the sonn must take for his wyfe his
mother-in-lawe; and the brother, the wyfe that was his brothers
wyfe; and make theyr beddes togyder. The Tartas be good men of
armes; to theyr lordes they be obedyent more than any other nation.
There lorde gyueth them no wages, but he may take from them
30 what it please hym. Nor for cost or ridynge theyr lorde is nat bounde
to gyue them anything, but they be fayne to lyue on their pray and
hauntyng that they take vpon their ennemis. Whan [E4r] the Tartas
ryde and passe by a passage there as they thinke to fynde no
vitayles, they bringe with them great plenty of beestes, kyne, and
35 mares; and lyue of the mylke and of the flesshe of these beestes
(and ete it and say that it is good flesshe). The Tartas be moch light in
dede of armes a horsbake, but a fote they be nat moche worth (for

they can nat go a fote). Whan thei be ordayned for to fyght, they
vnderstande shortly theyr captayns wyll and knowe what they
haue to do; wherfore the captayns rule theyr men lightly without any
labour.

5 The Tartas be subtyll for to take townes and castels. The Tartas
seke euer there aduauntage vpon theyr ennemys in batayle, and
wyll do none other thynge to theyr profet. The Tartas haue more
vauntage than other men: for if they be in a felde togyder for to
fyght agaynst theyr ennemys, if it please them thei shall fight; and if
10 the batayle pleased nat them, theyr ennemis can nat fyght agaynst
them nor come nygh them. The Tartas batayle is moche mortall; for in
one lytell batayle of the Tartas there shulde be more men slayne
and wounded than in a great batayle of other men, and that is for the
bowes and arowes that they ocupyed. Whan the Tartas be ouer-
15 com, they ronn all togyder as nigh as it can be possible. And is a
peryllous thinge to folowe them; for in goyng they kyll with their
bowes horses and men, and shote backwarde as thei do forward.
And if thei se that their ennemys folowed folysshely, they torne
vpon them; and somtyme it happened that they that ran after them
20 be kylled and slayne. The Tartas hoste is nat of grete mustre bycause
that they go nygh one with another, so nygh that x thousande Tartas
shewe nat v hunderde.

The Tartas be of fayre speking to their hoostes, and courtesly they
spende theyr meate; and lykewise that they shulde ben done with
25 them, or els they wolde take some parforce. The Tartas can well
conquere the strange things, but they can nat kepe it; for they
loued better to be in tentes and in the feldes thanne in the townes.
The Tartas be moche couytouse, and occupied moche to take other
mennes goodes, and they can nat kepe theyr owne, and nought thei
30 wyll spende. Whan the Tartas be in company there as they may be
maisters, they be of great corage and proude; and whan they se that
thei can nat haue the mastry, thei be courtes and honest. The
Tartas wyll euer take thinges to theyr profet, and shortly they be vp.
And in ii thinges they dare nat make a lye, nor say that they had
35 done any good dede of armes yf they had nat done, nor deny theyr
euyll dedes if they had done any. The other, before the lorde or
the iuge in iugment he dare nat deny the trouth, though he shulde be
condempned or lese his lyfe. And as moche as is sufficyent the
Tartas speketh.

[BOOK FOUR]

The maner howe a kynge or a prince shulde order them to warre

[E4v] Reason requireth that whosoeuer wyll moue warre agaynst his ennemys ought to considre iiii thinges: first, he ought to haue iust
5 and resonable cause or good tytell to moue the warre; the seconde thyng, that he ought to se to his power, if he be sufficient for all the cost and furnyssh, other thynges belongyng to the warre to be-gynne, maynteyn, and finysshe; the thyrde is that he ought wisely enquere of the condicyon and maner of his ennemis: the fourth is that
10 he ought to begyn warre in a conuenyent season and tyme.
    And [I], Frere Hayton, that by the commaundement of Our Lorde the Apostle ought to speke of this matter, I may say truely that the Christen men haue iust and resonable cause to moue warre agaynst the Sarasyns, to the valyaunt kynred of Mahomet. For they haue
15 occupyed theyr owne herytage that is the Holy Lande, the whiche almyghti God promysed to the Christen men, and there they fynde the Sepulture of Our Lorde Ihesu that is the begynnynge of the Christen fayth; and for the great dishonesty and great losse of blode that the Christen men haue had by the Sarasyns and euyll lyuers
20 in tyme passed; and for other dyuers reasons that shulde be long to reherse. The seconde reson, I say that no man ought to be in doute, for the holy Church of Rome, which is lady and maistres of all the world, hath wyll power by the grace of God, and with the helpe of the good kynges and princes of the Cristen fayth and the seruauntes
25 of Christ, to delyuer the Sepulture and the Holy Lande from the Sarasyns power, the which lande they holde and occupy by our synnes.

Of the thyrde reason and the fourth I speke – it is to knowe the
maner and condicion of his ennemys, and to chose tyme, place,
and season conuenyent for to begyn warre – I must speke more at
length. For a good surgyen that ought to knowe the syckenes of
5 the which he wyll gyue helth, likewyse a kyng or a prince ought to
enquere thintent, condicyon, and state of his ennemys to thintent
that he may begyn his warre wisely, maynteyn, and bringe to a goode
ende. To a prince in dedes of ware the secrete of his ennemys
ought nat to be hydde from him; for the thynges that be proued be-
10 forehande can do no grefe, and in the maters unpurueyed, somtymes
trouble many men coragious in dedes of armes and batayles whan
they haue no tyme nor rome to beware of the people and dangers that
be redy to come. In all other maner of warkes a remedy may be
founde except in batayle, if it be any faute in; for soone after the
15 payn, foloweth after the cost. Wherfore, to thintent that more
euydent vnderstandyng shulde be vpon our sayeng, we shal speke
of the passage of the Holy Lande, and also we shall say some
thinges of the state and condicyon of the lande of Egipt, the hoost of
Babylon, and of the ennemys power. [E5r]

20 ## How the Sowdan ordereth his barownes and his knyghtes

The Sowdan that holdeth nowe the realm of Egypt and of Syrie is
named Melcuaser and is a Cumany by his natyon. The knyghtes
and the hoost of Egypt be men of dyuers partes and of straunge
landes; for the men of that countrei be nought bowed a fote nor an
25 horsbacke, nother by see nor lande. The Sowdan of Egiptes power of
fotemen is nat great, but of horsmen is mighty. Verily the moost
part of them be sclauys that haue ben bought and solde, the which
the euyl Cristen men brought there for to sell them for couetise of
money; and other be they that were taken in batayle, which be con-
30 strayned to forsake the lawe of Christe. But the sclauys that be
solde be more praysed and more honoured, and dyuerse tymes it
happened that many wolde be solde bycause that they shall be the
better beloued of theyr lorde and maister. The Sowdan of Egypt is
euer in great dout and suspection of his men; for thei be of such
35 condicyon that they euer take the lordshyppe of their prynce, and by
reason of that many sowdans hath ben slayne. The hoost of Egypt
may be about xx thousande knyghtes, and some of them be good

warryours and vsed to do; verily, the grettest parte is but of small
price. Whan the Sowdan goeth with his hoost, he taketh with hym a
great quantyte of stoffe and of laden horses for the warre. They
haue resonably of goodes, and lyght for to ronne. Theyr horses and
5 mules be but small, nor they can nat do moch labour, and thei haue
great nede of good kepyng. The hoost of Egypt is euer redy and
apparylled to the Sowdans commaundement, for all they inhabit in
the cyte of Cayre.

The condicyon of the hoost of Egypt is suche: euery man of armes
10 hath his wages whiche passeth nat vi skore floryns, and euery
man is bounde to kepe iii horses and a camell for to bere his stoffe;
and whan the Sowdan bringeth his men out of the realme of Egypt
he gyueth them somwhat more if it please hym. The Sowdan departeth his wages and offices, and gyue them in kepynge to his
15 barownes that be called admiralles. To some he gyueth a hunderde;
to some ii honderde, more and lesse, after that he wyll do more
honor and profet to one than to another. For if the Sowdan gyue
power to one admyrall to kepe an hunderde or two honderde knightes,
he shall gyue hym for all, the hole wages as moche as it shall come to,
20 in a hole somme. And by reason this, the Sodan hath great faute in
his seruice. For this admyrall that gyue seruyce to an hunderde or
two hunderde knyghtes, thei be sclauons of their owne money, and
delyuerd [them] harnes and horses, and put them in seruyce for men
of warre, and receyued theyr wagis. And syke men of small price,
25 [E5v] and gaue them some thinges, and delyuerd them horses and
harnes, and receyue wages for them, and all the remenant thei put
in their purses. Wherfore diuerse tymes amonge suche men is founde
but fewe valyant men.

Of the subtyltie of the Sowdan of Egypt to
30 conquere cyties.

The myght of the Sowdan in the realme of Syrie may wel be V M
knightes, that haue thyr lyueng vpon the rentes of the lande. And
yet there is a great nombre of Bednyns and Turkmens, that be wood-
men, and do great helpe to the Sodan whan he wyll put sege to
35 any lande; for if he wyll, without any wages but gyueng them some,
he may haue them. For to go in batayle or for to defende his lande
the aboue sayd Bednyns and Turkmens wolde do nothyng for the

Sodan without gret wages; and yf the Sowdan wolde cause them
to do by force they shulde go away, the Turkmens ioyned to the
mountayns and the Bednyns ioyned to the desertes of Arabe. Yet
the Sowdan hath a sergeantre afote in the countreis of Moyllebech
5 and about the Mount Lyban and in the lande of the Assasyns; and
myght haue helpe of them to put the sege to a cyte or to a castell, or
for to kepe the lande in their countrey. But out of theyr countrey
they wolde nat go for the Sowdan, nor he can nat constrayn them, for
the great mountayns there as they be. The Sowdan of Egypt is
10 moch subtyll for to take cytyes and castels, and in diuers maners they
set vpon the landes: for by crosbowes, stones, and mynes vnder
the grounde, and by fyre that can nat be put out, and by other maner,
that thei take the landes lyghtly without any peryll.

Why they of Egypt yelded them to the Sarasyns

15 Themperour of Grece kept the lordshyp of Egypt, and gouerned the
lande by dukes and by officers that he sende euery yere to receyue
the rentes of the landes and sende them to themperour of Constantinople. And so the lordshyppe of the Grekes was in the lande of
Egypt tyll in the yere of Our Lorde God VII C hunderde and iiii. They
20 of the land of Egypt coude nat suffre the wronges that the Grekes
dyd vnto them; and than they yelde them to the Sarasyns, and chose
a lorde amonge them of Mahometz kynred, and named hym calyfe.
And all theyr lordes were called calyfe. And kept the lordshippe of
Egypt those of Mahometz kynred CCC xlvii yeres. After that, the
25 Sarasyns toke the landes, and the Medyens that be called Cordins
ocupied the lordshyppe of Egypt, as we shall say hereafter.

How the Christen men were driuen out of Egypt

[E6r] In the yere of Oure Lorde God, a thousande liii, Kyng Almaur,
Kynge of Hierusalem, of good mynde, gathered his hoost in all the
30 lande of Hierusalem, and entred into Egypt and conquered many
landes and cytes, as it is wrytten in the boke of the Holy Lande
conquestes. The Calyfe, seynge that he coude [not] abyde agayn the
Christen mens power, sende his messangers to the Sowdan of
Halap, that kept Mahometz lawe and thought to haue a great tresour
35 of the Calyfe, that was called Saraton. He and a great company of

men a ware came to helpe the Calyfe, and those men dyd so moch
that they droue the Christen men out of the lande of Egypt riche
and delectable. And the power of the Calyf was smale. The Sowdan
coueyted the lordship; wherfore he toke hym and put hym in pry-
5 son. And than after he set vpon the lande valyantly, and put it in his
subiection, and made hym sodan and lorde of Egypt. This Paraton was
of the Corasmyns nacion, and was the fyrst lorde in Egypt of his nation.
　　After the dethe of Saraton, one of his sonnes was made lorde of
Egipt that was called Salzadin. And this Salzadyn dyd so moch
10 that he vndyde the Kyng of Hierusalem and toke his cyties by force;
and toke dyuers other landes of the Cristen mens, as it apperith by
the boke of the conquestes of the Holy Lande.
　　After the deth of Salzadyn, his brother and one of his neuiewes,
one after another, kept the lordship of Egypt tyll the sowdans
15 tyme that was called Mellecasa. This Mellecasa was Sowdan of Egypt
at that tyme that the Tartas toke the realme of Cumany. The Sowdan herde say that the Tartas solde the Cumayns that they had taken
to a good shyppe; and than he sende dyuers marchauntes with a
great quantite of good for to by some of the sayd Cumayns, and in
20 specylly of the yongest. And many of them was brought into Egypt.
Malacasa dyde norysshed them and loued them moche, and lerned
them to ryde and to the armes, and trusted them well and kept
them euer nygh him.
　　And in that tyme that the Kyng of Fraunce, Loys, passed ouer the
25 see and was taken of the Sarasyns, the aboue sayd Cucumans (that
were bought and solde) kylde there lorde Malecasa, and made one of
them lorde that was called Turkmen. And by the reason of this, the
Kyng of Fraunce and his brother, that were in the Sarasyns pryson,
were the soner bought agayn and delyuerd out of pryson. In this maner
30 began the Cucumans to haue lordship in Egypt. This kinred of the
Cucumans is called Chapchap into the Orient partes nat many dayes.
　　After, one of this sclauons which was called Cochos kylled the
sayd Turkement, and made hym sowdan, and was called Melomees.
This man went [E6v] into the realme of Syrie and driued out Gynbago
35 and x thousande Tartas, the which Halcon had left for to kepe the
lande of Syrie. As he retorned to Egypt another of the sayde Cucumans kylde hym; which was called Bendocdar, and made hym
sowdan and made hym calle Meldaer.
　　This was moche wise and valyant to the armes and to his power.
40 He rose moche the Sarasyns power in the realme of Sirie and Egypt,

and toke many cyties and landes that the Christen men kept. And
toke by force the noble cyte of Antyoch in the yere of Our Lorde
God M CC lxviii. In the realme of Armeny this man dyde moch harme.
In this Bendocdar dayes, whan Syr Edwarde, Kyng of Englande,
5 passed ouer the see, the Sowdan thought to haue kylde hym by an
Assasyn; by the which Assasyn the Kyng was hurt with a knyfe
that was poysoned, but he was hole agayne by the grace of God.
Than after, it happened that the Sowdan had a drinke with mortall
venym and dyed in the cyte of Damas.
10   After his deth his sonne that was called Melecsart was made sowdan, but he kept nat long the lordshippe of Egypt; for another
Cucumant that was called Elsy dryue hym oute of the lordship and
the lande of Egypt, and made him sodan. This Elsy was he that
layd sege before the cyte of Triple, and toke it by force in the yere of
15 Our Lorde God a thousande two hondrede foureskore and nyne.

How Elsy was poysoned

In the yere after, the sayd Elsy brought all his power togyder nygh
Babylone, taryenge for to put sege afore Acre. Vpon a day, as he
put hym in a plesaunte place for to ease hymselfe, yt fortuned that a
20 seruaunt (the whiche he trusted well, and had made hym constable
of his hoost) gaue hym poyson to drynke; and dyed soone after. This
constable occupyed the lordshyp, but the other ran vpon hym and
cutte hym all to pecys. After that, one of Elsy sonnes was made
sowdan, that was named Melecasseraph. The which toke the cytie
25 of Acre, and put out of the landes of Syrie all the Christen men; this
was in the yere of Our Lorde God a thousande CC lxxxxi.

How Melcuaser was made Sowdan of Egypt

Whan Melecasseraph was retorned into Egipt, vpon a day he went a
huntyng, and there a seruaunt kylde hym in the wode. And soone
30 after, the seruaunt was kylde by the other. And after that he that is
Sowdan nowe was made sowdan in Egypt, that is called Melcuaser
(which was Melecasseraph brother). And bycause that this Melecuaser
was yonge, he was put vnder an ouersear, which was of the Tartas
nacion and was called Ginboga. This Gynboga putte away this chylde
35 [F1r] Melecuase, and put hym inwarde into the Crake of Mount Royall;
and toke the lordship and made hymselfe sowdan, and was called

Melecadell. In this Melechadels dayes was so grete nede of vitayles
that all the Sarasyns dyed for hunger if it had nat ben for the false
Christen men that brought them vitayle inough for couytes of money.
After that, it happened that tidynges came of the Tartas commynge;
5 than Ginboga gathered his hoste and went into the realme of Syrie
for to defende the lande agaynst the Tartas. This Ginboga honoured
moch those that had ben Tartas and kept them nere hym. Of this the
Cucumans had great enuy; wherfore it happed that as Ginboga
retorned to Egypt the Cucumans put hym out of his lordeship, and
10 made one of them sowdan that was called Lachyn (and was called
after Melecuaser).

This Lachyn wolde nat kyll Gynboga bycause that he wolde be his
felowe, but gaue him a countrey that was called Sarta. And after
that, he gaue hym the lordshyp of Haman, but he wolde nat suffre
15 that Ginboga shulde dwell in Egypt. This Sowdan taryed iii yeres
in the castell of Cayre for fere of his men, except a day that he came
downe to the playn and came there to play at the foteball. His
horse fyll vnder hym and brake his legge. After, it happed that vpon
a day this Sowdan Lachyn played at cheker; and had putte his
20 swerde nygh hym, and one of his owne seruauntes toke the swerde
and strake hym. And sone after, the other ran vpon hym that had
done the dede, and cut hym all in pecis. And after that, the Sarasyns
were in great debate for to make a sowdan, but in thende they
agreyd and put Melecuaser afore sayd in the lordship, the which
25 Ginboga had laft in the Crake of Mount Royall. This Sowdan is he
that ouercame Casan in the felde and is yet Sowdan of Egipt.

It shal be forgyuen me yf I speke to longe of the Cucumans, that be
subgettes bought and solde, and of the sowdans of theyr kinred;
for I do to shewe that the Sarasins can nat be long without such a
30 fortune shuld come vnto them, by the whiche they might nat come
out of Egipt nor go with an hoost in another lande.

How the lande of Egypt is watred with the water of flud Gyon

The realm of Egipt is moche riche and delyctable; it is xv dayes iourney
35 of length and thre dayes iourney in brede. The land of Egipt is a yle;
for by both the sydes is desertes and sandis, and of the other part is
the see of Grece. Towarde thorient is more nygh of the lande of
Syrie than of any other lande; verily betwene the ii realmes is well viii

dayes iourney of way. And all landes towarde thoccydent finysshed to one of the Barbare prouynce that is called Darta, and betwene
these two landes is well xv dayes iourney of desertes. Towarde mydday
fynisshed with [F1v] the realme of Nubye, which be Cristen men (and
5   all blacke for the hete of the sonne); and betwene the two landes is
well xii dayes iourney, and all sandes. In the realm of Egypt be v
prouinces: the first is called Sayth; the seconde, Meser; the thyrde,
Alexander; the iiii, Rychy (this countrey is closed of the see and
fluddes of an yle); and the other, Damyette. The chefe cytie of the
10 realme of Egypt is called Cayre, and is nygh of an olde cytie that is
called Meser. These two cyties be vpon the flud of Nyll syde (which
ronneth by the lande of Egypt) that is called Gion.

This fludde is moch profitable; for it watreth all the landes there as
it passeth, and maketh all the landes fruitfull and habondaunte of
15 all maner of goodes. In the flud of Nyll be fysshes ynough; and bere
great shippes, for it is great and depe. And aboue all the fluddes
the Nyll may be prased yf it were nat that there is a maner of beestes
that be called dragons, and deuoured horses and men that be vpon
the water and vpon the see whan thei may haue them; these beestes
20 be called cocalx. The fludde of Nyll riseth ones in a yere; and
begynneth to ryse at myddes of August, and so risynge tyll Saynt
Michaels day. And whan it is so high that it can no more, the men
of the countrey let the water ron by dykes and smale ryuers so that
they water all the countrey. And so the water tarieth there xl
25 dayes, and whan the grounde is dry, the peple sowe and set all the
grounde. And bycause of the sayd watryng, all maner of goodes
growe in that lande; for in these partes is neuer rayne nor snowe, nor
ye can nat knowe the winter from the somer. Yet the habytauntes
of Egypt hath put a colombe of marble in the myddes of the flude of
30 Nyll in a lytell yle that is called Meser, and haue made tokens in
the sayd colombe. And whan the fludde is flowen as moche as it may,
they loke vpon the colombe tokens; and after the risyng of the
water they shall knowe yf they shall haue great plenty of goodes that
yere or to skant, and vpon that, thei set price vpon theyr mar-
35 chaundyse. The water of the fludde of Nyll is holsome to drinke; but
whan it is taken out of the fludde it is to hote, but they put it in a
vessell of therth, and than it is clere, colde, and holsome.

In the realme of Egypt be two see portes or hauens; the one is
called Alexander and the other, Damyette. In Alexanders porte
40 may well come in shippes and galyes, and the cyte is strong and well
walled. The waters that they drinke in Alexandre cometh in cun-

dittes from the flude of Nyll, of the which they fylled their cesterns
that thei haue ynough in the cyte; they haue none other water that
thei might drynke. Wherfore yf the water that ronned in the cun-
dytes myght be stopped, they shulde be in great payne, and long
5 they coude nat lyue; by any other wise it shulde be harde to take
Alexander bi force. The cytie [F2r] of Damyette is vpon the flude of
Nyll, which was well closed in the olde tyme. But it was taken twyse
by the Christen men: ones by the Kyng of Hierusalem and by the
other Crysten men of thorient, and the other tyme by the Kyng of
10 Fraunce, Saynt Loys. And bycause of that, the Sarasins brake it
downe, and transported ferre from the see; and they made no walles
nor stronge place, and called this newe lande Newe Damyette; and
the olde Damyette is all wasted. With the portes of Alexandre and
Damyette the Sowdan hath great goodes.
15   The lande of Egypt yelde great haboundance of socour and of al
maner of goodes. They haue nat moch wines, but the wine that
groweth there is very good; the Sarasyns dare nat drinke wyn because that is forbydden them by theyr lawe. Moten, hennes, and
gottes thei haue ynough; but thei haue nat moche befe, and ete
20 horsflesshe. In the realme of Egypt be some Christen men dwellynge
there that be called Kepty, and holde the maner of the Iacobyns;
and in that parties they haue dyuers abbeys, and holde them fre and
in peace. And these Keptys were the oldest heyres of the lande of
Egypt, for the Sarasyns began to inheryt the lande sythe that they
25 had the lordship. The thynges that they can nat fynde in Egypt,
and that the Egipciens coude nat fynde if they shulde nat haue of
other men, they shulde haue great nede – as yron and other thinges.
Bycause and faute of that, they coude nat lyue longe. In all the realme
of Egypt is no cytie nor castell walled but the cyte of Alexandre,
30 the which is well walled. The Sowdan dwelled in the castell of Cayre,
whiche was nat stronge. All the lande of Egypt is kept and defendede
by knightes. Than, syth the hoost of Egipt was ouercome, the lande
might be shortly conqured and without any danger.

Whan tyme is to moue warre

35 In fewe wordes I say that I may say these wordes: 'Ecce nunc tempus
acceptabile, ecce nunc dies salutis.' For verily it is conuenyent
tyme, and acceptable and couenable tyme, to moue warre agaynst his
ennemys of the holy faith. Nowe is tyme couenable to gyue helpe
to the Holy Lande, the which hath ben longe in the euyll beleuers

handes; nowe is tyme conuenyent in the which the corages of
Christes louers ought to be in mynde to the Holy Landes passage, to
thintent that the Holy Sepulture of Our Lorde may be delyuerd out
of thennemys handes – that is the begynnynge of our fayth. Nor we
5 haue nat remembred in times passed of suche conuenyent tyme as we
haue nowe, as God by His pyte and mercy shewed vs in dyuers
maners. For first, God almighty, full of mercy, hath gyuen vs pastoure and right Holy Father right Christen and full of vertue; which,
syth that he was sette in the holy Apostolyque Sete, both night
10 and day thought [F2v] and desyred how he might socour the Holy
Lande for to haue it out of the ennemys of the holy faythes handes
(which blamed the name of Crist and the Holy Sepulcre of Our Lorde).
And bycause that they may truely beleue that God hath torned His
mercyfull eyen to beholde the Holy Lande, and hath gyuen him vpon
15 the erth his redemer (it is the Father Apostell), in the which dayes,
by the mercy of God, the Holy Lande of Hierusalem, that hath ben
long tyme kept vnder the seruage of our ennemys by our synnes,
shal be delyuered and brought to the fyrst fraunches and to the fyrst
power of the Christen men.

20 Why they go into the Holy Lande

Now is the tyme conuenyent and acceptable in the which God hath
shewed vs clerly that the Holy Lande shal be delyuerd out of the
ennemys power. For by the grace of God the kynges and the princes
of Christen landes be now in good state and in peace betwene
25 them, and haue no more warre nor debate as they were wont to haue
in the olde tyme. Wherfore it is lyke that God almyghtie wyll delyuer the Holy Lande. And yet all Christen men of dyuers landes and
of dyuers realmes by fayth and deuocyon be apparelled to take the
crosse and to passe ouer the see into the Holy Landes helpe, and to
30 put theyr body and goodes for the honour and reuerence of Our
Lorde Ihesu Crist valyauntly and with a good wyll.

How the ennemis of the Christen fayth was mynisshed and put down

Now it is conuenient tyme and acceptable by the which God shewed

to the Christen people that the power of the Christen faithes ennemys is dimynisshed: also by the Tartas warre by the whiche they
were ouercome and loste men without nombre in batayle: also for
this Sowdan that raigned those dayes in Egypt, that was a man of no
5 goodnesse and nothyng worth. Moreouer, all the Sarasyns prynces
be deed (that were wont to gyue helpe to the Sowdan) by the power
of the Tartas, and one was lefte alone, that was named Sowdan de
Meredyn, the which is tourned lately to the Tartas subiection. And
therfore, at this tyme without any daunger or payne the Holy Lande
10 myght be recouered and the realm of Egipt and of Syrie conquered;
and also, withall, the power of the ennemys might be the more easly
brought downe nowe than in tymes passe.

How Carbanda, Kyng of the Tartas, profered hymselfe and his power to go to the Holy Lande

15 Yet is conuenyent tyme the which God shewed to the Christen men,
bycause that the Tartas hath proffered themselfe to gyue helpe to the
Christen men agaynst the Sarasyns. And for this reason Carbanda,
Kyng of the Tartas, [F3r] sende his messangers, profferinge to putte
all his power to vndo the ennemys of the Cristen lande. And so, in
20 this tyme, the Holy Lande myght be recouered by the helpe of the
Tartas and the realme of Egypt conquered lyghtly without peryll or
daunger. And so it were nede that the Christen men shulde set
vpon the Holy Lande without any taryenge, for in the taryenge is
great daunger: for fere of Carbanda, that is nowe frende, shulde
25 fayle, and another might come that shulde vse the Mahometz wayes
and that shulde agre with the Sarasyns. And so it myght tourne to
great dammage and peryll of the Christen lande and of the Holy
Lande ouer the see.
    Before Your Reuerence, Holi Father, I say and confesse that I am
30 nat of sufficyent scyence to gyue counsell without great doyng as
the maker of the passage ouer the see to the Holy Lande. But bycause
that I haue yet the payne of the inobediente soone, I wyll obey to
the commaundement of Your Holynesse (against the which no good
Christen men ought to go). Than, requyring first pardon of any-
35 thyng that I shulde say, more or lesse, I shall say myne aduysement
after my lytell knowlege, all as the wyse men counsell.

Of the aduersytes and prosperiteys of the ennemys

To the honour of Our Lorde Ihesu Christe I trust to accomplysshe my
faute. I say, to the entent that the Holy Lande may be conquered
with leest payne and trouble, it is conuenyent that the Cristen men
5 shall entre into the lande, and that thei shulde set vpon their
ennemys in the sayd tyme that their ennemys shal be troubled of
some fortune. For if the Christen men wolde do this enterprise at
that tyme that theyr ennemys shulde be in prosperytie, they coude
nat fulfyll theyr enterprise without great daunger and payne. We
10 shall deuyse truely which is the prosperytie and whiche is the
aduersytie. The aduersyte of ennemys is this: whan the Sarasyns
haue a sowdan and a lorde wyse and valyaunt, and such that he
may without any fere of his rebellynge holde and kepe his lordshippe: the other prosperytie of the ennemys may be whan thei haue
15 ben longe in peace and without any warre of the Tartas or other
men: and yet whan they haue great haboundaunce of corne and
other goodes in the realme of Syrie: and yet whan the wayes be
sure by the see and by the lande and open, and such thynges that the
ennemys haue nede may be brought to them without any contradit
20 out of straunge countreis: and yet whan the Sarasyns be in peace
with Nubiens and with the Bednins of Egipt desert, so thei moue
no warre nor querell: and yet whan the Turqueniens and Bednyns
that dwelled [F3v] in the realme of Egypt and Syrie [be] obedyent to
the Sowdan of Egypt. Bycause of the aboue sayd thynges and
25 prosperites, the ennemys power shulde ryse so moch that it shulde
be impossible to ouercome them.

The names of the ix sowdans that were slayne and poysoned

By the contrary, aduersytes it myght come to the ennemys in dyuers
30 maners: it is whan the ennemys do ryse and kyll theyr sowdan or
lorde as they haue done in tymes past, and do often tymes. For, syth
the kynred of the Cucumans beganne to haue the lordshippe in
Egypt, ix haue ben ordayned sodans and lordes vpon them. And of
these ix sowdans that haue ben in Egypt, they haue ben slayne by
35 swerde: it is to knowe: Turquenien, Chocas, Lachyn; and ii other
that were poysoned, that was Bendocdac and Elsy; the two other,

Melecuaser and Gynboga, were putte in exyle. And this Melecuaser
that is nowe sowdan was ons putte out of his office and lordship,
and his lyfe in variaunce tarienge to an yll ende.

Prouision agaynst the Sowdan of Egypt

5 Item, the ennemyes myght come to aduersyte: it is whan the flude of
Nyll riseth nat so moch that they may water the grounde as nede
is; than the Sarasyns of Egypt shulde haue great nede and hunger.
And yet it is nat longe that it came so moch that, yf it had nat ben
for Christen men that brought them by the see for couytouse of
10 money, they had ben deed for hunger. And whan suche a nede
shulde come to thennemys, they shulde become poore, and shulde
be fayne for to sell theyr horses and brynge away theyr chyldren and
seruauntes; and by this reason, they shulde nat haue power to
depart out of Egipt nor come into Syrie. Euery one must cary with
15 hym all suche thynges and baggage that they haue nede of for viii
dayes – for hymselfe, his beestes, and his housholde; for thei fynde
but sandes and downes in the sayd viii dayes iourney. Wherfore
he that shulde nat haue horses nor camels shulde nat haue power to
departe out of Egypt, and by this maner the Sowdan shulde be so
20 troubled that he coude nat com to socoure the realme of Syrie. Yet
whan thennemys haue had longe tyme warre, yet great aduersytes
and thoughtfull to thennemys yf the wayes vpon the see were kept
that nothynge shulde be brought into theyr countrey of suche
thinges as they haue moste nede to: as yron, stele, and other thinges
25 that they coude nat haue but it were brought vnto theym out of
straunge countreis. And without such thinges they coude nat longe
endure. Yet whan the Nubyens or the Bednyns moued warre to
the Sowdan, he myght be by suche warre so troubled that he coude
nat depart [F4r] out of Egipt nor go in Syrie. Yet whan the lande of
30 Syrie hath nede and nat good season by drynes or by warre of the
Tartas or in other maner. For if the wayes shuld fayle, the hoost of
Egipt coude nat come for to dwell in Syre; for out of Egipt and other
landes thei coud bringe nothinge into Syrie, and by this reason the
hoost of thennemys coude nat departe out of Egipt. Than if then-
35 nemys shulde haue some of these aduersytes, without any faute
they coude nat depart out of Egypt for to come to Syrie. Than the

Christen men myght occupy the realme of Hierusalem; and myght repare the cyties and castels, and garnysshe them in suche maner that they shulde neuer fere the power of theyr ennemys.

How imbassadours were sende to Carbanda, a kynge of 5 the Tartas, that the ennemys shulde haue nothinge brought to them

Sith that we haue resonably spoken and deuised of the prosperites and aduersites that myght come to thennemys, we shall say in this party the begynnynge of the passage of the Holy Lande. I thinke, for
10 the suerti and the profet of the passage, that at begynnynge a certayn nombre of horsmen and fotemen myght knowe the power of thennemys; and as me semeth, for this present tyme it shulde be sufficient to the nombre of a thousande knyghtes, x galeys, and thre thousand dykers. And vpon this men shulde be sende a legate by
15 the Church and a wyse captayn and a valyaunt, that shulde passe with them ouer the see to the yle of Cypres in the realme of Armeny, as they shulde thinke the best to do. After that, without any tarienge, by the Kyng of Armenys counsell they shulde sende messangers to Carbanda, a kyng of the Tartas, requiring two thynges:
20 the one shuld be that Carbanda shulde defende in all his landes that nothyng shulde be brought in the lande of the ennemis; the other was that he shulde sende his messangers and of his men a warre into the countreis of Meletur that they shulde ronn and waste Halaps landes. After that, we pylgrims and them of the realm of Cypres and
25 of Armeny, by see and by land, we shulde moue warre and vndertake valyantly the ennemys landes; and that they shulde take payne to kepe the see in suche maner that nothynge shulde be brought into the ennemys landes. Yet our Christen men myght garnysshe the yle of Corcose, which is in a good place for to receyue the galleys,
30 and there they myght do a great dammage to the ennemis. Now verily I shall leue to speke of the maner of the beynnynge of warre and to sette vpon the ennemys; for after the condicyon and state of the ennemys shulde be nedys to chaunge counsell and vse, by the wyse mens counsell that shulde be present to the dede. [F4v] The
35 proffettes and the goodes that might come of this first vyage and passage I shall shortly herafter declare.

How the Sowdan of Egypt shulde be brought subget to the Christen men and to the Tartas

The first profet shulde be: for this fyrste passage might be ordayned
so that thennemis myght be so sore troubled by the helpe of the
5 other Christen men that be in the parties of thorient, and by the
Tartas, that thei coude haue no rest, but they shulde suffre great
thoughtes and great damages. For if by the Christen men and by the
Tartas the warre was done to the Sowdan of Egypt by see and by
lande into the realme of Syrie, the Sowdan shulde be fayne to sende
10 his men for to kepe and defende the passages and cyties that be
nygh of the see, and all other that myght be assayled. And if by the
Tartas the ware was moued in the parties of Meleton in the landes
of Halap, the Sowdans men shulde be saynt to come where it is well
xxv dayes iourney, and that they shulde come from Babylone to
15 this seruice; shulde be in short tyme afote, and shulde lose their
horses and theyr harnes, and shulde be so wery and so trobled
that they coude nat endure. In iii or foure maners thennemys shulde
lese theyr goodes and shulde suffre many great dammages. Yet by
the fyrst passage the ennemys myght haue moch trouble; for with the
20 commynge of the x galeys of the passage, with the helpe of these
that myght be arryued of the realme of Armeny and of Cipres, thennemys landes myght be roned all, and the galeys myght retorne
safe into the yle of Corcose. And if the Sowdan wolde kepe and
defende the sayd landes, he shulde be fayn to come hymselfe in
25 person, and with hym all his power of Babylon in Syrie, or he coude
haue sufficiently men to giue helpe to all the landes that be nygh of
the see. The commyng out of the realm of Egypt to come in Syrie
shulde by peryllous and damageable to the Sowdan: for fere of his
men trayson full of enuy; for by the setynge of the Christen men they
30 myght be so troubled that they shulde haue no rest damageable;
for he shulde consume and wast all his tresoure, so moche that it was
harde to beleue the great some of good that the Sodan and his men
spende and consumed euery tyme that they came out of Egypt landes
for to come in Syrie. Yet by the sayd galeys the wayes and the portes
35 of the sayde see mygt be kept in suche maner that it shulde be
brought nothinge to thennemys of such thynges that they haue
more nede and that they coude nat endure long without – as yron,
stele, and other thinges that be brought vnto theym out of straunge

countres; yet more, thennemys shuld lose the rentes of the see portes,
that is a great some of good and tresure. [g1r]

Yet, yf it shulde happen that the ennemys were troubled by some
aduersite and that they coude nat departe out of Egipt nor gyue
5 helpe to the landes of Syrie, than the pylgryms of this fyrst passage,
with the helpe of other Christen men of thoryent partes, myght
well redresse the cyte of Triple. And to the Mount Lyban be Cristen
men dwellynge, good sergeantes about xl thousande, that shulde
gyue the pylgrymes great helpe; and many tymes they haue rysen
10 agaynst the Sowdan, and do hym and to his men gret harm and
dammage. And than if the cytie of Triple shulde be formede, the
Christen men myght holde it tyll the commynge of the passage
generall, and myght take all the countrey about and kepe the
countrey of Triple. And might retorne easly by the men that shuld
15 come to the generall passage, for thei shuld fynde the port redy
there they might surely come.

Yet yf it shulde hapen that the Tartas shulde occupie the realme
and the Holy Lande, the Christen men of the fyrst passage shulde
be redy to recyue the Tartas landes and to kepe them in such maner.
20 And I, that knowe resonably the Tartas wyll, I beleue that all the
landes that they shulde conquere vpon the Sarasins, that with a gode
wyl they shulde gyue them in kepyng to the Christen men, franke
and quyte; for the Tartas coude nat dwell in that countrey for the
great hete that is there in somer. Wherfore they shulde be glad that
25 the Christen men shulde holde the landes and kepe them. The Tartas
do neuer fyght withe the Sowdan of Egypt for couytous to gette
landes and cyties, for they haue all Asie in theyr subiection; but thei
fight for cause that the Sowdan hath euer ben theyr princypall
ennemy and hath done them more harme and dammage than any
30 other (and specially whan thei haue had warre agaynst theyr neyghbours). And for this reasons aboue sayd I trust that the nombre aboue
is sufficyent: it is to knowe, a thousande knyghtes, x galleys, and
III M sergeantes. And many thinke that in this begynnynge that they
shulde nat make so many men that this shulde do, and the exspen-
35 ces and cost shulde multiply moche.

Yet by this fyrst passage might come iii other profettes. For syth
that the pylgryms of the first passage hath taryed in the partes
be-ende the see a season, and had knowen the condicyon and maner
of the lande and of the ennemys, they might gyue warnynge to the
40 other pylgrims that shulde come to the generall passage. Yet take we

the Tartas, for warre or for other thynges or for excuse, that they
wolde nat gyue helpe to the Christen men agaynst the Sarasyns, and
that the Sowdan and his men were in there prosperite, and that it
shulde nat be an easy thinge to conquere the Holy Lande and to
5 delyuer it out of the ennemyes power; Your Holy Paternite, knowyng
the condicyon [G1v] of the Holy Lande and seynge the generall
passage, myght haue better counsel and aduertisment vpon suche
thynges that shulde be conuenyent for to do: or for to passe ouer the
generall passage or to tary for conuenyent tyme. And by the reason
10 of this all the daungers of the ennemyes may be auoyded.
    Yet Your Holynesse shall pardon me, I dare say two other wordes.
The one is that Your Holynes wolde wryte to the Kyng of the
Georgiens, that be Christen men, and that they may be more deuout
peple than any other nacyon to the pylgrimages and to the holy
15 relykes of the Holy Lande, that they shulde gyue helpe and socour to
the pylgrims to recouer the Holy Lande. I beleue verily, for the
honour of God and for the reuerence of Your Holynes, they fulfill
your commaundement, for thei be deuout Christen men and men
of great power and valyant men of armes and neighbours of the realm
20 of Armeny. And yet that Your Holy Paternyte wolde write to the
King of Nubiens, which be Christen men and were conuerted to the
fayth of Christ by Saynt Thomas in the holy lande of Etyope, sen-
dynge that they shulde moue warre agaynst the Sowdan and his
men. And I beleue verily that the aboue sayd Nubyens, for the
25 honoure of Our Lorde and for the reuerence of Your Holynes, they
shulde moue warre agaynst the Sowdan and his men, and shulde
do them harm and dammage to theyr power; and that shulde be great
trouble for the Sowdan and for his men. And the sayde letters
myght be sende to the Kyng of Armeny, that shulde translate them in
30 theyr langage and sende them by your messangers.
    Deuoutly and truly I haue rehersed after my lytell vnderstanding
suche thinges as is nedefull to the begynninge of the passage and
helpe of the Holy Lande; and after, wyllyng to obey the comaunde-
ment of Your Holy Paternyte, vpon this that is nede to the generall
35 passage ouer the see.

Of the generall passage

The generall passage may be in iii wayes. The one shulde be by the

way of Barbary, but this way I wolde nat gyue counsell to them
that knowe the condicion of the countrey. The other shulde be by the
way of Constantynople, it is to knowe, by the way that Godfray de
Bullyen and other pylgrims in that tyme kept. As I beleue parfetly,
5 the passage generall myght go lightly to the cytie of Constantynople.
But goynge ouer the Braz of Georgie and goyng by the Turkes the
way shulde nat be sure, for the Turkmens that be Sarasyns and
that dwell in Turky. Truely the Tartas may delyuer and ensure the
way, and might ordayne that in the lande of Turkey shulde be
10 brought vitayles ynough into the pylgrims [G2r] hoost, and horses of
a resonable price. The other way that euerybody knoweth, it is by
the see.

    Therfore, if the passage wyll go by the see, there must be at euery
port of the see shippes redy apparelled and other necessary thynges
15 to passe with the pylgrims; and moreouer it shuld be conuenyent to a
prefeke terme and a couenable season that all the pylgrimes shulde
be redy to go in the shippes and passe togyder. And so they might
come to Cipres and rest them and their horses of the see labour. After
that the passage generall shulde be aryued in Cipres and shulde be
20 refresshed a certayn dayes, yf the pylgrims of the first passage had
closed the citie of Triple or another vpon the see in Syrie, the passage
myght come thyder, and that shulde be to them great ease. And yf
the pylgrims of the first passage had nat closed some lande in Syre, it
shulde be nede that the passage generall shulde take the way by
25 the realm of Armeny; in this maner it is to knowe that the pylgrimes
shulde refreshe them and their horses in the realme of Cipres tyll
Mychelmas day, that they might passe surely to the realme of Armeny. And there they shulde fynde such thinges as they shulde
nede to; verily thei myght tary in the cytie of Tersot more easely
30 bycause that they shulde fynde there great plente of waters and
pastour for their horses, and from the realme of Turkey that is nygh
they shulde bringe vitayle and horses and such thinges that they
shulde haue nede of – in the lande of Armeny also. And they myght
tary all the wynter in Armeny. And whan the pasture shulde be
35 comming, the pylgrims hoste might go to Antioch (that is from the
lande of Armeny a dayes iourney), and from thens the shippes
myght go by the see to the port of Antioch, and so the see hoost and
the lande hoost shulde be neyghbours.

    After that the pylgrims shulde haue occupied the cytie of Antioche,
40 the which they shulde shortly take with the helpe of God, the

pylgrimes myght refresshe them in this lande certayn dayes. And myght ronn and rauysshe their ennemys landes that be thereabout, and therewith they might knowe the condicyon, state, and wyll of their ennemis that be thereabout. And in this parties of Antioch
5 there be Christen men dwellyng that be good sergeantes, and shulde come with a good wyll to the Christen mens hoost and myght do them good seruyce. After that the pylgrims shulde depart out of Antioch, they myght go by the see syde to the cite of Lyche; this way shulde be shorter and better for the see doth flowe to the hoost
10 of the lande. Verily, nygh to the Margat by the see syde is a passage that troubleth moche the people that passe by. And yf it shulde happen that the ennemys had garnysshed this passage in suche maner that the pylgrems might nat passe, our men might retorn without any daunger into Antyoche. And myght go by the way of Ephemye
15 towarde Cesar by the syde [G2v] of the flude of Renell vpward; and by that way the hoste shulde finde gode pasture and good waters and the ennemies landes garnisshed with vytayle and other goodes, of the which the hoost myght haue great ease. And by this way our men myght go by the cyte of Haman, which is a riche cytie;
20 the which the Cristen men might occupy shortly. And if it shuld happen that the ennemis wolde defende Haman for bycause it is a riche cyte, and that thei shulde nat come to the batayle agaynst the Christen men, they shulde haue a great vauntage to fight in that place and shulde lightly ouercome their ennemies.
25   And yf the Christen men might ones ouercome the Sowdans hoost, after that they shulde fynde nothyng agaynst them; and so they myght go streight to the cytie of Damas, the which they shulde take, or they shulde yelde themselfe by some treatie. For syth the Sowdan shulde be ouercome, they of Damas shulde nat holde; but they
30 wolde yelde them with a good wyll, there lyue safe, as they dyd to Halcon and to Casan after that they had ouercome the Sodan. And than yf the Cristenmen had taken Damas, they shulde lightly conquere the remynaunt. And yf the ennemies shulde lose the batayle, the Cristen men might come to Tryple in iiii dayes from Damas, and
35 might make agayne the cite of Triple; and with this, the Cristen men that be of the Mount Lyban shulde gyue great helpe to the pylgrimes. And so, yf the Christen men myght kepe the cite of Triple, they might conquere the cite of Iierusalem with helpe of God.
  Of the company of the Christen men and of the Tartas, I thynke
40 that a certayne nombre, about xx thousande Tartas, myght do great

ease and proffet to the Christen men goynge by the countres; for fere
of the Tartas, the Bednyns nor Turkemens durst nat come nygh to
the Christen mens hoost. The other ease shulde be that the Tartas
shulde puruay for vitayle to the Christen mens hoost, and shulde
5 come out of ferre countreis for to gette money or some other thinge.
Yet by the Tartas they might enquere and knowe the communyca-
tion of the ennemyes; for the Tartas be lyght for to ronn in and out,
and can well entre and come out night and day of their frewell. To
batayle and to bete cyties the Tartas myght be thrifty, for they be
10 moch subtyll in suche thinges. And yf it shulde happen that Carbanda, or another in his rome, with men shulde come for to entre in
the lande of Egipt, than it shulde be well done to shyft and go ferre
from their company. For the Tartas wolde nat do after the Christen
mens wyll, and the Christen men myght nat folowe the Tartas
15 wyll, that be a horsbacke and go hastly, and the Christen men myght
nat folowe them for the fotemen. Yet whan the Tartas know that
they be stronge and haue power, they be moche proude and without
reason, and [G3r] coude nat be without doynge harme to the Christen
men, the which thing the Christen men might nat suffre; wherof
20 myght come great sklaundre and euyll wyll amonge them. But
vpon this thei might put good remedy: it is to knowe, that the Tartas
shulde go by Damas way, as they be vsed to do euer, and the Cristen
men shulde go in the parties of Iherusalem. And in this maner, goyng
ferre one from another, it shuld be good peace betwene the Tartas
25 and the Christen men, and loue kept; and the myght of the ennemies
shulde be confounded rather by two than by one.
　　Yet another thinge I wyll remembre to Your Holynesse: it is this:
the Christen mens counsell shulde be kept wysely. For in tyme
passed they wolde nat kepe their counsell; wherfore they haue hadde
30 many great sorowes, and the ennemys haue skaped many great
daungers and haue taken from the Christen men the maner to accom-
plyssh their desyres. And yf it be so that the passage generall
name might nat be kept close, for thei shulde go by the vniuersall
worlde, neuerthelesse, that coude nat torne to no daunger nor
35 losse to ennemies. For they coude nat haue no helpe of no port, and
in dyuers maners the Christen mens counsell myght be kept, doynge
maner to do a thing and do another. And the cause that the Tartas
coude nat kepe their counsell, which thinge hath done them oftentymes grete harme. The Tartas hath such a maner that at first mone of
40 Ianuarii they take counsell of all such thynges that they haue to do in
that yere. Wherfore, yf it fortune that they wyll moue warre agaynst

the Sowdan of Egypt, soone after, their counsell is knowen of all.
And so the Sarasyns sende worde to the Sowdan, and vpon that
the Sowdan maketh hym redy agaynst them. The Sarasyns can kepe
well their counsel, which thyng hath done them many tymes good.
5 And so it is sufficiently spoken and sayde for this present tyme vpon
the dede of the passage generall of the Holy Lande byende the
see.

After all this, I pray humbly that [Your] Blessyd Holynes wyll receyue this that my deuocyon writeth vpon the passage of the Holy
10 Lande. And yf I haue sayd more or lasse that it shulde be, I put it to
your correctyon. For I had nat ben so hardy to giue counsell vpon
so great a mater as the passage of the Holi Lande yf it were nat by the
commaundement of Your Holy Paternite. Which, sythe that it was
sette to the sege pastorall by the commaundment of God, of all his
15 hurt desyred, procured, and laboured how the Holy Lande, that
was a rose of the precyous blode of Our Lorde Ihesu Chryst, shulde
be delyuerd fro the euyll lyuers. And for this reson all Cristen
kynges and princes be called to his counsell, to thintent that he may
haue counsell and be aduertysed vpon the helpe of the Holy Landes
20 passage. Howbeit that Our Lorde is full of mercy, which hath shewed
vs by very experience that [G3v] he wyll delyuer the Holy Lande
out of thennemis handes to the tyme of Your Holy Paternite, we
ought all to pray humbly that longe lyfe and good gyue hym that
reigneth in saecula saeculorum. Amen.
25 Here endeth the boke of Thistoris of Thorient Partes (compyled by
a relygious man, Frere Hayton, frere of Premonstre order, somtyme
lorde of Corc, and cosyn german to the Kyng of Armeny) vpon the
passage of the Holy Land, by the commaundement of the Holy
Fader the Apostle of Rome, Clement the V, in the cite of Potiers.
30 Which boke, I, Nicholas Falcon, writ first in French as the Frere
Hayton sayd with his mouth without any note or example; and out of
Frenche I haue translated it in Latyn for our Holy Father the Pope,
in the yere of Our Lorde God M CCC vii in the moneth of August.
Deo gracias.

35 [I4v] Here endeth a lytell cronicle, translated out of Frenche into
Englysshe at the cost and charge of Richarde Pynson, by the com-
maundement of the right high and mighty prince, Edwarde, Duke of
Buckyngham, Erle of Hereforde, Staffarde, and of Northamton.
And imprinted by the sayd Richarde Pynson, printer vnto the kinges
40 noble grace. Cum priuilegio a rege in dulco.

Commentary

7/14 *some in naturs of thinges*: Hetoum may be referring to the popular Hindu folk belief in spirits and local gods manifesting themselves in certain localities, trees, monuments, etc, or perhaps to the more primitive animism practised in various islands in the East Indies.

8/29 *this realme of Tarsey*: Both M.C. Seymour, ed *Mandeville's Travels* (Oxford 1967) 253 n 184/3, and Kohler (*RHC Arm* II 122 notes a, b) gloss Hetoum's 'Tharsey' as the country called Telas or Teras situated between the Ili and Tarim rivers and inhabited by a Turkish tribe, the Uighurs. Seymour suggests that Hetoum confused this country with the biblical Tarshish, traditionally identified as the home of the Three Wise Men because of Psalm 72.10. The biblical Tarshish was used generally to indicate a remote corner of the world, sometimes eastern, sometimes western. Because of an early alliance in 1209 between the Uighur ruler and Genghis Khan, literate Uigher officials quickly rose to prominence in the early Mongol bureaucracy. This, and the fact that a Uighur captive was the first tutor to the sons of Genghis Khan, led to the adoption of the Uighur script by the illiterate Mongols (as Hetoum records 33/14–15). For a brief summary of Uighur history see J.J. Saunders *The History of the Mongol Conquests* (London 1971) 31–4. However Hetoum's linking of the biblical Tarshish and the Three Wise Men with the Uighur nation is unusual, and probably derives from his uncle Sempad's account of his visit to the Mongol capital of Karakorum. Cf Sempad's letter to his brother-in-law, King Henry I of Cyprus: printed in *Recueil des historiens des Gaules et de la France* ed Martin Bouquet et al, XX (Paris 1840) 361–3; and by Sir Henry Yule *Cathay and the Way Thither* 2nd ed rev H. Cordier, The Hakluyt Society Second Series No. 38 (London 1915) I 162, 262–3 (French text of letter with English translation). In this letter, Sempad claims that the Mongols have been converted to Christianity by Eastern Christians, including those from 'Tanchat' who are descended from the Three Wise Men. Sempad's 'Tanchat' refers most probably to the land of the Tanguts (which included many Uighurs).

9/29–32 *for the moost parte ... leters of Arrabyans*: The oasis cities of Turkestan (including Samarkand and Bukhara) were conquered in the early eighth century by the Arabs.

10/28 *the see of Reme*: The Sea of Azov was called Tana by the Latins (the original spelling of Hetoum's French text).

11/30 *the long and great desert of Inde*: Probably classical Gedrosia (ie the region of Makran in southwest Pakistan) which Alexander the Great crossed as he returned from the Indus river to the southeastern provinces of Persia

11/33–5 *Saynt Thomas the Apostle ... Christen fayth*: Cf *Marco Polo. The Description of the World* ed and trans A.C. Moule and Paul Pelliot I (London 1938) 388, 397–8. The presence of Christians in India was more probably the result of Nestorian missionary work in the sixth and seventh centuries than of the legendary efforts of St Thomas the Apostle. Cf the apocryphal *Acts of St Thomas*, a Nestorian writing existing in, among others, an Armenian version.

12/8–12 *which yle is named Celan ... for excellence and royaltie*: Marco Polo says that the king of Ceylon has the biggest ruby in the world, with which he rubs his face daily in order to retain his youthful looks (*Marco Polo* I 379–80).

12/32–3 *a fludde named Physon ... Paredise Terrestre*: The Phison, one of the four rivers flowing out of Paradise (Genesis 2.11) and identified in the Middle Ages with various rivers, is taken by Hetoum to be the Oxus or Amu-Darya.

13/4–5 *In auncyent tyme ... the fyre for theyr god*: Hetoum is referring to Zoroastrianism, the original religion of Persia before its conquest by the Arabs in AD 652. See Mary Boyce, *Zoroastrians: Their Religious Beliefs and Practices* (London 1979). By Hetoum's time, of course, Persia was almost entirely Moslem.

13/34–14/1 *the great cytie ... the Yren Gate*: Cf *Marco Polo* I 98; also E. Bretschneider *Medieval Researches from Eastern Sources* (London 1888) II 115–19. Derbend (on the western shores of the Caspian), by means of its famous wall, guarded the major route into Persia through the Caucasus mountains. The Persian Emperor Khusrau I Anoshirwan (AD 531–79) is said to have built the city and its wall (which extends on the one side into the sea for a mile, and on the other, one hundred and twenty miles into the mountains). Certainly it was not Alexander the Great who built the city. This legend arose because the wall at Derbend was taken to be the site of the great gate of iron and brass which according to legend Alexander erected to shut out the barbarian peoples of Gog and Magog. See *The Life and Exploits of Alexander the Great* trans E.A. Wallis Budge (London 1896) II 236–8, 451–3, for examples from the *Ethiopian Version of the Pseudo-Callisthenes* and the *Ethiopian Christian Romance of Alexander*. According to Andrew Runni Anderson in *Alexander's Gate, Gog and Magog and the Inclosed Nations* Monographs of the Medieval Academy of America No 5 (Cambridge, Mass. 1932), this legendary association probably began in the twelfth century when the memory of the city's real founder had faded. See also J.A. Boyle 'The Alexander Legend in Central Asia' *Folklore* 85 (1974) 217–28, rpt as No XXIV in J.A. Boyle *The Mongol World Empire 1206–1370* (London 1977).

14/14–15 *they folowe the maner ... vnder their lorde*: In 1237–8 the Mongols conquered northern Iraq, the Caucasus, the Crimea, and most of Russia. The defeat of the Seljuk sultan of Iconium in the campaigns of 1241–3 forced most of Anatolia to submit to Mongol rule. Thus by Hetoum's time all of the ancient kingdom of Greater Armenia would have been under direct or indirect Mongol rule for over fifty years.

14/16 *the other, Alcen*: Kohler (*RHC Arm* II 128 note b) identifies the original French *letres aloen* as the Uighur alphabet of the Alans. But Paul Pelliot, in *Notes on Marco Polo* I (Paris 1959) 25, corrects Kohler and says that 'Aloen' in fact represents the Caucasian Albanians (not to be confused with modern Albania in the Balkans), a totally different people from the Alans. Elsewhere in *RHC Arm* II (128, 139, 268, 593, 628), 'Aloens' is correctly glossed as the Aghouans or Caucasian Albanians, one group of whom lived in Greater Armenia under the religious rule of the Armenian catholicus.

14/26 *it is named the countrey Alayne*: Ie Alania in the Caucasus region north and east of Derbend. The Alans (also called As or Aas) first appeared in this area in the first century. Originally their tribal confederation extended from the lands north of the Aral Sea to the Don river basin, but in Mongol times they dwelled, as Hetoum implies, in the eastern Caucasus (although the name of their country was often extended to include the entire area northwest of the Caspian sea). The Alans were Greek Orthodox Christians, but some, carried off by the Mongols to serve in their armies in China, were later converted to Roman Catholicism by John of Montecorvino in the early fourteenth century. Cf Pelliot *Notes* 1 16–25 and Saunders *The Mongol Conquests* 59 note 26.

14/31 *the other, Abcas*: Cf *Marco Polo* 1 98–9. Abazia (modern Soviet Abkhazskaya) lies north and west of Georgia and borders on the Black Sea. Iberia (ie Georgia) and Abasgia (ie Abazia) were originally themes or administrative units in the Byzantine empire. Cf William of Tyre *A History of Deeds Done beyond the Sea* trans E. Babcock and A.C. Krey (New York 1976) 1 490. The Abazians are a Circassian people, converted to Christianity by the Byzantines in the seventh century, and remaining so until conquered by the Turks in the fifteenth century.

14/37 *a prouynce which is called Haynsen*: According to Seymour (*Mandeville's Travels* 254 note 188/1) this is probably the district of Hamschen between the Black Sea and the Balkhar Dagh mountains, and the darkness is probably the seasonal fogs that visit the steppe of Mughan, west of the Caspian and lying about the lower Kur river. See also Pelliot *Notes on Marco Polo* II (Paris 1963) 621. In *Marco Polo*, and in medieval geography generally, the province of darkness refers to the subarctic regions of northern Russia and Siberia (also occasionally to the darkness that occurred when the people of Gog and Magog were enclosed by Alexander). Pelliot (II 620) provides an interesting parallel to Hetoum's story in a tale told by Pian Carpine about an expedition of Genghis Khan in the East, where Genghis Khan is prevented from advancing because of dense clouds which blinded him and his army. Persecution of the Christians in Persia began under Shapur II (AD 309–79) when Christianity became the official religion of the Roman Empire. These persecutions continued throughout the next two centuries, and during the reign of the emperor Firuz (AD 457–83) there were rebellions in Christian Armenia and Georgia. But no Persian emperor died in pursuit of fleeing Christians (although many fled to Byzantine protection). See P.M. Sykes *A History of Persia* (London 1915) 1 414–15.

15/30–3 *This Ninyue ... nowe all wasted*: Cf Jonah 1–4. Nineveh fell to the Medes c 606 BC.

15/37 *called Babylone*: Babylon on the Euphrates (modern Hilla) was the ancient capital of Mesopotamia. The city gave its name to the region, which is perhaps the reason why Hetoum confuses it with the new Abbasid capital of Baghdad on the Tigris (founded in AD 762 by Caliph Abn Jafar Mansur).

15/37–16/2 *In this lande ... Iherusalem*: Nebuchadnezzar, king of Babylonia, defeated Necho II of Egypt at Carchemish in 604 BC, thereby gaining Syria and Palestine.

16/4–5 *be called Nestoryns ... false lawe of Mahomet*: P omits *e ont letres caldées* after *Nestorins*. It is of course the Moslems who use Arabic in their worship; the religious language of the Nestorian church was Syriac. The Nestorian church is more properly known as the church of the East (although at times it has been influenced by the teachings of Nestorius who died AD 451). The Nestorians claim uninterrupted descent from the church established by King Abgar v of Edessa (who was reportedly converted by one of Christ's disciples after the Ascension). After the condemnation of Nestorius by the Council of Ephesus in AD 431, the Eastern bishops gradually came together as a separate church centred in Persia. Since Nestorians made up much of the merchant class throughout Asia, the church enjoyed wide support there. Missions were sent to India in the sixth century and to China in the seventh to ninth and twelfth to fourteenth centuries. It is the Nestorian church which constituted the Christian church in Asia until the arrival of the first Roman Catholic missionaries in the fourteenth century.

16/11 *the vernicle*: Hetoum seems to be conflating two similar but different legends concerning a miraculous image of Christ, one associated with St Veronica, and the other with King Abgar v of Edessa. St Veronica supposedly offered her headcloth to Christ to wipe the blood and sweat from his face on the way to Calvary, and when he returned it his features had been miraculously impressed upon it. A portrait of Christ in Rome since the eighth century was said to be this same headcloth and was translated to St Peter's in 1297, where it was greatly venerated throughout the Middle Ages. There was also a tradition, accepted as authentic in the East, that King Abgar v of Edessa (4 BC–AD 50) received from Christ his portrait miraculously imprinted on canvas.

16/12–16 *the lande of Baram ... in the Bible*: Cf Genesis 11.30–2, 12.1–6. Harran is the land where Terah, Abraham's father, stopped after leaving Ur of the Chaldees, and from which Abraham and his family set out for the Promised Land of Canaan (cf William of Tyre I 456).

17/22–3 *the cyte of Trapesonde ... within fewe yeres*: In 1204 (the same year as the fall of Constantinople to the Latin Crusaders) two grandsons of the Byzantine emperor Andronicus I (1183–5) seized the area around Trebizond on the southeast coast of the Black Sea, and established the empire of Trebizond. The independence of this empire lasted until 1214 when the sultan of Iconium greatly reduced its territory and put the emperor under his suzerainty. The empire continued in this reduced state for two and a half centuries, exercising considerable influence in the Crimean and Black Sea regions because of its commerce, until the empire fell to the Ottoman Turks in 1461. Cf A.A. Vassiliev *History of the Byzantine Empire 324–1453* (Madison, Wisc. 1958) I 15, II 468, 506–7, 530–1; and W. Miller *Trebizond, the Last Greek Empire* (London 1926).

17/35 *Iacobins*: The Syrian Monophysite community (who rejected the teaching of the Council of Chalcedon on the Person of Christ) were called Jacobite after Jacob Baradeus, the man instrumental in making Monophysite the national church of Syria.

18/11 *Sein*: Cham was the Arab name for Syria, and, in particular, the province of Damascus.

18/15–16 *The sayd Silyce ... Armeny*: See Introduction xiii–xix.

18/24–6 *The Maronyns ... Mount Lyban*: The Maronites are a Syrian church, most of whose members still live in Lebanon. Although they claim descent from the monastery established by St Maro (d. AD 507), it is more likely that they arose as a separate body in the seventh century because of their acceptance of the Monothelite doctrine (a political compromise worked out by the emperor Heraclius with the Monophysites) which resulted in their excommunication by the Council of Constantinople (AD 680). After the arrival of the Crusaders in 1181, the Maronites entered into formal communion with Rome, although retaining their own liturgy.

19/7 *As Saynt Luke sayth in his Gospell*: Cf Luke 2.

19/11–15 *This Emperour ... CCC yeres*: Hetoum appears to be referring generally to the rise of the Sassanid dynasty in Persia. In AD 226 the last Parthian King of Kings was defeated and killed by his vassal-king Ardeshir, the first Sassanid emperor of Persia. The Sassanids ruled for four centuries until the rise of Islam and the Arabian conquest of Persia in the mid-seventh century. However, Hetoum's 'Cosserossath' resembles the name of two later Sassanid rulers, Khusrau (or Chosroes) I Anoshirwan ('Immortal Soul') (531–79) and Khusrau II Aparwez ('the victorious') (591–628). In 540 Khosru I devastated Antioch and the cities of northern Syria, and during his reign the centre of power within the Persian empire shifted from the Iranian plateau to the Mesopotamian plain (throwing the Persian empire into greater conflict with the Byzantine empire). Under Khosru II the Persians occupied Egypt, Syria, and Palestine, for a time threatening Constantinople itself. See Peter Brown *The World of Late Antiquity* (London 1971) 154, 159–69.

19/18–19 *In the yere ... realme of Syri*: By AD 632 Arabia was once more united under the first caliph abu-Bakr (632–34) after the fighting that had broken out after the death of the Prophet Mohammed in 631. But the invasion of Syria did not begin until 633, and Damascus fell in September 635. In 636 the Byzantine emperor Heraclius (who had just succeeded in recovering Syria from the Persians in 628) sent an army of 50,000 men under his brother Theodorus to meet the Arab invaders. The Byzantines were decisively defeated in a battle that took place on 20 August 636 at the juncture of the Yarmuk river and its tributary the al-Ruqqah. Hetoum may be conflating this battle with the battle for Antioch in the same year, fought outside the walls of the city on the plain of Possena (?Hetoum's 'Pofferit'), but the battle of Yarmuk decided the fate of Syria. In the same year the Arabs conquered the rest of Syria, stopping only at its natural boundary, the Taurus mountains (cf P 20/8–10). Between 639 and 646, the Arabs added Egypt, Mesopotamia, and Persia to their conquests.

20/10–11 *Wherof they rose ... to Constantynople*: Hetoum appears to be conflating three major Arab naval campaigns against Byzantium between AD 649 and 717. The first conquered Cyprus in 649, pillaged Rhodes in 654, and in 655, off Phoenix on the Lycian coast, annihilated the Byzantine navy commanded by Emperor Constans II. The second Arab offensive occurred from 674–80. The Arabs conquered the peninsula that projects from Asia Minor into the Sea of Marmora, called Cyzicus by the Byzantines and the Isle of Arwad by the Arabs (?Hetoum's 'yles of the Rhomayns,' P 20/17). Byzantium was saved from the Arabian siege by the energetic efforts of the emperor Constantine IV (668–85) and, according to legend, by the newly invented Greek fire. The most severe attack on Byzantium took place betweeen 715–17. When the besieging forces finally withdrew, a terrible storm (?Hetoum's 'tempest of wynde and rayne,' P 20/21–2) wiped out nearly the entire fleet. See Philip K. Hitti *A History of Syria* (London 1951) 443–7.

20/13–14 *Saynt Barnabe the Apostle*: Cf Acts 4.36, 13.16. According to tradition St Barnabas founded the Cypriot church.

20/30–3 *After that ... realme of Persy*: The Arabian invasion of Persia began in AD 633 but the capture of Mesopotamia was not completed until 637, after the battle of Cadesia in 636 (probably Hetoum's 'battle of Maraga'). The conquest of the rest of Persia followed quickly after the great Arabian victory in 642 at the battle of Nahavand south of Hamadan. But Yezdigird III, the last Sassanid emperor, was not killed at Mervin until 652. As Hetoum records (P 20/38ff),

Yezdigird's cause was taken up briefly by the Turks, who had by now crossed over the Oxus and settled in the eastern parts of Khurasan province.

21/18–19 *a lorde, the which they called the sowdan*: Hetoum is probably thinking in terms of the terminology of his own time. The leader of the Arabs was actually called caliph. The first four caliphs, elected in the years immediately following the death of the Prophet, were followed by various hereditary dynasties: first the Umayyid (661–749) based in Damascus, and then the Abbasid (750–1258) based in Iraq. After the murder of the last Abbasid caliph by the Mongols in 1258, the title was taken up by descendants of the House of Abbas in Egypt. When the Ottoman Turks conquered Egypt in 1517, the Turkish sultan adopted the title of caliph. Sultan is a Turkish title meaning 'him with authority,' and was first applied to Toghrul, Seljuk emperor of Persia. Thereafter the title became standard, and was adopted by most Moslem rulers.

22/3–14 *in this maner abode ... were made all Sarasyns*: Between AD 663 and 671 Caliph Mu'awiyah completed the subjugation of Khurasan province, crossed the Oxus river, and captured the major cities of Transoxiana and Turkestan. But it was not until the campaigns of the caliphs 'Abd-ad-Malik (685–705) and Welid (705–715), and the crossing of the Jaxartes river, that the Turks were really incorporated into the Arabian empire and converted to Islam. Turcoman or Turkman is the name given to the nomadic people belonging to the southwestern branch of the Turkic linguistic group (stretching from Siberia to modern Turkey). The name was also occasionally used to distinguish between the established Seljuk ruling class and the warlike nomadic Turkmen who had fought with them, and who continued to seek military expansion in Asia Minor and elsewhere. However these Turkmen and the Seljuk Turks were all of the same racial stock.

22/22 *In that tyme ... Sarasyns*: By the mid-ninth century, with the Abbasid dynasty in decay, various regional magnates gained power. One such local dynasty was the Hamdamid, which controlled northern Syria. The most notable Hamdamid was 'Ali Hasan Saif-al-Sawlah, who fought against the Byzantine emperor Nicephorus II Phocus (?Hetoum's 'Diogines'). After Saif's death, Nicephorus managed to recapture Aleppo, Antioch, and Homs. Antioch remained in Byzantine hands until 1084. See Hitti *History of Syria* 564–5.

22/33–4 *In the yere ... lordshyp in Asye*: Cf a similar account of the Turks and the election of Seljuk in William of Tyre I 71–4. By 1037 the Seljuk Turks under Toghrul and Chakir (grandsons of their tribe's eponymous founder Seljuk, ?ie

Hetoum's 'Salyoth') had conquered Khurasan. In 1055 the caliph of Baghdad was forced to recognize Toghrul as sultan of Persia. See Claude Cahen 'The Turkish Invasion: The Selchükids' in *A History of the Crusades* gen ed Kenneth M. Setton, II (Philadelphia 1962) 135–76.

23/14–17 *the great Artothe ... made hymselfe sowdan*: Ibn-Urtuq was a Turkman officer in the Seljuk army who in 1117 gained possession of Aleppo. The dynasty that he established was based in Mardin. Urtuq was a noted opponent of the Crusaders.

23/19–26 *This Alpasselem ... Turky*: Alp Arslan (1063–72), nephew and successor of Toghrul, extended the Seljuk empire to the east and the west. In 1071 he defeated a much larger Byzantine army at Manzikert in Asia Minor, capturing the emperor Diogones Romanus. After Alp Arslan's death, in 1077 a cousin named Sulaiman established himself in Asia Minor, with his capital (after 1084) at Iconium (Rum). It was Sulaiman's son, Kilij Arslan, whom the first Crusaders encountered in 1096 as they crossed Asia Minor. Cf William of Tyre I 107–10, 153ff.

24/1–2 *and not long after thei toke it*: Under Sultan Malik Shah the Seljuks conquered Antioch in 1084.

24/4–9 *Melacacerath, themperour ... Emperour of Asye*: With the death of Malik Shah in 1092 the unity and peace of the Seljuk empire ended. Despite what Hetoum says, Malik Shah had four sons (all of whom reigned at some point): Mahmud (1092), Barkiyaruk (1092–1104), Mohammed (1104–17), and Sanjar (1117–57). Initially, Mahmud and Barkiyaruk fought for the throne, ending with the death of Mahmud in 1092. But civil war continued afterwards and the empire broke up into various regional dynasties under the nominal rule of the sultan.

24/21–3 *the founde that ... and kylde hym*: Antioch fell to the Crusaders in 1097, but Barkiyaruk did not die until 1204. From 1099 until shortly before Barkiyaruk's death, his brother Mohammed had been in rebellion against him. Barkiyaruk's son and successor, Malik Shah, was deposed in 1204 by his uncle Mohammed, who then reigned until 1217. While Hetoum is correct about the discord among the Seljuk Turks and the disintegration of central authority, no Greeks or Armenians 'chased' the Seljuk Turks out of Persia.

24/33–25/14 *In the realme of Corasmyns ... slayn in batayle*: Hetoum here is compressing the history of the Khwarizmian empire, which ruled eastern Persia and the land of Khwarizm to the north from the time of the Seljuks to the time of the Mongol invasions (ie, from 1150 to 1231). The Khwarizm shahs began as vassals of the Seljuk sultans but quickly rose to prominence with the decline of Seljuk power, and in 1194 overthrew Toghrul III, last Seljuk sultan of Persia. Under the last shah, Ala-ad-Din Mohammed (1200–20), the Khwarizm empire stretched from Iraq to Chinese Turquestan, and from India to Transoxiana. But when Genghis Khan invaded Transoxiana in 1219, Mohammed declined to fight. Resistance was centred in his son Jalal-ad-Din (Hetoum's 'Ialadyn'). After an initial victory in 1220, Jalal-ad-Din was forced to retreat west. In 1225 he defeated the Caliph and occupied Azerbaijan province, including its capital Tabriz (Hetoum's 'Torys'). In 1231 Jalal-ad-Din was finally defeated by a Mongol force under Chormaghun, and was killed shortly after by Kurdish tribesmen. See Saunders 40–2, 60–1, 77–8.

25/15–17 *there they toke ... by a lady*: According to Kohler (*RHC Arm* II 146 note a), this 'lady' is Safia Khatun, widow of al-Malik al Aziz Giat-ad-din and regent of Halap during the minority of her son.

25/30–1 *the Corasmins duke ... Beretall*: Ie Berke Khan, a chief of the Khwariz-mians, who in 1244–7 led his people in aid of the Ayyubid rulers in Syria against Egyptian forces

26/1–2 *The lande ... Beligian*: The original homeland of the Mongol tribe is the country near the source of the Onon river in the Great Kentai range of mountains. According to J.A. Boyle ('Sites and Localities Connected with the History of the Mongol Empire' *Proceedings of the Second International Congress of Mongolists, Ulan Bator 1972* 75–9, rpt as No XVI in *The Mongol World Empire*), as a result of a German-Mongolian expedition in 1961, it was found that Burqan Qaldun (?Hetoum's 'Beligian'), the sacred mountain of Genghis Khan's youth, is actually Kentei Khan, a peak in the Great Kentei range. As for Hetoum's reference to 'wylde men,' he has probably connected this Far Eastern mountain with the frequent references in the Alexander-romance to 'wild men' dwelling in these parts.

26/8–16 *Dyuers natyons of Tartas ... before sayd*: 'Malgothz' comes from a variant French spelling of the original *Mogols* (ie 'Mongols'). Hetoum in this passage may simply be distinguishing the various Mongolian tribes from other nomadic (eg, Turkish) ones. He does go on to list all the other Mongolian tribes:

Tartars, Tangut, Oirat, Chelair, Sunit, and Merkit. However, by 'Malgothz' Hetoum may also be alluding to the existence of an elite sub-group within the Mongol tribe itself, claiming descent from Alan Qu'a, widow of a Mongol chieftain, who after being impregnated by a divine ray of light gave birth to three sons. See René Grousset *Conqueror of the World* trans D. Sinor and M. MacKellar (Edinburgh 1967) 8. Genghis Khan was descended from one of these sons, and the group was known by the surname Niroun (ie 'kept apart') in order to distinguish the purity of their origins. Cf C. d'Ohsson *Histoire des Mongols depuis Tchinguiz-Khan jusqu'à Timour Bey ou Tamerlan* (The Hague 1834) I 23–5, 425–7. At the time of Genghis Khan the Mongol tribe was in fact leaderless and subject to the other Mongolian tribes, as Hetoum relates. For a brief history of the Mongolian tribes, see E.D. Phillips *The Mongols* (London 1969) 25.

26/16–23 *a poore olde man ... theyr neighbours*: Despite what Hetoum says, Genghis was not an old man when he became leader of the Mongols. Genghis was born c 1167, probably became leader of his father's clan by 1175, and was confirmed as Great Khan in 1206. There are a number of legends accounting for his name and title, all generally involving some form of divine intervention; see Pelliot *Notes* I 298. In several of them, a bird singles out Genghis to be the leader of the Mongols and from the bird's cry comes the title Genghis Khan. Hetoum's account of a White Knight may simply reflect a similar desire to claim divine sanction for Genghis Khan's rule, and to emphasize for a Western audience the supposed pseudo-Christian monotheism of Mongol religious beliefs. But Hetoum appears to be drawing on a Mongol legend more closely connected to fact. According to Mongol religious beliefs, a ruler could only learn the will of Tengri (the ruler of Heaven) through the medium of a shaman. At the great gathering of the Mongols in 1206 which approved the election of Genghis as Great Khan, one such shaman, named Kokocu Tab-tengri, claimed to have ridden up to heaven on a white horse, where he learnt that Tengri had appointed Genghis as Great Khan (cf d'Ohsson I 98–100 and R.P. Lister *The Secret History of Genghis Khan* [London 1969] 191–5). However, when Kokocu later attempted to dominate Genghis, the Great Khan ordered Kokocu's brothers to kill him. The fact that Kokocu's father remained a loyal and trusted follower of Genghis might be the factual basis behind Hetoum's later account of how Genghis commanded all his lords to kill their first-born sons as a test of their loyalty to him (P 29/5–14). The exact meaning and derivation of the name Genghis is unclear. According to Pelliot (*Notes* I 296–303), it comes from the Turkish *tengiz*, ie 'ocean,' and thus means 'oceanic or universal.' The Mongol form is 'Chinggis.' The more familiar European forms of 'Genghis' and 'Jenghiz' come via Arabic, which has no 'ch' in its alphabet (Saunders 50 note 11). I have used the more familiar English form 'Genghis.' For a description of Genghis Khan's abilities as a soldier and administrator, see Saunders 63–70.

27/19 *twyse haue ... Tartas emperour*: It is unlikely that Hetoum would actually have witnessed the election of a Mongol Great Khan, since this would have occurred in Mongolia. But it is possible that he may have been present at the elections of two of the Persian ilkhans, given the close links between Cilician Armenia and the Persian ilkhanate at this time and the relative proximity of Cilicia to the ilkhans' capital of Tabriz.

27/33–4 *forthe withal ... warkes and dedes*: Mongol religion was shamanistic, so-called because it requires a shaman or prophet to mediate between ordinary men and the world of the spirits. Although there was a great god of the heavens called Tengri, more attention was paid to the lesser natural and ancestral spirits. This shamanism was easily accommodated to the more superstitious forms of Nestorian Christianity and Lamaist Buddhism, the latter generally adopted by later Mongol leaders. See Phillips 33–4 and J.A. Boyle 'Turkish and Mongol Shamanism in the Middle Ages' *Folklore* 83 (1972) 177–93, rpt as No xxii in *The Mongol World Empire*.

27/36–28/1 *ordayned that ... thoman*: This kind of decimal organization is characteristic of most of the central Asian nomadic tribes and dates back at least to the third century BC. Apparently Genghis Khan's major innovation was in creating new military units of mixed races and tribes; whereas before decimalization had been used to divide individual tribes and clans (Saunders 63). The term 'thoman,' from Turkish *tümen*, indicates the debt owed by the Mongols to their former Turkish overlords for providing much of Mongol military and social terminology (Phillips 22–4).

28/32–29/2 *as they wolde ... sayd busshe*: Cf Lister 43–52, for a similar story which may lie behind Hetoum's account. There Genghis also hides in a thicket for several days and nights in order to escape his pursuers, although he is eventually forced out by hunger and captured. Later he escapes and is aided by a friendly family, one of whom says 'When a bird, escaping from its cage, flies into the bush, the bush gives it shelter' (50). When the other captors come looking for Genghis, he hides in a cart of wool, which his pursuers do not look into, saying, 'You think a man could lie under all that wool for three days, in this weather' (51). Thus Genghis Khan escapes.

29/23–8 *thou passe ... with all thy men*: It is uncertain which of Genghis Khan's early campaigns is referred to here. It might be the first major western campaign of the Mongols against the Karakhitai in 1209. Lake Baikal was known as 'the Sea' to the Mongols, and it is thought that Hetoum's Mt Belgian refers to the sacred mountain of Burqan Qaldun in the Kentai range. Hetoum might therefore be using the two great landmarks of the original homeland to indicate the Mongols' departure from it. He may also be referring, as Seymour suggests (*Mandeville's Travels* 251, note 164/1), to the campaign of 1219 against the Khwarizmian empire. In that case Mt Belgian would refer to the Altai mountains, and the sea, to Lake Balkash, between which the main Mongolian army passed as they moved from their camp in the upper Irtish valley to the cities of Bukhara and Samarkand. It was shortly after this campaign that Genghis Khan died (as Hetoum records, P 31/10–1).

30/20–31/2 *and gaue theym ... shall nat contynue*: This story is also told by Juvaini in *The History of the World-Conqueror* trans J.A. Boyle (Manchester 1958) I 41. Ultimately the story derives from *The Secret History of the Mongols* (see Grousset 8), where it is told, not of Genghis Khan, but of his legendary ancestress, Alan Qu'a. The story is also common in the West, coming originally from Aesop. Cf the first dumb show in Thomas Sackville and Thomas Norton's *Gorboduc or Ferrex and Porrex* (ed I.B. Cauthern Jr [London 1970] 8).

31/2–4 *Dyuers more commaundementes ... great reuerence*: These commandments probably allude to the Mongol laws codified by Genghis Khan and called the *yasa*. Generally the code involved the complicated observances connected with Mongol shamanism. But it also prescibed a policy of religious toleration and non-involvement of Mongol overlords with their conquered subjects, designed to ensure the survival of the Mongols as a separate race. Genghis Khan's *yasa* remained for several generations after his death a potent force in preventing the assimilation of the Mongols by the generally more advanced cultures that they ruled. See d'Ohsson I 408ff and Saunders 69.

31/11–12 *his sonne ... after hym*: Ogedei was elected Great Khan at the meeting of the Mongol tribes in 1229, probably because of his recognized shrewdness and good-nature. Ogedei died on 11 December 1241 (not c.1243 as Hetoum says) from excessive drinking and debauchery.

31/13–21 *we shal say ... vnto this day*:The number nine was traditionally held sacred by the Mongols. When Genghis became Great Khan, he set up his famous *tuk* or standard in imitation of the Turkish khans, which consisted of a pole surmounted with nine white yak tails hanging from its head (Phillips 40).

31/31-2 *Than Hoctoca ... named Gebesabada*: Hetoum's 'Gebesabada' sounds most like the Mongol general Subedei, who, with Batu, from 1236–42 invaded and conquered the Crimea, the Ukraine, southern Russia, Hungary, and Poland. But the campaign that Hetoum describes corresponds to that led by the Mongol general Chormaghun in 1230–1, to recover Persia from the Khwarizmian forces of Jalal-ad-Din. The Mongols occupied northwestern Iran and Azerbaijan. From 1236–9 Chormaghun invaded Transcaucasian Albania, Greater Armenia and Georgia, defeating the army of the Georgian queen Rusadan (cf P 32/22–6). Chormaghun continued to govern this area until 1241, basing himself in the great grazing lands of Azerbaijan and the steppes of Mughan and Arran. See Saunders 77–9.

33/5–11 *commaunded to his sonn Iochi ... prouynces*: What Hetoum appears to be describing here is the territorial division that occurred after Genghis Khan's death between his sons Jochi, Chagatai, Ogedei, and Tolui. Jochi and his heirs were assigned the lands west of the Irtish river and Aral Sea to Russia. Since Jochi had died six months before Genghis, it was his son Batu who first conquered and ruled this land of Kipchak. Chagatai was given the lands of Turkestan and Transoxiana (between Mongolia and the Oxus river), except for the area east of Lake Balkash which became the Great Khan Ogedei's personal domain. Tolui received the Mongolian homeland. A more detailed and accurate account of this division occurs in Juvaini I 42–3. Cf Saunders 73–4. Hetoum's Jochi seems to refer not to Genghis Khan's eldest son Jochi but to the house of Ogedei (since 'Chapar' at P 35/8 is descended from Ogedei not Jochi, and the territory in question is part of Ogedei's patrimony).

33/19–25 *After that, themperour ... Sowdan of Turkey*: This 'Bacho' is not the previously cited 'Bacho' (ie Batu, son of Jochi), conqueror of Kipchak, but rather Baiju, son and successor of the Mongol general Chormaghun (cf Commentary 31/13–21. After the defeat of Ogedei, Baiju invaded the sultanate of Iconium, defeating the sultan Kai-Khusrau II (Hetoum's 'Giriacadyn,' P 33/33) at the battle of Köse-Dagh (Hetoum's 'Asadache,' P 34/4). Thereafter, the sultan of Iconium was a vassal of the Mongols (and after 1260, of the Persian ilkhans).

34/10–12 *after hym one of his ... long after hym*: Ogedei died in December 1241, but his son Guyuk was not elected until the great meeting of the Mongols in 1246. Guyuk's reign was cut short by his early death in April 1248.

34/12–14 *One of his cosyns ... lordships*: After the death of Guyuk in 1248, the opposition party led by Batu and Tolui's widow ensured the election of her son Mongke as Great Khan in July 1251. Under Mongke the third great wave of Mongol expansion occurred. His brother Hulagu conquered the remainder of Persia, Iraq, and northern Syria. And Mongke himself led the first of many invasions of southern China. In 1254 Mongke was also the recipient of the second Western mission to the Mongols, that of William of Rubruck on behalf of King Louis IX of France. Despite what Hetoum says (P 34/14–23) Mongke died in 1259 while campaigning in southern China. Hetoum's account may refer to one of the invasions of Japan mounted in 1274 and 1281 by Mongke's brother and successor, Qubilai Khan. Both times the Mongol fleets were destroyed, either by the Japanese or by storms. Cf *Marco Polo* I 358ff and Saunders 122.

34/24–9 *and made his brother ... of his dayes*: After Mongke's death in 1259 there followed a struggle for the succession that ended in 1262 with the victory of his younger brother Qubilai. Under Qubilai, the Mongols finally completed the conquest of southern China (by 1279), even invading Tibet and Indochina. Qubilai's growing preoccupation with China can be seen in his removal of the Mongol imperial capital from Karakorum in Mongolia to Khanbalik (ie Beijing, Hetoum's 'Ioing') in China. Indeed Qubilai was the last Great Khan in anything more than name, and after him the Mongol world empire divided along national and religious lines. See Saunders 120–7.

34/34–35/9 *Iochy, the first sonne of Hoctoca ... rest and peace*: This and the following two chapters amplify Hetoum's earlier account of the division of the Mongol empire after the death of Genghis Khan (cf Commentary 33/5–11). Although the eldest son of Genghis Khan was called Jochi, the territory controlled by Hetoum's 'Iochy' corresponds to that claimed by the House of Ogedei. See Saunders 171–2.

35/12–13 *Bacho ... partyes of septentrion*: The invasion of Russia and eastern Europe from 1237–41 by Batu, son of Jochi, is probably the most famous Mongol campaign from the Western point of view. After sweeping through the Ukraine and most of Russia, in 1240 the Mongol forces split into three groups: one advanced against the Poles, another against southern Hungary, and the main force under Batu and Subedei against Gran and Pesth, the major cities of Hungary. After the fall of Hungary, a large German and Polish army was defeated near Liegnitz in Poland, and the Mongols penetrated as far as the Adriatic in the south. The rest of Europe was saved by the untimely death of Ogedei in 1241, which demanded Batu's presence in Mongolia to ensure the election of his candidate as Great Khan (see Saunders 87–8). The Mongols never returned to Europe, and the boundaries of Batu's kingdom (known as the khanate of the Golden Horde or Kipchak) remained fixed, stretching north of the Black, Caspian and Aral Seas, from Moscow to Lake Baikal (Saunders 80–9).

35/25–35 *The Tartas ... to the other syde* : Saunders (86) records an interesting parallel to Hetoum's account. In April 1241, during Batu's invasion of Hungary, King Bela held a bridge on the river Sayo near Tokay. While Batu attacked the bridge, Subedei crossed the river upstream and surprised the Hungarians from behind. Although King Bela escaped, most of his officers and men were killed. However Batu did not die until 1255 or 1256.

36/27–37/2 *send before for his brother ... into Armeny*: Sempad went to the Mongol capital of Karakorum in 1247, returning to Armenia in 1250. He may perhaps have arrived in time for the election of the Great Khan Guyuk in 1246, to which the grand duke of Russia, the sultan of Iconium, the caliph of Baghdad, the sultan of Egypt, and the king of Georgia sent envoys. Cf Saunders 93–4 and John of Pian Carpine's account in *The Journey of William of Rubruck to the Eastern Parts of the World* trans William W. Rockhill, The Hakluyt Society Second Series No 4 (London 1900) 20; and in *Mission to Asia* ed Christopher Dawson (London 1955; rpt Medieval Academy Reprints No 8, Toronto 1980) 62–6. Sempad described some of his experiences during this visit in a letter to King Henry I of Cyprus: see *Recueil des historiens des Gaules* xx 361–3; and Yule *Cathay and the Way Thither* I 162, 262–3.

37/4–12 *the Kynge apparylled ... themperour of the Tartas*: In 1254 Hetoum I set out from his capital Sis, for the Mongol capital of Karakorum (not for Hetoum's 'Molch,' ie Almalic in Central Asia). Kirakos of Ganjak provides a contemporary account of the journey: see J.A. Boyle 'The Journey of Het'um I, King of Little Armenia, to the Court of the Great Khan Möngke' *Central Asiatic Journal* 9 (1964) 175–89 rpt as No IX in *The Mongol World Empire*. According to Saunders (79), Hetoum I may have been encouraged to initiate this trip and his policy of a Mongol-Christian alliance by the success of a Georgian embassy in 1240 and that of a Nestorian Armenian ecclesiastic named Simeon in securing from the Great Khan complete religious freedom and security for the Christians of these areas under Mongol suzerainty. Cf J.A. Boyle 'Kirakos of Ganjak on the Mongols' *Central Asiatic Journal* 8 (1963) 199–214 rpt as No XIX in *The Mongol World Empire*. See Saunders 97–8 for a summary of the unfounded rumours that Guyuk was Christian, which may also have encouraged Hetoum I's missions to the Mongols.

39/13–26 *Halcone occupyed ... no other thyng*: In 1255 Mongke's younger brother,

Hulegu, began the conquest of Persia and the caliphate of Baghdad. In preparation he sent his general Ketboge to attack the Assassins of northern Iran. The fortress of Gird-Kuh, one of the Assassin strongholds, held out for a period of eighteen years (until 1271), and is probably Hetoum's 'Tygado.' See *Cambridge History of Iran* vol v *The Saljuq and Mongol Periods* ed J.A. Boyle (Cambridge 1968) 341–5 for a description of the campaign. Hetoum's title 'Old Man of the Mountain' is that given by Latin writers to the head of the Syrian branch of the Assassins (destroyed by Sultan Baibars by 1273). For a brief history of the Assassins, see Bernard Lewis 'The Isma'ilites and the Assassins' *History of the Crusades* gen ed Setton II 99–135. Cf also *Marco Polo* I 128ff.

39/33–40/15 *and beseged the cyte … calyfe in Baldache*: Hulegu captured Baghdad in 1258, ruthlessly killing many of its inhabitants (see *Cambridge History of Iran* v 345–9). Hetoum's version of Caliph Mostassem's death is that given by most Western accounts (including Joinville and Marco Polo) and derives ultimately from the Persian historian Nasur-ad-Din. See J.A. Boyle 'The Death of the last 'Abbasid Caliph: a Contemporary Muslim Account' *Journal of Semitic Studies* 6 (1961) 145–61 rpt as No XI in *The Mongol World Empire* for a description of the differing versions of the caliph's death, as well as a translation of Nasir-ad-Din's account. In the Moslem version the caliph is rolled up in a carpet and trampled to death by Mongol horsemen, the standard Mongol execution for royalty.

40/20 *A woman that was called Descotacon*: Dokuz Khatun had been the wife of Hulegu's father, and she held pride of place amongst Hulegu's wives. Because she was a Nestorian Christian, Dokuz used her influential position to aid the cause of Persian Christians. She built many churches and during her lifetime Christians were predominant in Persia. Dokuz died a few months after Hulegu in 1265.

41/16–18 *And so Halap … threskore*: At this time Syria was divided into various small principalities ruled by descendants of Saladin, chief of whom was Nasir Yusuf, sultan of Aleppo. Aleppo fell in 1260 with the customary slaughter of its inhabitants. Sultan Nasir abandoned Damascus (which surrendered without any resistance) but was captured by Ketboge at Gaza. See Saunders 113.

41/31–4 *Halcon dyd send … the Sarasyns*: Bohemond VI succeeded his father as prince of Antioch in 1252 at the age of fifteen. Two years later at the request of King Louis IX of France, he married Sybil, daughter of Hetoum I. Probably as a result of his father-in-law's influence, Bohemond was the only Latin prince to acknowledge Mongol suzerainty and to enter into an alliance with them. In recognition of his help in the Syrian campaign of 1260, Hulegu returned to Bohemond Moslem lands formerly belonging to the principality of Antioch (in particular, the port of Latakia). In return, Bohemond agreed to reinstate the Greek patriarch of Antioch. However, Bohemond's co-operation with the Mongols outraged the other Latins in Outremer. See Steven Runciman *A History of the Crusades* III (Cambridge 1952) 306–7, 319.

42/9–10 *After that, he went ... Agaba*: Because of the power struggle that followed Mongke's death in 1259 (cf Commentary 34/24–9), it was essential that Hulegu direct his forces to the east (in order to support Qubilai, his candidate for Great Khan) and north (to defend himself from his enemy Berke and from Arik Boge, the rival claimant to the position of Great Khan).

42/16–26 *there cam newe tydinges ... theyr frendes*: Relations between Hulegu and Berke had been strained for some time, in particular by their support for rival sides in the war of succession between Arik Boge and Qubilai (lasting from 1259–62). But Berke, a convert to Islam, had also been incensed by the treatment accorded to the caliph after the capture of Baghdad, and by what he considered as Hulegu's ungrateful treatment of Berke's contingent of troops there. Thus in January 1263 Berke invaded the Caucasus and won a great victory over Hulegu's forces on the frozen Terek river. Cf Rashid-ad-Din *Histoire des Mongols de Perse* trans E.M. Quatremère, I (Paris 1836) 391–401 and *Marco Polo* I 478–82.

42/33–43/18 *the deuyll put ... declared hereafter*: Hetoum is describing the raid in 1260 made by Julian, lord of Sidon and Beaufort, on some of the neighbouring Moslem countryside recently conquered by the Mongols. The 'yle' to which the people of Sidon flee (P 43/13) is the Castle of the Sea, which during the sack of Sidon by Ketboge's forces was relieved by Genoese ships from Tyre. See Runciman III 308–9.

43/21–8 *the Sowdan of Egipt ... Christen men kept*: On 3 September 1260 at 'Ain Jalut' or 'Goliath's Spring' just south of Nazareth, the Egyptian army led by Sultan Kutuz decisively defeated the Mongol forces under Ketboge. The latter was taken prisoner and beheaded, while the remnants of his army fled back over the Euphrates into northern Iraq (not Armenia as Hetoum says).

43/37–44/5 *After hym .... thousande CC lxiiii*: Abaga became khan on his father's death in 1265. He hastened to obtain confirmation of his title from his uncle the Great Khan Qubilai, and Abaga is probably the first Mongol ruler of Persia to be given the title ilkhan or 'obedient khan' (see Saunders 121 note 5). For modern histories of the ilkhans, see B. Spuler *Die Mongolen in Iran* 3rd ed (Wiesbaden 1968); R. Grousset *L'Empire des Steppes* 4th ed (Paris 1952) 420–68; and in English, *The Cambridge History of Iran* v which deals with the Seljuk and Mongol periods. Much in these modern histories is derived from the contemporary Persian historian Rashid-ad-Din, part of whose universal history has been translated into English by J.A. Boyle *The Successors of Genghis Khan* (New York 1971).

44/9–11 *and was moche fortunat ... an ydolatrer*: Abaga was probably a Buddhist like his father, but favoured the Christians in his kingdom because of the influence of his Christian wife Maria, natural daughter of the Byzantine emperor (Runciman III 331–2).

44/11–3 *he made warre ... the Sodan of Egipt*: From 1266–9 Abaga was drawn into the fighting between the Great Khan Qubilai, with Borak, his candidate for Transoxiana and grandson of Chagatai, and Kaidu, the other claimant for Transoxiana and grandson of Ogedei (cf *Marco Polo* I 447–57). In 1266 an invasion from the north by Berke, khan of Kipchak and Kaidu's ally, was repelled by Abaga's forces. And in 1269, after peace had been restored between Borak and Kaidu, Borak invaded Khurasan and was not finally repelled until his death in 1270 (see *Cambridge History of Iran* v 357–60). Abaga did try twice to invade Syria, in 1278 and 1279, both times unsuccessfully.

44/20–2 *for that cause ... of the Holy Lande*: Baibars captured Antioch in May 1268. Cf *Continuation de Guillaume de Tyre* in *RHC Occ* II 456–7; and Runciman III 325–6.

44/23–33 *Bendonedar, which was Sowdan ... moche enhaunced*: Al-Malik Rukn-ad-Din Bibars Bunduqdar, or Baibars, became sultan of Egypt in 1260, after the murder of the former sultan, Kutuz. In 1266 Baibars invaded Cilician Armenia, and on 24 August that same year defeated the Armenians at the battle of Darbsak (cf Runciman III 322–3). King Hetoum's eldest son Leo was captured and a younger son, Toros, killed. The 'castell of the lande of Halap' (P 45/7) which Hetoum mentions are the castles of Darbsak, Behesni, and Raban. Thanks to the intercession of Sonqor al-Achqar (Hetoum's 'Sangolagar'), King Hetoum was allowed to keep Behesni. Leo was returned in 1268 and succeeded his father in 1270, when the latter abdicated to become a monk.

45/29–34 *At that tyme the Sowdan ... out of Turky*: At the time of Baibars' invasion of Turkey in 1277, the Seljuk sultanate of Iconium was ruled by a child, Kai Khusrau III. Real government rested with Sulaiman, the 'pervaneh' (ie 'keeper of the seals'), and with the large Mongol garrison stationed there. Baibars, it seems, had been invited to invade Turkey by a group of barons, possibly including Sulaiman. When Baibars defeated the Mongol army at Abulistan in 1277 and occupied the city of Caesarea, Abaga hurried to meet him. Baibars then withdrew to Damascus, and Abaga proceeded to punish those officials whom he felt had shirked their duty, in particular Sulaiman, whom he executed in July 1278. Hetoum repeats (P 46/12–16) the popular rumour current at the time that Abaga had Sulaiman's flesh served to him at a state banquet. There is no record of Abaga inflicting a defeat on the retreating Egyptian army (as Hetoum reports, P 46/1–7). Hetoum may be thinking of Abaga's later attempts to invade Syria in 1278 and 1279.

47/6–7 *Bendonedar was poysoned ... of Damas*: Baibars was poisoned in 1277 and was succeeded by his eldest son al-Malik as Sa'id (Hetoum's 'Mellecset'), who reigned for only two years. He was in turn succeeded by his brother Malik al-Adil, who was deposed after several months by Malik al-Mansur Saif-ad-Din Kalawun al-Elfy (Hetoum's 'Esly'). Kalawun reigned from 1279–90.

47/20–48/20 *Mangadamor rode ... M CC lxxxii*: Hetoum's exact and detailed account of the battle suggests an eye-witness account. According to Kohler (*RHC Arm* II 184 note a) the Armenian army was destroyed during its retreat from Homs by bands of Turkmen and Kurds, who then ravaged the coast of Cilician Armenia and sacked the city of Ayas. Cf a letter from an English Hospitaller, Joseph de Chauncey, to Edward I of England, giving an eye-witness account of the battle of Homs and its aftermath that is similar to Hetoum's: 'A Crusader's Letter from "The Holy Land"' trans William B. Sanders, Palestine Pilgrims' Text Society No 5 (London 1888) 7–13.

48/26–31 *it happened that ... foureskore and two*: Abaga died in April 1282 after he fell into a delirium brought on by excessive drinking. The rumour of poisoning was raised by Abaga's son Arghun, and directed against the Juvaini brothers, grand viziers under Abaga and his successor, after Arghun failed to secure the succession (*Cambridge History of Iran* v 364–5).

48/32–7 *After the dethe of Albaga ... Mahomet Can*: Abaga had meant his son Arghun to succeed him, but after Abaga's death in 1282, his brother Teguder secured the election. On assuming the throne, Teguder converted to Islam and took the name Ahmed. Shortly after, civil war broke out between him and Arghun, and the Mongol generals, alarmed at Teguder's pro-Moslem policies, eventually declared for Arghun, killing Teguder in 1284. Boyle, however, attributes Teguder's downfall simply to ineffective government (*Cambridge History of Iran* v 368). The 'myghty man' (P 50/2) who frees Arghun is the Mongol general Bukka, who later rebelled against Arghun after he became khan. The 'constable' (P 49/35) commanded to guard Arghun is the same Georgian general 'Ameleth/ Halmach Bech' (ie Alinaq) whom Hetoum mentions earlier in his description of the battle of Homs (P 48/6ff). Cf also *Marco Polo* I 457–65 for the conflict between Arghun and Teguder.

50/13–14 *In the yere ... lorde of the Tartas*: Arghun's reign (1284–91) saw the return to many of the traditional policies of Hulegu and Abaga. Arghun was pro-Buddhist and also showed great favour to the Christians (perhaps because he saw the desirability of an alliance with the West). His son was baptized Nicholas in 1289 in honour of Pope Nicholas IV. Arghun wrote to Pope Honorius IV in 1285 to suggest a combined attack against Egypt, and in 1287–8 he sent a Nestorian ecclesiastic, Rabban Sauma, on an official mission to Rome, Paris, and the English court at Bordeaux. See *The History of Yahballaha III and Bar Sauma* trans J.A. Montgomery (New York 1927; rpt 1966), and *The Monks of Kublai Khan* trans E.A. Wallis Budge (London 1928). In 1289 Arghun made a final appeal to the West for aid in his projected attack on Damascus in 1291. For a translation of this letter, see A. Mostaert and F.W. Cleaves *Les Lettres de 1289 et 1305 des Ilkhans Arghun et Oljeitu à Philippe le Bel* (Cambridge, Mass. 1962). Arghun appears to have been a less able administrator than his predecessors, in particular, unable or indisposed to check the rapacity of the Mongol overlords who exploited the native Moslem population. Arghun died in March 1291 after a long illness.

50/34–5 *In the yere ... Kalgato helde the lordship*: Perhaps because of his youth, Arghun's son Ghazan was passed over, and Arghun's younger brother Gaikhatu was elected khan. His reign (1291–5) was marked by excessive profligacy and financial folly, and eventually Gaikhatu was strangled by his generals in April 1295. Cf *Marco Polo* I 467–8.

51/5–6 *After the deth ... which was called Baydo*: Baidu, a first cousin of Gaikhatu, reigned for only a few months, until deserted by his generals in favour of Ghazan. Although Baidu was not a Christian, his pro-Christian policies may have contributed to his downfall. Baidu was the last ilkhan to seek confirmation of his title from the Great Khan, for Qubilai's successors in China were no longer recognized as Great Khans by the other Mongol rulers.

51/27–31 *After Baydos deth, Casan ... the Sarasyns*: On the advice of a Moslem general named Narwaz, Ghazan (1295–1304) was converted to Islam, taking the name of Mahmud and the title of sultan. Under the pressure of the fanatical Narwaz, for two years Christians, Jews, and Buddhists were cruelly persecuted. Finally Ghazan, who himself favoured religious tolarance, purged these fanatical Moslem elements within his government. However, while Ghazan strongly supported an alliance with the Christian West, he never abandoned Islam, and all future ilkhans were Moslem. In domestic affairs, Ghazan's reign was the most brilliant of all the ilkhans. He reformed taxation, supported education and the arts, and embarked on an ambitious building programme, assisted by his able grand vizier, the historian Rashid-ad-Din. See *Cambridge History of Iran* v 379–97 and Saunders 135–8. Hetoum's description of Ghazan as short and ugly (P 54/20–1) echoes other Western impressions of Mongolian physical features (cf Sempad's description of the Mongols in Yule-Cordier *Cathay and the Way Thither* I 262).

52/2–53/18 *Whan Casan came ... Wednisday before Christmasse*: In 1299 Sultan al-Malik al Nasir invaded north Iraq. In a counter-attack Ghazan crossed the Euphrates with an army of 90,000 men, defeating the Egyptian army at Homs on 24 December 1299.

55/32–8 *Whan the sommer ... all the countres*: In January 1299 Kipchak, governor of Damascus, deserted to the forces of Ghazan. Thus, after Ghazan's conquest of Damascus in 1300, he was reinstated as the city's governor. But the same year, after Ghazan had returned to Persia to deal with an invasion of Khurasan, Kipchak led the rebellion in Syria which drove out the small Mongol force of occupation led by Ghazan's general, Mulai.

56/15–16 *tydinges came ... Casan* : In fact heavy rains and floods kept Ghazan and his army in Iraq and were the reason that the combined expedition was cancelled.

57/7–12 *he herde tidynges ... the realme of Syrie*: It is unclear why Ghazan returned to the east bank of the Euphrates and did not lead the 1303 campaign in person. It is also unclear whom Hetoum means by 'Baydo.' For it was in 1301, not 1303, that Ghazan was forced to return to Persia to defend an invasion of Khurasan by Kutlughshah, the Chagatai khan.

59/35–60/17 *For the Sowdan sende ... the King of Armeni*: In 1305 the Egyptians invaded Cilician Armenia, sacking the capital of Sis. But on 18 July an Armenian army, aided by a company of Mongol soldiers, defeated the Egyptian invaders and a temporary truce was negotiated with the sultan of Egypt. See Serarpie Der Nersessian 'The Kingdom of Cilician Armenia' in *History of the Crusades* gen ed Setton II 657.

60/28 *Our Lady Delepiscopie chirch of the order of Premontrey*: The Premonstratensian monastery of Lapais or Bellapais was situated on the north shore of the island of Cyprus close to the capital of Nicosia. It was one of the more powerful and prestigious of the island's monasteries. For a description, see T.S.R. Boase 'The Arts in Cyprus: Ecclesiastical Art' in *History of the Crusades* gen ed Setton IV (Madison, Wisc. 1977) 183–4.

60/32–3 *the realme of Armeny ... than it was*: For a discussion of the civil unrest and dynastic disputes that divided Cilician Armenia from 1292–1305, see *History of the Crusades* gen ed Setton II 656–8; *The Cilician Kingdom of Armenia* ed T.S.R. Boase (New York 1978) 28–33; and Fr H. François Tournebize *Histoire politique et religieuse de l'Arménie* (Paris [1910]) 220–8.

62/7–8 *Carbanda helde his power ... of Toris*: Mohammed Kharband Oljeitu (ie 'the Fortunate') reigned from 1304 to 1316. Despite what Hetoum says, relations between Persia and Chagatai were relatively quiet during Oljeitu's reign (until an invasion of Khurasan in 1314), and in the Caucasus Tokhta's threatening movements of troops did not result in war. Oljeitu completed the construction of the new city of Sultaniya which replaced Tabriz as capital (despite what Hetoum says). And he sent embassies to Philip of France and Edward I of England to announce that there was now peace amongst the Mongols and to urge a Western-Mongol alliance and crusade (see Mostaert and Cleaves *Les Lettres de 1289 et 1305*). For a summary of the relations of the ilkhans with the West, see J.A. Boyle 'The Il-Khans of Persia and the Christian West' *History Today* 23 (1973) 554–63 rpt as No XIII in *The Mongol World Empire*.

62/35–63/9 *Albaga dyde make ... the sayde passage*: After Abaga's battle with Berke in the valley of the Kur river in 1266 (cf Commentary 44//11–13), Abaga dug a huge ditch beyond the Kur which he fortified and garrisoned (Sykes II 101). Hetoum has apparently misunderstood the Mongol word *siba* (ie 'palisade, wall') as a 'place named Ciba' (see *Cambridge History of Iran* v 356). According to J.A. Boyle in 'Ghazan's Letter to Boniface VIII: Where was it written?' *Proceedings of the 27th International Congress of Orientalists* (Wiesbaden 1971) 601–2 rpt as No XII in *The Mongol World Empire*, the nearby steppe of Mughan is noted as a resting-place for migratory birds and was probably known in Hetoum's time as

'Bird Gate.' The word 'seyserach' (Fr *seiserach*) is not recorded other than by Hetoum and is probably a borrowing from the Armenian *sarsarak* (a bird of unidentified species proverbial for its anxiety). See J.A. Greppin *Classical and Middle Armenian Bird Names, a Linguistic, Taxonomic and Mythological Study* (Delmar, New York 1978) 89–90.

66/22–67/28 *The knyghtes and the hoost ... fewe valyant men*: Hetoum gives a brief but accurate summary of Mamluk feudalism. Kipchak and Circassian slaves were introduced by later rulers of the Ayyubid dynasty in Egypt to bolster the sultan's power (cf P 69/15–23). But in 1250 Aybak, one of these slaves, gained power and began the Mamluk slave dynasty which ruled Egypt until its conquest by the Ottoman Turks in 1517. See Philip K. Hitti *History of the Arabs* 10th ed (London 1979) 671–82; Mustafa M. Ziada 'The Mamluk Sultans, 1291– 1517' in *History of the Crusades* gen ed Setton III 486–512; and David Ayalon *L'Esclavage du mamelouk* Oriental Notes and Studies No 1 (Jerusalem 1951). The conditions for being a Mamluk were not to have been originally Moslem, to have been born outside the Mamluk state, and to have been bought at an early age. The slaves were placed in a special school in Cairo for military and religious training until they reached manhood. Then they were freed, becoming members of the royal Mamluk corps and ascending through the ranks. Power outside the royal household was controlled by various emirs, themselves former royal Mamluks, who were given the rents of lands in return for a promise to maintain a certain number of fighting men for the sultan. Officially Mamluk status and an emir's lands could not be passed on to descendants, although exceptions occurred.

68/21–4 *than they yelde ... CCC xlvii yeres*: The Arabs conquered Syria between 640 and 646 AD. For the various dynasties which controlled the caliphate, see Commentary 19/18–19.

68/25–6 *and the Medyens ... Egypt*: In 1171 Saladin, a Kurd, seized power in Egypt from the last Fatimid sultan al-Adid.

68/28–32 *In the yere ... Holy Lande conquestes*: In fact King Amalric I of Jerusalem (1163–74) invaded Egypt four times – 1163, 1164, 1167, 1169. The first two invasions had little success, but the third prompted the Fatimid sultan's appeal for help from Nur-al-Din, Turkish atabeg of Syria. This call in turn led to the dispatch of Shirkuh (Hetoum's 'Saraton') and his nephew Saladin to Egypt. In 1167 Amalric besieged Fustat (Babylon or Babilyun) south of Cairo, and in the same year surrounded Shirkuh in Alexandria. Amalric's invasion of 1168 led to the seizure of power in Egypt by Shirkuh. Cf William of Tyre II 302–5, 314–43, 349–56, 362–90.

69/8–12 *After the dethe ... Holy Lande*: Al-Malik al-Nasir Sala-ad-Din Yusuf, or Saladin, succeeded his uncle Shirkuh as grand vizier. Upon the death of the last Fatimid sultan in 1171, Saladin became sultan of Egypt (1171–91), establishing the Ayyubid dynasty (named after Saladin's father) which ruled Egypt from 1171 to 1250. After seizing Syria from Nur-al-Din's young son, Saladin devoted his attention to crushing the Crusader states. These were reduced to a small coastal strip between Tyre and Tripoli, along with Antioch, after the battle of Hattin in 1187 (Runciman II 403–73). After Saladin, Syria was divided amongst his decendants, who ruled there until the rise of the Mamluks.

69/24–9 *in that tyme ... out of pryson*: Louis IX took the cross in 1244. Two months earlier a combination of Egyptian and Khwarizmian mercenaries had recaptured Jerusalem. By 1249 Louis was in the Holy Land and ready to attack Damietta in the Nile delta. Initially the Crusaders were successful, and Damietta fell without a battle in June of the same year. But the Crusaders remained the summer in Damietta, and when they did embark, chose to attack Cairo instead of Alexandria, the more logical objective. Because of mismanagement by the king's brother, the army was trapped in the Nile delta by the Egyptians and forced to surrender. The king and his nobles were eventually released for a massive ransom of 800,000 ducats. In May 1250 Mamluk slaves assassinated the young Ayyubid sultan Turan-Shah, installing in his place a fellow slave, Aybak (Hetoum's 'Turkement'). Louis remained in Outremer for four more years, improving fortifications and settling disputes in an effort to ensure the safety of the kingdom of Jerusalem. Cf Joinville *Vie de Saint-Louis* in *Joinville & Villehardouin, Chronicles of the Crusades* trans M.R.B. Shaw (Harmondsworth 1963) 163–353; *Continuation de Guillaume de Tyre* in *RHC Occ* II 566–71, 589–630; Joseph R. Strayer 'The Crusades of Louis IX' *A History of the Crusades* gen ed Setton II 255–92; and Runciman II 255–92. Louis was also in contact with the Mongols, receiving a Mongol embassy in December 1248 and himself sending Andrew of Longjumeau in January 1249 to the Mongol Great Khan (see Denis Sinor 'The Mongols and Western Europe' *History of the Crusades* gen ed Setton III 522–4 rpt as No IX in *Inner Asia and its Contacts with Medieval Europe*).

69/32–3 *After, one of this sclauons ... called Melomees*: Izz-ad-Din Aybak, a Turk (Hetoum's 'Turkement'), was assassinated in 1257 by his wife, the widow of the last Ayyubid sultan. Aybak was succeeded by his son al-Malik al-Mansur 'Ali, who reigned for two years, until deposed by his regent, al-Muzaffar

Saif-ad-Din Kutuz (1259–60). It was Kutuz who defeated the Mongols under Ketboge at the battle of 'Ain Jalut (cf Commentary 43/21–8). As he returned to Egypt, he was assassinated by his emirs.

69/37–70/3 *which was called ... M CC lxviii*: Cf Commentary 44/23–33, 44/20–2, 45/29–34, 47/6–7.

70/4–7 *In this Bendocdar dayes ... grace of God*: Edward, when still Prince of Wales, decided to take the cross after the fall of Antioch in 1268. He arrived in the Holy Land in the spring of 1272. With his small force of men, Edward could accomplish little, and a truce was negotiated in May 1272 with Sultan Baibars. Despite this, Baibars sent an Assassin (disguised as a native Christian) who stabbed Edward with a poisoned knife. Like Louis IX, Edward saw the advantages of a Western-Mongol alliance, and on his arrival sent an embassy to the Persian ilkhan Abaga. The latter, however, was preoccupied with fighting in Turkestan and was able to send only a small raiding party against Baibars. See Runciman III 335–8; *History of the Crusades* gen ed Setton II 517–18.

70/10–13 *After his deth ... made him sodan*: See Commentary 47/6–7.

70/20–1 *a seruaunt ... dyed soone after*: Despite what Hetoum says, Sultan Kalawun (ie 'Elsy') died of natural causes while preparing to attack Acre in 1290.

70/30–2 *after that ... Melecasseraph brother*: See Commentary 52/2–53/18. Al-Malik al Nasir Mohammed, Kalawun's son, had one of the more turbulent reigns in Mamluk history. He first ruled from 1293–4, when he was deposed by his Mongol regent, Ketboge (Hetoum's 'Ginboga'), who ruled from 1294–6 under the title Malik-al-Adil. When Ketboge was deposed by his emirs in 1296, they appointed another son of Kalawun, Malik al-Mansur Husam ad-Din Lajin (Hetoum's 'Lachyn'), who was assassinated in 1298. Al Nasir Mohammed was then reinstated, and reigned until 1340.

71/17 *to play at the foteball*: The original French 'la Solle' is, according to Kohler (*RHC Arm* II 230 note c), a corruption of the Arabic 'soldjan' or 'savledjan.' This was a ball-game played on horseback and resembling polo, which originated in Persia but was immensely popular as a sport of princes from Mongolia to Byzantium. Of all the rulers of Egypt the Mamluks were most attached to the game, and built lavish establishments in which to play it. Players were frequently blinded by the ball or injured by a falling horse. See Taki-Eddin-Ahmed Makrizi *Histoire des sultans mamlouks de l'Egipte* trans E.M. Quatremère, I (Paris 1837) 121 note 4.

72/11–12 *the flud of Nyll ... that is called Gion*: See Genesis 2.13 and Commentary 12/32–3.

72/28–34 *the habytauntes ... to skant*: The *meqias* or nilometre was built at the southern end of the island of Rawda, opposite Old Cairo or Misr el-Atiqah (Hitti *History of the Arabs* 453).

73/7–10 *But it was taken twyse ... Saynt Loys*: The attempt by Amalric I, king of Jerusalem, to take Damietta in 1169 was unsuccessful. But in 1219, members of the Fifth Crusade under John of Brienne, king of Jerusalem, did capture the city, which they held until September 1221 (Runciman III 149–70). King Louis IX of France took Damietta in 1249 and the Crusaders held the city until April of the next year (cf Commentary 69/24–9).

73/20–1 *In the realme ... be called Kepty*: The Egyptian (and Ethiopian) Monophysite Christians are known as Copts (cf Commentary 17/35).

73/35–6 *Ecce nunc ... dies salutis*: Cf Vulgate 2 Corinthians 6.2.

74/7–8 *pastoure and right Holy Father ... vertue*: Ie, Pope Clement V (1305–14)

75/17–19 *Carbanda ... the Cristen lande*: See Commentary 62/7–8.

78/28–9 *Yet our Christen men ... the galleys*: After the fall of Acre in 1291, all that remained in Crusader hands of the former mainland states was the waterless island fortress of Ruad, two miles off the coast and opposite the city of Tortosa. This island was the base used in the abortive campaigns of 1300–1 and 1303, but was abandoned by the Templars that same year.

83/28–31 *syth the Sowdan ... to Halcon and to Casan*: Cf P 41/19–24, 54/29–33.

84/39–41 *The Tartars hath ... in that yere*: Hetoum is probably thinking of the great assembly of all Mongols called a *kuriltai*, which dealt with everything from the planning of war strategy to the election of a new Great Khan. During the reigns of Genghis and his first successors it was customary to hold an annual *kuriltai* at which the entire year's strategy would be decided. By the time of Hetoum, because of the fragmentation of the Mongol empire, these international gatherings no longer occurred. But similar organizational *kuriltai* were held by the ilkhans of Persia. See Runciman III 319 where he describes those present at Hulegu's last *kuriltai*.

Bibliography

The bibliography contains only those works mentioned in the Introduction and Commentary.

Abel-Rémusat, J.P. 'Mémoires sur les relations politiques des princes chrétiens et particulièrement des rois de France, avec les empereurs mongols' *Mémoires ... de l'Académie des Inscriptions et Belles-Lettres* 6 (1882) 396–467; 7 (1884) 335–438

Adams, Robert P. *The Better Part of Valor: More, Erasmus, Colet, and Vives, on Humanism, War, and Peace, 1496–1535* (Seattle 1962)

Akelian, S. *Chronicle of the General Sempad* [in Armenian] (Venice-San Lazzaro 1956)

Akopian, A. *Short Chronicles: XIII-XIV Centuries* [in Armenian] 2 vols (Erevan 1951–1956)

Amadi, *Chronique d'Amadi* ed René de Mas Latrie. *Collection de Documents Inédits sur l'histoire de France* première série (Paris 1891)

Anderson, Andrew Runni *Alexander's Gate, Gog and Magog and the Inclosed Nations* Monographs of the Medieval Academy of America No 5 (Cambridge, Mass. 1932)

Anglo, Sydney *The Great Tournament Roll of Westminster: A Collotype Reproduction of the Manuscript* 2 vols (Oxford 1968)

– *Spectacle, Pageantry and Early Tudor Policy* (Oxford 1969)

Atiya, Aziz S. *The Crusade in the Later Middle Ages* (London 1938)

Ayalon, David *L'Esclavage du mamelouk* Oriental Notes and Studies, No 1 (Jerusalem 1951)

Baluze, S. *Vitae paparum Avenioniensium* 2 vols (Paris 1693)

Barclay, Alexander *The Ship of Fools* ed T.H. Jamieson, 2 vols (Edinburgh 1874)

Baumer, Franklin L. 'England, the Turk, and the Common Corps of Christendom' *American Historical Review* 50 (1944) 26–48

Beazley, C. Raymond *The Dawn of Modern Geography* 3 vols (Oxford 1906)

– *Prince Henry the Navigator* (London 1895)

Bennett, Josephine W. *The Rediscovery of Sir John Mandeville* (New York 1954)

Biblia sacra juxta vulgata Clementinam (Tournai 1956)

Bibliotheca Grenvilliana ed John T. Payne and Henry Foss, 3 vols (London 1842–72)

Bibliotheca Heberiana, Auction Catalogue of his Library 4 vols (London 1834–7)

Boyce, Mary *Zoroastrians: Their Religious Beliefs and Practices* (London 1979)

Boyle, J.A. *The Mongol World Empire 1206–1370* (London 1977)

Bretschneider, E. *Medieval Researches from Eastern Sources* 2 vols (London 1888)

Briquet, C.M. *Les Filigranes* ed Allan Stevenson, 4 vols (Amsterdam 1968)

Brown, Peter *The World of Late Antiquity* (London 1971)

Bryer, A. 'Edward I and the Mongols' *History Today* 14 (1964) 696–704

Budge, E.A. Wallis, trans *The Life and Exploits of Alexander the Great* 2 vols (London 1896)

– *The Monks of Kublai Khan* (London 1928)

Calendar of State Papers (Venetian) ed Rawdon Brown Vol II (London 1867); Vol III (1869)

The Cambridge History of Iran Vol V *The Saljuq and Mongol Periods* ed J.A. Boyle (Cambridge 1968)

The Cambridge Medieval History Vol IV, Part I *Byzantium and its Neighbours* ed J.M. Hussey (Cambridge 1966)

Caoursin, Gulielmus *The Siege of Rhodes* trans John Kay. (London c 1482; rpt English Experience No 236, Amsterdam 1970)

Capystranus (London: Wynkyn de Worde [nd])

Catalogue of Western Manuscripts in the Old Royal and King's Collection ed George F. Warner and Julius P. Gilson, 4 vols (London 1921)

Chauncey, Joseph de 'A Crusader's Letter from "The Holy Land"' trans William B. Sanders *Palestine Pilgrims' Text Society* No 5 (London 1888)

Continuation de Guillaume de Tyr in *Recueil des historiens des croisades: Documents Occidentaux* Vol II ed Philippe le Bas et al (Paris 1859)

Dawson, Christopher, ed *Mission to Asia* (London 1955; rpt Medieval Academy Reprints No 8, Toronto 1980)

Der Nersessian, Serarpie 'Armenian Chronicle of the Constable Smpad' *Dumbarton Oaks Papers* No 13 (1959) 145–68.

Fifty-Five Books Printed Before 1525, An Exhibition from the Collection of Paul Mellon ([New York] 1968)

Gage, J., ed 'Extracts from the Household Book of Edward, Duke of Buckingham, 1508–9' *Archaeologia* 25 (1834) 311–41

Giustiniani, Sebastiano *Four Years at the Court of Henry VIII* trans Rawdon Brown, 2 vols (London 1854)

The Great Chronicle of London ed A.H. Thomas and I.D. Thornley (London 1938)

Greppin, J.A. *Classical and Middle Armenian Bird Names: A Linguistic, Taxonomic and Mythological Study* (Delmar, New York 1978)

Grousset, René *L'Empire des Steppes* 4th ed (Paris 1952)

– *Conqueror of the World* trans D. Sinor and M. MacKellar (Edinburgh 1967)

Hall, Edward *The Union of the Two Noble and Illustre Famelies of Lancastre and York* ed Henry Ellis (London 1809)

Helyas, Knight of the Swanne trans R. Copland (London: Wynkyn de Worde 1512; STC 7571; rpt New York: The Grolier Club 1901)

Hetoum *La Flor des estoires de la terre d'Orient* and *Flos historiarum terre orientis* ed C. Kohler et al in *Recueil des historiens des croisades: Documents arméniens* (Paris, 1906)

– *La Flor de la Ystorias de Orient* ed Wesley Robertson Long (Chicago 1934)

– *History of the Tartars* Armenian trans Br P. Mkrtitch Avkerian [Jean-Baptiste Aucher] (Venice 1842)

– *Table chronologique* in *Recueil des historiens des croisades: Documents arméniens* Vol I 469–90 ed E. Dulaurier et al (Paris 1869)

A History of the Crusades [Gen ed Kenneth M. Setton, 5 vols] Vol I *The First Hundred Years* ed Marshall W. Baldwin (Madison, Wisc. 1969); Vol II *The Later Crusades 1189–1311* ed Robert Lee Wolff and Harry W. Hazard (Philadelphia 1969); Vol III *The Fourteenth and Fifteenth Centuries* ed Harry W. Hazard (Madison 1975); Vol IV *The Art and Architecture of the Crusader States* ed Harry W. Hazard (Madison 1977); Vol V *The Impact of the Crusades on the Near East* ed Norman P. Zacour and Harry W. Hazard (Madison 1985)

Hitti, Philip K. *History of the Arabs* 10th ed (London 1979)

– *A History of Syria* (London 1951)

Hodnett, Edward *English Woodcuts, 1480–1535* (Oxford 1973)

Iwamura, Shinobu *Manuscripts and Printed Editions of Marco Polo's Travels* (Tokyo 1949)

Joinville, Jean de *Joinville & Villehardouin, Chronicles of the Crusades* trans M.R.B. Shaw (Harmondsworth 1963)

Juvaini, 'Ala-ad-Din 'Ala-Malik *The History of the World Conqueror* trans J.A. Boyle, 2 vols (Manchester 1958)

Langlois, V. *Revue de l'Orient* 3ᵉ série, 15 (Paris 1863)

Letters and Papers, Foreign and Domestic, of the Reign of Henry VIII ed J.S. Brewer. Vol I rev R.H. Brodie (London 1920); Vol II (1864); Vol III (1867)

Lister, R.P., trans *The Secret History of Genghis Khan* (London 1969)

Lydgate, John *The Minor Poems: Part II, Secular Poems* ed Henry N. MacCracken EETS OS 192 (Oxford 1934)

McKerrow, Ronald B *Printers' and Publishers' Devices in England & Scotland, 1485–1640* (London 1913)

Makrizi, Taki-Eddin-Ahmed *Histoire des sultans mamlouks de l'Egipte* trans E.M. Quatremère, 4 vols (Paris 1837–45)
Mandeville, Sir John *Mandeville's Travels* ed M.C. Seymour (Oxford 1967)
Marco Polo. *The Description of the World* ed A.C. Moule and Paul Pelliot, 2 vols (London 1938)
Mattingly, Garrett *Renaissance Diplomacy* (London 1955)
Metlitzki, Dorothee *The Matter of Araby in Medieval England* (New Haven 1977)
Mézières, Philippe de *Epistre au Roy d'Angleterre* British Library MS Royal 20.B.6
– *Letter to King Richard II, A Plea Made in 1395 for Peace between England and France: Original Text and English Version of 'Epistre au roi Richart'* trans G.W. Coopland (Liverpool 1975)
Middle English Dictionary ed Hans Kurath and Sherman M. Kuhn (Ann Arbor 1952–)
Miller, W. *Trebizond, the Last Greek Empire* (London 1926)
Montgomery, J.A., trans *The History of Yahballaha III and Bar Sauma* (New York 1927; rpt 1966)
Moseley, C.W.R.D. *'Mandeville's Travels*: A Study of the Book and its Importance in England (1356–1750)' Diss East Anglia 1971
Mostaert, A., and F.W. Cleaves *Les Lettres de 1289 et 1305 des Ilkhans Arghun et Oljeitu à Philippe le Bel* (Cambridge, Mass. 1962)
D'Ohsson, Mouradja *Histoire des Mongols depuis Tchinguiz-Khan jusqu'à Timor Bey ou Tamerlan* 4 vols (The Hague 1834–54)
The Oxford English Dictionary ed Sir James Murray et al, 12 vols (Oxford 1933)
Palmer, J.J.N. *England, France and Christendom, 1377–99* (London 1972)
Parkes, M.B. *English Cursive Book Hands (1250–1500)* (Oxford 1969)
Parry, J.H. *The Age of Reconnaissance* (London 1963)
Pelliot, Paul 'Les Mongols et la papauté' *Revue de l'Orient Chrétien* 23 (1922) 2–20; 24 (1924) 225–335; 28 (1931) 3–84
– *Notes on Marco Polo* 3 vols (Paris 1959–73)
Penrose, Boies *Travel and Discovery in the Renaissance 1420–1620* (Cambridge, Mass. 1952)
Perrat, Charles 'Un Diplomate gascon au XIVe siècle: Raymond de Piis, nonce de Clément V en Orient' *Mélange d'Archéologie et d'Histoire* XLIVe année (1927) 34–90
Phillips, E.D. *The Mongols* (London 1969)
Plomer, Henry R. *Wynkyn de Worde & his Contemporaries* (London 1925; rpt 1974)
Rashid-ad-Din *Histoire des Mongols de Perse* trans E.M. Quatremère [1 vol published] (Paris 1836)
– *The Successors of Genghis Khan* trans J.A. Boyle (New York 1971)

Rasmussen, Jens *La Prose narrative française du XVe siècle: Etude esthètique et stylistique* (Copenhagen 1958)

Rawcliffe, Carol *The Staffords, Earls of Stafford and Dukes of Buckingham 1394–1521* (Cambridge 1978)

Recueil des historiens des Gaules et de la France ed Martin Bouquet et al, Vol xx (Paris 1840)

Regestum Clementis papae V, anni secundus et tertius (Rome 1886)

Richard, Jean 'The Mongols and the Franks' *Journal of Asian History* 3 (1969) 45–57

Rubruck, William of *The Journal of William of Rubruck to the Eastern Parts of the World, 1253–55, as Narrated by Himself, with Two Accounts of the Earlier Journey of John of Pian de Carpine* trans William W. Rockhill, The Hakluyt Society Second Series No 4 (London 1900)

Rüdt-Collenberg, William Henry, Count *The Rupenides, Hethumites and Lusignans: The Structure of the Armeno-Cilician Dynasties* (Paris: Calouste Gulbenkian Foundation Armenian Library 1963)

Runciman, Steven *A History of the Crusades* 3 vols (Cambridge 1951–4)

Russell, Jocelyne G. *The Field of Cloth of Gold* (London 1969)

Sackville, Thomas, and Thomas Norton *Gorboduc or Ferrex and Porrex* ed I.B. Cauthern, Jr (London 1970)

Saunders, J.J. *The History of the Mongol Conquests* (London 1971)

Schwoebel, Robert *The Shadow of the Crescent: The Renaissance Image of the Turk (1453–1517)* (Nieuwkoop 1967)

Setton, Kenneth M. *Europe and the Levant in the Middle Ages and the Renaissance* (London 1974)

– 'Pope Leo X and the Turkish Peril' *Proceedings of the American Philosophical Society* 113 (1969) 367–424

Short-title Catalogue of Books Printed in England, Scotland, & Ireland, and of English Books Printed Abroad, 1475–1640 ed Alfred W. Pollard et al (London 1926); 2nd ed rev W.A. Jackson et al, 2 vols (London 1976)

Sinor, Denis *Inner Asia and its Contacts with Medieval Europe* (London 1977)

– 'Les Relations entre les Mongols et l'Europe jusqu'à la mort d'Arghoun et de Bela IV' *Cahiers d'Histoire Mondiale* 3 (1956–7) 39–62

Skelton, R.A. *The European Image and Mapping of America A.D. 1000–1600* The James Ford Bell Lectures, No 1 (Minneapolis, Minn. 1964)

Spuler, Bertold, *History of the Mongols, Based on Eastern and Western Accounts of the Thirteenth and Fourteenth Centuries* trans Helga and Stuart Drummond (London 1972)

– *Die Mongolen in Iran* 3rd ed (Wiesbaden 1968)

Sykes, Percy *A History of Persia* 2 vols (London 1921)

Tipping, H. Avray *English Homes* Vol 1 *Period II: Early Tudor, 1485–1558* (London 1924)

Tournebize, Fr H. François *Histoire politique et religieuse de l'Arménie* (Paris [1910])

Vassiliev, A.A. *History of the Byzantine Empire 324–1453* 2 vols (Madison, Wisc. 1928; rpt 1952)

Vaughan, Dorothy M. *Europe and the Turk: A Pattern of Alliances 1350–1700* (Liverpool 1954)

Wagner, Anthony 'The Swan Badge and the Swan Knight' *Archaeologia* 97 (1959) 127–38

William of Tyre *A History of Deeds Done beyond the Sea* trans E. Babcock and A.C. Krey, 2 vols, Columbia Records of Civilization, No 35 (New York 1943; rpt 1976)

Williams, Sheila 'The Lord Mayor's Show in Tudor and Stuart Times' *The Guildhall Miscellany* 1 (1959) 3–18

Workman, Samuel K. *Fifteenth Century Translation as an Influence on English Prose* (Princeton 1940; rpt New York 1972)

'Wynkyn de Worde and his 1512 Edition of *Helyas, Knyght of the Swanne*' ed Stanley Daniel Lombardo, Diss Indiana 1976

Yule, Sir Henry *Cathay and the Way Thither* Rev H. Cordier, 4 vols, The Hakluyt Society Second Series Nos 38, 33, 37, 41 (London 1913–16)

Textual Notes

These notes record obvious compositorial errors and omissions that have been silently emended, along with the original readings. Editorial emendations necessary to clarify the sense of the Pynson translation are also noted, along with the original English and French readings.

3/5 Hereforde] P1 (Bodleian Auct. QQ supra II 24); Gloucestre P2 (BL 148 c. 1), P3 (BL G 6789)

3/12 themperours] themperous P1–3

4/30 were] P1; wear P2–3

9/7 reuerence] renerence P1–3

11/7 reminaunt] remiuaunt P1–3

11/10 begyninge] begynnge P1–3

11/11 the countray] they countray P1–3

14/20 wynter] wnyter P1–3

15/6 fludde] fuldde P1–3

15/9 Sauorelx] Sanorelx P1–3

16/15 Promysson] promyssson P1–3

17/8 Turkey] Cipres P1–3; Fr 'Turquie,' var 'Cyppre'

17/32 Trapesonde] Tarpesonde P1–3

17/36 lordship] lorship P1–3

18/10 depar[t]ed] depared P1–3; Fr 'devisé,' ?compositorial omission of 't'

20/3 there] thrre P1–3

21/38 they] the P1–3

22/2 where they] where the they P1–3

22/15 deceyu[er]ed] deceyued P1–3 ?compositorial omission of 'er' abbreviation

23/3 space] shace P1–3

23/9 Constantynople] Constantyple P1–3

23/11 one of] one ot P1–3
24/13 brought] brough P1–3
25/29 Hames] Harmes P1–3
25/31–2 [he] send] send P1–3; *Fr 'il manda'*
27/3 commaundementes] commaundementcs P1–3
27/26 wolde] wode P1–3
29/33 Cangius] Cangins P1–3
30/20 gaue] gane P1–3
31/16 all the] all they P1–3
31/17 commaundement] commaundcment P1–3
33/12 hoost] P1–2; hoest P3
33/30 [They] went] went P1–3
34/28 emperour] emperonr P1–3
35/1 gyue] Pl; gyuen P2–3
37/5 armes] armens P1–3
37/7 of Turkey] P1–2; or Turkey P3
38/4 [he] answered] answered P1–3
38/17 Christen] threisten P1–3
38/37 we gyue vnto [hym]] we gyue vnto P1–3; *Fr 'li donons'*
39/5 fynisshed] fyuisshed P1–3
39/16 [that] a lord,] a lorde P1–3
41/40 brother] brotheh P1–3
42/1 sought] fought P1–3; *Fr 'queroient,' ie 'sought'; ?misreading of long-tailed initial 's' as 'f'*
42/8 Christen] cstristen P1–3
43/37 Halcon] Halcou P1–3
47/30 Sarasyns] sarasyus P1–3
48/37 putte] pntte P1–3
49/19 that is] the is P1–3
49/32 neuiew] neniew P1–3
50/18 strong] storng P1–3
52/21 Chapchap] Chapcha P1–3
52/29 [ba]tayle] tayle P1–3 ; *Fr 'la bataille'; ?compositorial omission*
54/4 thought] though P1–3
54/7 Frere] fere P1–3
56/20 honderde] houderde P1–3
56/29 the which thei] they which thei P1–3
56/30 they brought] the brought P1–3
56/31 the remenant] they remenant P1–3
56/32 horses] horess P1–3
58/6 dispraysed] dspiraysed P1–3

58/17 enemys] enenmys P1–3
59/1 coude] counde P1–3
59/28–9 M other knightes] C other knightes P1–3; *Fr 'M chevaliers'*
60/14–15 xviii day] viii day P1–3; *Fr 'xviii jors'*
60/27 into Cipres] into Egipt P1–3; *Fr 'en Chipre,' var 'en Egipte'*
61/6–7 [he] rehersed [it]] rehersed P1–3; *Fr 'le recontoit'*
61/7 dyd vs put [it]] dyd vs put P1–3; *Fr 'les nous faisoit mettre'*
61/23 Capar] P1; Tapar P2–3
62/2 Kynge of Hungarie] kynge of Bulgarie P1–3; *Fr 'roiaume de Ungarie'*
62/31 the] they P1–3
63/5 lyces] Lyces P1–3; *Fr 'lices,' ie 'palisades, fortification walls'; ?compositorial error*
63/7 lices] Lices P1–3; *?compositorial error*
64/20 be kylled] by kylled P1–3
64/21 thousande] housande P1–3
65/1 shulde] shlude P1–3
65/5 tytell] lytell P1–3; *Fr 'cause ou occasion'*
65/11 [I], Frere Hayton] frere Hayton P1–3; *Fr 'je, frere Haiton'*
66/5–6 to enquere] te enquere P1–3
66/11 in dedes] is dedes P1–3
67/23 delyuerd [them] harnes] delyuerd harnes P1–3; *Fr 'lur donent armes'*
68/20 coude nat] coude uat P1–3
68/32 he coude [not] abyde] he coude abyde; *Fr 'il ne se pourroit defendre'*
69/30 to haue] to hane P1–3
69/31 Chapchap] P1–2; Chapchan P3
70/3 Armeny] Cucumanie P1–3; *Fr 'Ermenie,' var 'Cumanie'*
71/13 countrey] P1–2; coutrey P3
71/35 iourney] iouruey P1–3
72/11 flud] fuld P1–3
74/20 they] thy P1–3
74/28 take] toke P1–3
75/2 Tartas] tartarus P1–3
76/4 trouble] tronble P1–3
76/15 without] withont P1–3
76/22 Turqueniens] truqueniens P1–3
76/23 [be] obedyent] obedyent P1–3; *Fr 'sont bien obeissanz'*
81/32 begynninge] begynnige P1–3
82/2–3 the way of] they way of P1–3
82/27 Mychelmas] Myhelmas P1–3
83/24 lightly] lighty P1–3
85/8 [Your] Blessyd Holynes] blessyd holynes P1–3; *Fr 'la Vostre Sainteté'*
85/27 lorde of Corc] lorde of court P1–3; *Fr 'seignor de Corc'*

French-English Variants

These notes elucidate obscurities in Pynson's translation or record significant omissions from the original French. Whenever possible, corrected English translations in the notes are taken from the Royal manuscript (indicated by an 'R' in parenthesis); otherwise they are my own.

7/21–6 And, as the Cathayns ... theyr subtylyte: *E dient les Catains que il sont ceus qui voient de II oils, e des Latins disent qu'il vioent d'un oil, mès les autres nacions dient que sont aveugles.* 'And the Cathains say that it is they who see with two eyes, and of the Latins they say that the Latins see with one eye, but the other nations, they [ie the Cathains] say that they are blind.'

10/1–3 This same realme ... iournay in length: *Cestui roiaume marche devers orient, qui dure bien cent journeés de lonc* 'This realm extends towards the east a good one hundred days' journey in length.'

10/9 letters proper vnto theymselfe: P omits Fr following *letres propres: Une maniere de Crestiens habitent en celes terres, qui sunt apellés Soldains, e ont letres e lengue propre* 'A group of Christians live in these lands, who are called Soldains [ie probably Nestorian Christians under the jurisdiction of the bishop of Sultaniyeh] and who have their own language and way of writing.'

10/20–3 no tree there groweth ... gardens and orchyards: *nul arbre n'i croît de que l'om face merain ne buche, for que en aucuns leus, où il ont aucuns arbres plantez por faire jardins* 'nor any tree grows there from which one might make timber or logs, except in some places where they have planted some trees to make gardens.'

11/2 gret byrdes of diuers kynde: *Ostours e autres oiseaus de proie* 'Goshawks and other birds of prey'

11/30–3 Towarde the north parte ... all the balayses: *Devers septentrion par long est le grant desert d'Inde, là où l'empereour Alisandre trova si grant diversité de serpens e de bestes, si com se contient en ses histoires* 'Towardes the north alonge is the grete desert of Inde where the Emperor Alexander founde so grete quantitie of serpentes and of beestes, as it is conteigned in his histories' (R). P (or his exemplar) perhaps omitted the verb of Fr sentence and consequently assumed that *devers septentrion* referred back to *contrée* in the previous sentence.

12/14 enuyroned or set aboute with the occean see: *environnée de desert, e de l'autre part de la mer occeane* 'enuironed with desert, and apon that other partie it is enuironed of the see occean' (R)

14/20 noyse and murmure: *la noif* 'snow.' P probably misread written long-stemmed final 'f' as long-stemmed 's,' producing Fr *nois* 'noise.'

15/37 Babylone: *Baldach, qui jadis fu dite Babiloine*

16/1 anthetinoyson: *en chetivoison* 'in captiuitie' (R). Because of similar written 't' and 'c,' and 'n' and 'v,' forms, P or his exemplar has misunderstood the Fr phrase or misread it as a proper name.

16/16 This is called Grioise and the land of Mesopotamy: *Ceste terre si est apellée Mesopotame, en lengue grizoise* 'this land thus is called Mesopotame in the Greek tongue.' P appears to have had an unrecorded variant in his exemplar containing *et* (rather than *en*) *grizoise*.

17/1–5 and with the realme of Georgy ... vpon the see syde: *et avec le royaume de Georgie. Devers occident s'estent jusques à la cité Satalie, qui siet sur la mer de Grece. Devers septentrion n'a nulles confines avec aucune terre, et s'estent de lonc en lonc sur la rive de la mer* 'and with the realm of Georgia. Towards the west it extends to the city of Satalia, which is situated on the See of Greece. Towards the north it has no boundaries with any country, and extends alongside the sea.'

17/16–7 of the great Cesar of Grece: *la cité de Cesarée la grant de Grece* 'citie of Cesaree the Graunte of Grece' (R)

21/9 there owne men: *leur volenté* 'their will'

21/10 to sende to the Kyng of Persy: *d'envair le roiaume de Perse* 'to enuade the royalme of Perse' (R). P or his exemplar probably misread *envair* as *envoier* (ie *envoyer* 'to send').

23/28–9 And of these men ... de Bullayns passage: *E cestui font mencion les estoyres du passage de duc Godefroi de Bouillon* 'And this [ie Soliman and his acts] is mentioned in the histories of the passage of Duke Godfrey of Bouillon.'

25/19–20 in the cyte of Halap ... of Eufrates cam: *à la cité de Halape, prés du flum Eufrates, et vindrent* 'in the citie of Halap by the flode of Eufrates, and come' (R)

26/20 he oweth to be: *tu doies*

26/21 by hym: *par toi* [*var lui*]

28/4–5 they sholde holde ... ordayn them: *ilz tenissent à payez de ce qu'il leur donrait* 'they should take as pay what he would give them.' P perhaps misread *leur donrait* as one word *l'ordonroit* because of similar written 'o' and 'e' forms.

28/10–4 And not for because that ... his sonnes heed: *ne por quant por que il doutoient le peuple et que il savoient que Changius Can estoit fait empereor par le commandement de l'immortel Deu, il n'oserent refuser son commandement, ains tailla chascun des sept chevetaines la teste de son filz* 'nevertheless, not only because they feared the people, but also because Changius Can was made emperor by the commandment of the immortal God, they would not dare refuse his commandment, but each one cut off the head of his son.'

28/26–7 And whan Cangius men ... in the prese: *Quant la gent Changius Can virent leur seignor à terre entre les presses*

30/13 moche water marese and the lande desert: *eives ameres e la terre deserte* [var *eaues et rivieres et la terre*] 'the waters bytter and the lande desert' (R). P perhaps followed Fr variant, in which case 'marese' would be a noun meaning 'lake, pool, stream.' But P or his exemplar perhaps misread original Fr *ameres* as *à mares* (ie either singular noun *marrese* 'marsh' or plural noun *mares* 'stagnant pools'). ME 'marese' also can mean 'marsh; pool,' (n) or 'marshy' (adj).

33/15–18 therfore the dwellers ... than the other: *por ce que les habitans de celes contrées estoient touz ydolatres, les Tartars comencierent aourer les ydoles; mès tout adès confessoient le Deu inmortel, plus grant que les autres* 'because the inhabitants of these countries were all idolators, the Tartars began to worship idols; but always they confessed the immortal God greater than any other gods.'

33/27–9 they sholde do ... began the batayle: *feüssent savoir à celui de ses enfans qui plus près de eaus seroit, que lur donast aide de genz d'armes, e après pourroyent ilz commencier la bataile* 'they should make known [their needs] to whichever of his children who would be closest to them, in order that he might give aid with men of war, and after that they would be able to begin the battle.'

34/15 vpon the see: *par mer au roiaume de Cathai* 'by the see into the royalme of Cathay' (R)

34/26 and made them Christen men: *e fu crestien* 'and Cobila [not his men] was a Christian'

36/17 there men: *leur heirs* 'their heirs'

36/26 to take ... frendes: *d'aquillir sa bienvoillance e s'amisté* 'to gete his good wyll and amitie' (R). P perhaps misread Fr as *bien e s'amis*.

39/16–7 saue that ... to beleue: *sauf ce que leur seignor, lequel est només le Viel de la montaigne, leur enseigna à croire* 'except what their lord, who is called the Old One of the Mountain, teaches them to believe.' P perhaps was confused by separation of Fr subject and verb, or P's compositor perhaps omitted the essential second 'that' in the translation.

39/27–8 and retorned ... a halfe after: *e retorna en Ermenie après III ans e demi* 'and retourned into Armenye after iii yeres and an half' (R)

41/3 of the Kyng of Anyne and of Syrie: *du roiaume de Surie* 'the royalme of Sirie' (R). Because of the similarity of minims in 'u' and 'm' of *roiaume*, P (or his exemplar) perhaps misread it as two words *roi anine* (cf 47/15–16 and 55/28 for same mistake).

41/32 sonne: *gendre* 'son, son-in-law' (the latter is historically accurate).

42/28–9 in the realme of Syri and went to the Palestines parte: *au roiaume de Surie e ès parties de Palestine* 'in the royalme of Sirie and in the parties of Palastine' (R)

43/16 nor his men: *ne ceaus de lui* 'nor they [ie the Christians] in him'

43/24–5 and so they fled ... in the bataye: *dont il tornerent en fuie, e leur chevetaine qui Ginboga avoit nom* [var *Gingoba avoit nom*] *fu mort en la bataille* 'from which they turned in flight, and their captain who was called Ginboga was slain.'

46/12 was put to dethe: *tranchier par mi* 'cut assondre in the mydill' (R). Cf 49/10, 70/30.

47/14 Mangadamor: *Mangodamor son frere* 'Mangadamor his brother'

48/14 Through faute of vitayle: *por la longue voie e por defaute de viandes* 'for by long waye and defaulte of vitailles' (R)

51/27 He shewed: *Al commencement de sa seignorie, il se mostra* 'And in the begynnyng of his reign he sheude' (R)

52/29 vndertake: *eschiver* 'evade, escape'

53/24 his commyng: *son comandement* 'his ferder commaundement' (R); cf 55/7.

53/34 into dyuers wodes: *ça et là par diverses parties e voies* 'here and there by diuers wayes' (R). P or his exemplar perhaps misread *voies* as *boies* (ie 'woods') because of similar written 'v' and 'b' forms.

54/14 his person: *sa poesté* 'his myght' (R)

56/29–30 With theyr beestes and catell: *les bles e les bestes*

57/20 the countrey: *jusques à la cité de Hames* 'vnto the citie of Hames' (R)

58/7 shulde take corage: *se meissent en conroi* 'should put themselves in order or disposition.'

58/9 betwene ii waters: *Il estoient environnés de II pars d'un lac e d'une montaigne* 'They were surrounded on two sides by a lake and a mountain.'

58/33–4 in the mornynge: *de la nuit* 'of the night'

59/15–16 to the entent ... lyke mater: *à ice que les perils puissent estre eschivés en semblant cas* 'to thende that the perell may be eschewde in lyke cas' (R)

59/17 good ende: *bone fin, e les oevres que l'on fait sans porveance acostuméement faillent à venir à leur proposement* 'good ende, and the workes that be done withoute purveyaunce many tymes fayle to come to their purpose' (R)

60/26 in that tyme: *en celui champ meismes* 'and in the same feld' (R). P or his exemplar perhaps misread *champ* as *tamp* (ie 'time')

60/29–30 and longe I ... my lyfe: *à ce que je, qui avoie esté lonc temps chevalier au monde, refusant les pompes de cestui siecle, peüsse servir en humilitei, le remenant de ma vie, à Nostre Seignor* 'to thende that I, which haue long tyme ben knyght of the worlde, refusyng the pompes of the same world, may serue in humylitie the remanent of my lyif to Our Lorde Ihesu Criste' (R)

61/28–9 Somtymes themperour maketh warre against Chapchap: *Aucune foiz la gent de l'empereor lur movent guerre. Aucune foiz Capar e sa gent movent guerre à Carbanda* 'Sometimes the people of the Emperor make war on them. Sometimes Capar and his men make war on Carbanda.'

62/13 Turke of Egypt: *soudan d'Egypte*

63/17 be moche dyuers: *sont molt divers des autres genz* 'haue many diuersities from other people' (R)

63/19 immortall: *inmortel, e en leur dit mettent Deu tot avant* 'immortal, and in their sayings put God before all other things'

63/22–3 if the byt ... deedly: *e se il laissoit le frein en la bouche de son cheval, quant il deüst paistre, il quideroit pechier mortelment* 'and if they leave the bit in the mouth of their horse when he is pastured, they think it a mortal sin'

63/30 cost: *ost* 'army, important war'

64/6–7 and wyll ... profet: *e n'en ont vergoigne de partir, o autre faire à lur profit* 'and they haue no shame to departe fro the bataill or sege and to do other thinges for their profyttes' (R)

64/33 The Tartars ... be vp: *Les Tartars a lur profit legierement mentent.* P probably mistook *mentent* as *montent* because of similar written 'o' and 'e' forms.

64/38–9 And as moche ... speketh: *Et à tant soufist à parler des Tartars* 'And so this sufyseth to speyke of the Tartars' (R)

65/14 to the valyaunt kynred of Mahomet: *e la pute lignée de Mahomet* 'and the foule sect of Mahomet' (R)

65/16 there they fynde: *e tienent* 'and [the Saracens] hold'

66/9–13 for the thynges ... redy to come: *car les choses porveues ne solent grever e les desporveües* [var *en celles desporveües*] *troblent sovent les corrages des gens, nomeement en fait de bataille, où l'om n'a luec ne temps de contrester as perils qui jà sont aparailliés* 'for things foreseen cause no grief, but things unforeseen often trouble the hearts of men, especially in the matter of battle, where a man has neither the opportunity nor the time to withstand perils for which he has not already prepared himself'

66/13–15 In all other ... the cost: *En toutes autres euvres, l'om puet miaus metre amendement qu'en fait de bataile si l'om i faut, car tantost la poine ensuit avec les coustemens* 'In all other things one can better make improvements than in the fact of battle, if one lacks anything there, for directly the pain ensues with the attendant costs'

66/24 be nought bowed: *ne valent riens en fait d'armes* 'be worth nothing in dedes of armes' (R). Possibly P's 'bowed' is past participle of ME 'bouen,' ie 'to incline toward something, to have a tendency to something.' Possibly P may have translated the Fr verb as 'be not lowed,' ie the aphetic form of 'allowed' ('praised, commended'). His compositor may then have mixed up 'l' and 'b,' producing 'be not bowed.'

67/3–6 of stoffe ... good kepyng: *de somage e de chamiaus* [var *chevaux] chargiés. Chevaus d'armes ont assez bons, e ont jumenz molt legier à courre; rocins e muletes ont petit. Leurs chevaus ne porroient sofrir* [var. *soustenir] molt grant travail, ains ont mestier de grans garde* 'of baggage and laden camels. They have enough warhorses and have very good running mares. They have few pack horses and mules. Their horses cannot withstand much labour and need much care taken over them.'

67/14 his wages and offices: *soldoiers* [var *souldées*], ie 'soldiers.' P has chosen an alternative meaning ('payment, wages') that does not fit the present context.

67/21–7 For this admyrall ... in their purses: *car ceaus amiraus qui doivent servir ou* [var omits *ou] C o CC chevaliers achatent esclas de lurs deners e lur donent armes e chevaus e les metent en servise por genz d'armes, e receivent por eaus les soldées, e il querent homes de petit pris, et leur donnent aucune chose et leur prestent armes et chevaulx, e les metent en servises, e receivent por eaus les soldées, e tout le remenant metent en leur bourses* 'for these emirs, who ought to serve with 100 or 200 knights, buy slaves with their own money and give them arms and horses and put them in service as men of war, and receive wages for them [from the Sultan], or they find men who will serve at a low cost, and give them a small amount of money and provide them with arms and horses, and put them in service, and receive for them wages [from the Sultan], and the difference they put in their own treasuries.'

67/35–68/1 for if he wyll ... without gret wages: *car il vont* [var *il les veult] sans soldées, soulement por gaignier aucune chose à defendre la terre ou à aler en bataille* 'for they go without wages, except for what they can gain [ie as plunder].' P follows variant Fr reading, which generally distorts his translation.

68/9 The Sowdan: *La gent du soudan* 'the Sultan's men'

68/25 the Sarasyns toke: *perdirent les Sarazins* 'thise Sarrasens loste' (R)

68/33–5 to the Sowdan of Halap ... Saraton: *au soldan de Halape, requerant aide. Le soldan de Halape* [var. omits *Le soldan de Halape], qui tenoit la loi Mahomet, e qui quidoit avoir grant quantité de tresor du calif, manda un sien chevetaine, qui avoit non Saraton* 'to the Sultan of Aleppo, requesting help. The Sultan of Aleppo, who kept Mohammed's laws and who thought to gain a great treasure from the Caliph, sent one of his captains called Saraton.'

71/35 is a yle: *ausi come une isle* 'is as an isle' (R)

71/38–72/1 viii dayes iourney of way: *viii jornées, e est tout sablon* 'viii iourneys, all in sande' (R)

72/8–9 countrey is closed of the see and fluddes of an yle: *contrée est environnée de mer e de flums si come une isle* 'country is surrounded by the sea and by rivers as if it were an island'

72/30 called Meser: *devant la cité de Meser* 'afore the citie of Meser' (R). P perhaps misread Fr as *devant cité* 'the before cited.'

73/20 horsflesshe: *char de chamel* 'flesh of camelles' (R)

75/30–1 to gyue counsell ... of the passage: *à conseillier sur si grant afaire come est la besongne du passaige* 'to counsell so grete a worke as is the busynesse of the passage' (R)

75/31–2 bycause that I haue yet the payne: *à ce que n'encorre* [var *encore*] *la poine* 'so that I will not incur the pain.'

76/2–3 I trust to accomplysshe my faute: *de la qui misericorde je espeir de complir ma faute* 'by whose mercy I hope to complete my task'

76/13 without any fere of his rebellynge: *sanz poour de relevement e de traison de sa gent* 'withoute drede of rebellion or treason of his people' (R)

76/35 Turquenien, Chocas, Lachyn: *Turquemen, Chotos, Melech Saraf e Lachim*

77/31 For if the wayes shuld fayle: *Car se au roiaume de Surie faussisent les rentes* 'for yf the royalme of Sirie shuld fayle in rentes' (R)

79/15 shulde be in short tyme afote: *en poi de temps seroient apovris* 'in a short tyme thei shuld be empoueryshed' (R)

79/28–31 shulde by peryllous ... his tresoure: *seroit au soldan ennuieuse et dommageuse e perilleuse pour la trahison de sa gent ennuieuse. Car par les envassemens de Crestiens porroit estre si troblés que ilz n'aroient repos si non damagiouse, car il consumeroit et gasteroit tout son tresor* 'should be to the Sultan troublesome and harmful and perilous because of the treason of his people. For he might be so troubled by the incursions of the Christians that his forces would have to go without any rest, something harmful to him because it would consume and waste all his treasure.'

80/33–5 And many thinke ... multiply moche: *E me semble que en ces comencement ne feroient plus de servise d'eulx tans de gens que ceaus feroient, e molteplieroient moult les despenses* 'And it seems to me that at the beginning more men would not be of any use, but would just greatly add to the expenses.'

81/33–5 and after, wyllyng ... generall passage: *Et après, vuillant obeir as comandemens de la Vostre Sainte Paternité, parlerai* [var omits *parlerai*] *sur que covient au passage general* 'And after, wishing to obey the commandment of Your Holiness, I will speak about what should take place in the general passage.'

82/1 I wolde nat gyue counsell to them: *je lais à conseiller* [var *je la conseille; je la à conseillier*] *à ceaus* 'I leve to the counseill of them' (R)

82/34–5 And whan the pasture shulde be comming: *Au temps du pascour venant.* P has mistaken Fr masculine noun *pascor* 'Easter, spring' as feminine noun *pascor* 'pasture.'

84/35 of no port: *d'aucune part* 'from any part'

84/37 And the cause that: *E ce que* 'And the fact that'

85/16 was a rose: *fu arosée.* Neither MED nor OED record a participial adjective 'arose' meaning 'moistened.' P perhaps borrowed the word from Fr, and his compositor, not understanding, printed it as 'a rose,' since it was common to refer to Christ's wounds as 'a rose.' Cf. Lydgate's poem 'As a Midsomer Rose,' in *The Minor Poems of John Lydgate: Part II, Secular Poems,* ed Henry N. MacCracken, EETS OS 192 (Oxford 1934) 785, where the poem's imagistic word-play on 'rose' culminates in the wounds of Christ.

Index of Proper Names and Places

Further information can be found in the relevant entries in the Commentary. The letter *y* has been treated as *i* throughout.

Glossary

This selective glossary records obsolete words and forms not obviously recognizable as modern words because of differences in spelling. Pynson's text uses *i/y* and *u/v*, and forms with and without final *e*, in free variation. In this glossary the letter *y* has therefore been included in *i* throughout, and *u* and *v* are used interchangeably.

ABBREVIATIONS

2, 3	2nd, 3rd person
adj	adjective
adv	adverb
comp	comparative
conj	conjunction
Eng	English
Fr	French
imper	imperative
intrans	intransitive
n	noun
OED	*Oxford English Dictionary*
p	participle
P	Pynson's translation/translator
pa	past
pl	plural
ppl	participial
pr	present
pred	predicate
prep	preposition

pron   pronoun or pronominal
refl   reflexive
sb   somebody
sg   singular
sp   spelling
sth   something
trans   translation of
v   verb
var   variant

a (prep) in, on
abasshed (pa p) upset, perplexed
abyde (v) wait for (sb, sth) to arrive
abyte (n) *abyte of relygion* monastic habit
abordreth (3 sg pr) approaches, adjoins, borders (*OED* first use in this sense 1611)
ab(o)undance (n) abundance
abrode (adv) abroad, widely
admirall (n) emir, Saracen lord
advertisment (n) warning, notification
aduys(e)ment (n) advice, counsel; consideration, reflection; *take aduys(e)ment* take
   thought, consider
affliccion, afliction (n) penance, mortification of the flesh
afor(e (adv) before
afote (adv & pred adj) on foot
afray(e)d (ppl adj) afraid, frightened
after (prep) according to; *after as* (conj) as
ayenst(e, agaynst (prep) against, to
Alcen (adj) Caucasian Albanian, Aghouan
aleuen (adj) eleven
al(l (adj) all
alway, al(l)wey(s (adv) always
anthetinoyson see French-English Variants
apparaunt (adj) visible
apparellyd, apparelled, apparylled, apperylled (pa p) prepared for, made ready for
   (action); equipped, provided with
appoyntment (n) agreement, treaty
ar(e, be (2 sg pr & 3 pl pr) are
Armenoses (adj) Armenian
armours (n pl) military equipment (esp siege engines), arms

auncetours, auncytours (n) ancestors
auncyent, aunsyant (adj) old

badde (3 sg pa) bade, commanded
bayly (n) king's officer
balayses (n pl) balas rubies
barowne (n) baron, lord
batayle (n) battle array
be see *ar(e*
be-ende (prep) beyond
be(e)st (adj) best
beestes (n) animals (domestic), beasts
beestysshe (adj) brutish, ignorant
beleue (n) religious faith, doctrine
berde (n) beard
bere (v) bear, carry (arms); contain, have (life); *bereth* (3 sg pr)
besinesse (n) enterprise, affair, business
bestiall (adj) brutish, ignorant
by (v) be
by (prep) in, throughout
blame (v) rebuke, scold
borde (n) side, border
borne (pa p) born
bounde (n) border, boundary
bowed (pa p) ?inclined (toward sth); ?praised, commended
braz (n) arm of sea
brede, bredthe (n) width, breadth
breke (v) break, crush; demolish, breach (a fortification); *brake* (3 sg & pl pa)
brende, brent (3 pl pa) burned
broder, brodre (n) brother
burges (n) full citizen, freeman (of town)

cam(e see *come*
cause (v) induce, compel
certayne, certen (adj) certain
cesterns (n pl) cisterns
chambre (n) room; private room ?=dwelling, abode 54/37
chaung(e (v) change; *chaunged* (pa p)
cheker (n) game of chess (of checkers)
chese, chose, chuse (v) choose; *chose* (pa p)

close (adj) enclosed
closed (3 sg pa) walled in, fortified; (pa p) surrounded
cocalx (n pl) crocodiles
coygne (n) money, currency
colombe (n) column
come, cum (v) come; *cometh* (3 sg pr); *cum, came* (3 pl pr); *cam(e* (3 sg & pl pa);
    com(e, comen (pa p)
compased (pa p) surrounded, enclosed
composicyon (n) contract, treaty
conde(m)pned (pa p) condemned
considre (v) consider
constable (n) governor of a royal fortress; chief executive officer of a ruler
constrenyd, constrayned (3 sg pa) constrained, compelled, obliged
contradictyon (n) opposition
contradit (n) prohibition, opposition
conuenable, couenable (adj) apt, appropriate
coude (3 sg pa) was able, could
counsayl(l)e, counsel(l (n) advice, counsel
counted (pa p intrans) included, considered; (trans) recounted, told
countray (n) country; *countreys* (n pl)
course (n) a run, battle-charge; *make a course* charge, attack
courtesly (adv) courteously, graciously
couenable see *conuenable*
couytes (n) greed, covetousness
couytus (adj) covetous
cricke [?error; trans Fr 'crac'] (n) inlet of the sea; small stream 18/6
cum see *come*
cundit(t)e (n) open channel, conduit
cuniuracyon (n) plotting, conspiracy

damageable (adj) injurious
dapart see *depart*
dar(r)e (v) dare; *durst* (3 sg pa)
debate (n) quarrel, dispute, strife
deceyu[er]ed see *disceuerd*
deed (pa p) dead
defaut(e (n) lack, insufficiency, absence
delectable (adj) pleasing to the senses, pleasurable
delycate (adj) delightful
demeane (v) guide, govern, behave

demonstracyon (n) sign, proof; *by demonstracyon* by the indication (of)

denteth (adj) delicious, rich, fine

depart (v) go away, depart; divide, separate; *depar[t]ed* (pa p)

depe (n) interior (of a country)

dere (adj) valuable, prized, expensive

deuise, diuise (v) tell, relate, describe; decide, determine; *deuisen* (3 pl pr)

dyamante (n) diamond

dyche (n) ditch, moat

dyker (n) ditch-digger, embankment-builder ?=worker in the army, builder of fortifications (?instead of Fr 'peons' ie 'foot soldiers,' P's exemplar contained var Fr 'peoniers' ie 'foot soldiers; workers in the army,' a reading closer to Eng 'dykers') 78/14

disceuerd, deceyu[er]ed (pa p) separated, isolated from

discomfyt, disconfyted (pa p) defeated in battle

disconfort (n) dismay, grief, distress

dishonesty (n) dishonour, disgrace, shame

disprayse (v) speak ill of, disparage, slander

distroyed (3 sg pa) ?harassed

dyuers (adj) different

diuise see *deuise*

doute (n) doubt, fear, anxiety

downe (n) sand-hill, dune (*OED* first use in this sense 1513)

draughte (n) drawing, writing

driue (v) drive; *driue, driued* (3 sg pa); *droue* (3 pl pa); dryued, dryuen (pa p)

duke[1], *duc* (n) duke, leader

duke[2] [trans Fr 'duc' ie 'great eagle, horned owl'] (n) duck; ?great eagle, horned owl (*OED* use in this sense only 1656)

durst see *dar(r)e*

eas(e)ly (adv) easily

eyen (n pl) eyes

els, elles (adv) else

emonges see *amonge(s*

encrease, encrees, encerase, encre(s)se (v) increase

ende (n) end; *at the later ende* finally, at last

engyn (n) mechanical device (used in warfare); talent, skill

enhaunced (p pa) enhanced

enquerre (v) inquire

entreprise (n) attack, invasion

enuyroned, inuyroned (pa p) surrounded, encircled

ete (v) eat; *eteth* (3 sg pr); *etyng* (pr p)
example (n) original, exemplar (of a book)
exchaunges (n pl) commerce, sale of goods
experience (n) demonstration, proof; practical experience

fayn(e (adj) forced (to)
famylyer (adj) household
farder see *farther*
farre, ferre (adv) far
farther, farder (adv) farther
faute¹, (n) task
faute² (n) deficiency, lack; fault; *withoute (any) faute* without
   fail
fawkon (n) falcon
feat (n pl) martial exploits, deeds
feder see *fether*
feyght see *fyght*
feldys (n pl) fields
fellowe (n) comrade, friend
felon (adj) wicked, cruel
feringe (pr p) fearing
ferme (adv) firmly, faithfully
fermed (pa p) established
ferre see *farre*
fesante (n) pheasant
fether, feder (n) feather
fyght, feyght (v) fight
flod(d)e, fludde (n) river
fludde see *flod(d)e*
folysshely (adv) foolishly, in a foolhardy manner
formede (pa p) made, constructed, fortified
frank(e (adj) free; *frank(e and quit* exempt, free from tax
fredom (n) liberality
frendes (n pl) ?friends, supporters, favourites 36/26
frere (n) member of a brotherhood, monk
furnyssh (n) provisions, supplies
furnysshed (pa p) fitted out, equipped

garnis(s)he (v) equip, furnish; fortify
geder (v) gather; collect; *gethared* (3 sg pa)
german (adj) near of kin; *cosin german* first cousin

gethared see *geder*
gyde (n) guide
gise, guyse (n) usage, fashion, way
goo (imper sg) go
good(e (n) possessions, wealth; produce, crop
grace (n) goodwill, favour; thanks
grefe, greve (n) harm, hardship, trouble
Greioise (n) Greek, the Greek language; (n pl) Greeks
greue (v) injure, harm, harass
grosse (adj) simple, crude
growe (v) grow; *groeth, groweth* (3 sg pr)
guyse see *gise*

habytauntes (n pl) inhabitants
habondaunte (adj) abundant
harnes(se, harnis (n) personal armour, weapons; *bere harnes(se* bear arms, fight
hauntyng [trans Fr 'de chace'] (n) spoils of the chase (in hunting) ?=plunder
hede (n) heed
heed[1] (n) head; most important
heed[2] (n) head; upper end, top (of a geographical area)
heer (n) hair
heerdmen (n pl) herdsmen, shepherds
hert (n) mind, will; *gret hert* nobility
heuy (adj) sorrowful
hyderto (adv) hitherto, until this time
hye (adj) high
hold(e (v) regard, consider; observe, keep; *holden* (pa p)
hole (adj) healthy, unharmed
holsome (adj) wholesome
honderd, hondred, hundreth (adj) hundred
house [trans Fr 'maisons'] (n) ?clan, ?household, family
hurt [trans Fr 'cuer'; *OED* lists as southwest var spelling for 'heart' but perhaps
    compositorial error] (n) heart, mind, will 85/15

idolater, ydolatour, idolatr(i)er (n) idolater
ye (adv) yes
ye (pron) you
yelde(d (3 pl pa) yielded
yll (adv) poorly
imbassadour (n) ambassador; messenger
impered (pa p) damaged, impaired

incontynent (adv) immediately, forthwith
ingenyous (adj) intelligent, resourcefull
ynough, inow (adj) enough, sufficient
inuyroned see *enuyroned*
ioyned (pa p) located near, adjacent to
iournay (n) day's journey or march
yse (n) ice; frozen surface of a river
iuge (n) judge
iug(ge)ment (n) judgment
iust (adj) just

kepar (n) defender, guard
kepynge (n) care, provision
kyne (n) cattle
kinred (n) race, lineage, descendants
knowle(a)ge (n) knowledge, awareness; learning

lawe, lay (n) religious law, belief
ledder (n) leather
lege (n) distance of three miles, league
lengar (comp adv) longer
length (n) length; *of length, in length* for the full length and distance
lese (v) lose
lette (3 sg pa) prevented; *latt* (pa p)
letter (n) writing, script
leue (v) leave
lycence (n) permission, agreement, approval
lices see *lysses*
lyft (adj) left
light (v) descend, alight; dismount
lightly(e (adv) easily
linage (n) lineage, offspring
lysses, lices (n pl) palisades, fences (in fortification)
lyuely (adj) life-giving, necessary for life
lyueng (n) livelihood, income
longyng (pr ppl adj) belonging

maynten (v) maintain
maister (n) master
marchaundise (n) trade, commerce
marcheth (3 sg pr) borders on, adjoins, extends to

marese (?adj) marshy; (?n) lake, pool, stream
marlyon (n) merlin (a small European falcon)
maruayle, marueyle, marueyll, meruayle (n) marvel
mean (n sg & pl) method, means; *by mean whereof* because of which
meate, mete (n) food, supplies
medell, med(d)yll, medle (v) engage in, be concerned with
mencyon (n) mention
mercy(e (n) mercy; thanks
mere (n) lake, sea
merily (adv) happily
meruayle see *maruayle*
mete (n) see *meate*
mete (v) meet; *mette* (3 sg pa)
metely (adj) proper, suitable
mydday (n) south
myddes (n) midst, centre
mynde (n) will
mynisshe (n) reduce, lessen; *mynisshed* (pa p)
myscheffe (n) misfortune, trouble, misery
mystlyn (n) maslin, mixed grain (esp rye mixed with wheat)
moche (adj) much, many
moneth (n) month
moued (3 sg pa) stir up, commence (war, etc)
murmure (v) complain, grumble
mustre (n) display, outward show

nacion, natyon (n) family, kindred; *after their nacion* according to the custom of their country
naturall (adj) rightful, legitimate
naturs (n pl) ?material world, material things
nede (n) need, necessity; *nedis* (n pl) pressing affairs, emergencies, perils
nede (adj) necessary
nedefull (adj) necessary
neuew(e (n) nephew
nygh (adj) near, close to; *nyghest* (superl)
nombre (n) number
nother (adv) neither
nought (n) nothing

ocupied (3 pl pa) practised
onely (adj) only; one, solitary

ons (adv) once
or (conj) before
ordayn (v) appoint
ordynaunce (n) battle-array
ordring (n) management, arrangement
orient (adj) eastern
orient (n) east
other (adv) either
ouersear (n) supervisor, guardian
oweth (3 sg pr) ought, shall

payne (n) suffering, punishment; trouble; *take payne* trouble oneself
panym (n) pagan
parfetly (adv) truly
parforce (adv) forcibly, by violence
paryll see *perill*
parlyment (n) speech, conference, consultation
passage (n) movement from one place to another
pas(se (v intrans) make one's way, proceed; (trans) go through, across; *pas(se out of (from) this worlde* die
paste (pa p) past
pastour¹ (n) shepherd
pastour², pasture (n) pasture
peace, peas (n) peace
peces, pecis (n pl) pieces
penure (n) want, scarcity, destitution
pepyll, peple (n) people
peraduenture (adv) perchance, perhaps
perlys (n pl) pearls
person (n) *of his person* by himself
personably (adv) in person
peuisshenesse (n) malignity, perversity
playn (adj) flat, level
plenty, plent(i)e (n) abundance
plesed (3 sg pa) pleased
poyntment (n) agreement, pact
popyngay (n) parrot
praied (3 sg pa) beseeched, supplicated
prayeng (pr p) praying, beseeching
prased (pa p) valued, extolled
prefeke [trans Fr 'nomé'] (adj) ?prearranged, fixed in advance

(?P borrowed Fr 'preficié' ie 'fixed in advance' or wrote 'prefix' –
rare ppl adj that *OED* records once 1500 – which compositor mistook as
'prefeke')

prey (n) booty, plunder
prese (n) thick of the fight; melee
price (n) price, rate; value, worth
pryde (n) pride; *pryde of this worlde* worldly pride, vainglory
pryuely (adv) in private, secretly
profet[1] (n) profit
profet[2] (n) prophet
prof(f)eringe (pr p) offering, presenting
proper, propre (adj) peculiar
proude (adj) arrogant, haughty
proued (pa p) attempted, striven
puysaunt, pusaunt (adj) mighty, powerful
puissaunce (n) power, might; an armed force
purpose (v) intend, resolve; *purposyng(e* (pr p)
purposlye (adv) intentionally, on purpose
puruey (v) foresee, prepare, arrange beforehand
pusaunt see *puysaunt*

quadrate (adj) square, rectangular
quyte (adj) free, clear; *frank and quyte* exempt, free from tax

raygne (n) reign
raygne (v) rule, reign
raygnyng (n) reign, period of rule
ran see *ron(n*[2]
ranne see *ron(n*[1]
rauysshe (v) plunder
recheth (3 sg pr) reaches
reclamed (3 pl pa) proclaimed, named (*OED* lists two examples of use in this
  sense, both 16th century)
reherse (v) say, relate, narrate
reysed (3 pl pa) raised
religion (n) monastic life
renne see *ron(n*[2]
rente (n) revenue, income
repare (v) repair, restore
reposed (3 pl pa refl) rested (themselves)
resorting (n) frequenting, haunting

ryde (v) ride; *rod(d)e, rydde* (3 sg & pl pa)
ris(s)e (v intrans) rise; (trans) increase
robed (3 pl pa) robbed
rod(d)e see *ryde*
rome (n) place
ron(n¹, rone (v) run; *ranne* (3 pl pa)
ron(n², renne (v) pursue, chase; overrun; *ran* (3 sg pa)
ronner (n) messenger, scout, courier
ronning(e (pr p) running
rought (3 sg pa) reached, came to

sacrifice (v) sacrifice (to), worship; *sacrified* (3 pl pa)
saffir (n) saphire
saynt see *sende*
salt(e (adj) salty
saruage see *seruag(e*
saue (prep) except, with the exception of
scaped (3 pl pa) escaped
science (n) knowledge
sclauys, slauons (n pl) slaves
se (3 sg & pl pa) saw
sect (n) principles (of) or adherents (to) a religion
sede (n) offspring, progeny
sege¹ (n) throne, seat of rule; ecclesiastical see; *sege pastorall* pastoral see, See of Rome
sege² (n) siege
seyserach (n) Armenian bird
semblable (adj) like, similar
sende (3 sg pa) sent; *saynt* (pa p)
sene (pa p) seen
septentrion (n) north
sergeantre (n) sergeants or squires collectively
seruag(e), saruage (n) servitude, slavery; feudal homage, allegiance
set(t (v) situate; plant *set(t* (pa p); *set(t about* surrounded by
sharp (adj) acute, violent
shepard(e, sheperde (n) shepherd
shew (v) show
shyppe (n) good bargain, purchase; *to a good shyppe* at low cost, cheaply
shytte (pa p) shut
syctynge see *syttyng*
syke (v) seek

sykeness (n) illness
syngynge (n) chanting, saying of mass
sith(e (prep & conj) since
sittying, syctynge (pr p) sitting
skant (adj) little
sklaundre (n) shame, slander
sklender (adj) slender, slight
slauons see *sclauys*
socour (n) sugar
sodaynly, sodenly(e (adv) suddenly
softly (adv) carefully, unobtrusively
solempne (adj) solemn
solempnyte (n) gravity, solemnity
somer (n) summer
somme (n) amount, sum
in sonder (adv phrase) asunder, into separate pieces
sondry (adj) different
soner (comp adv) sooner
sonne (adv) soon
sonne¹, soone (n) son
sonne² (n) sun
sorye (adv) sorry
sparois (n pl) sparrows
specylly (adv) particularly; *in specylly* especially
spredynge (pr p) spreading
stedfaste (adj) firm
stedfastly (adv) firmly
sterre (n) star
styll (adv) continually; *styll and well* continually and rapidly
stoffe (n) soldier's baggage; stock of food
strake (3 sg pa) struck
straunge (adj) foreign
streight (adv) straight, directly
subgection, subiection (n) dominion, control; state of being subject
subget, subiett (adj) under the rule of, owing allegiance to
subgette (n) slave
subtylytie (n) cleverness
subtyll (adj) cleverly devised; cunning, clever
suerti (n) certainty; *for suerti of* in order to ensure (that)
suspection (n) suspicion

swerde, sworde (n) sword

terme (n) appointed period of time
terrestre (adj) earthly, terrestrial
thankynges (n pl) thanks
the (pron) they
their, thi(y)r (pron adj) their
then, than (adv) then
thens (adv) there, to that place
thider (adv) thither, to that place, there
thiyr see *their*
thir see *their*
this(e (pron adj) these
thoman (n) toman, cavalry division of 10,000 men (*OED* first use 1599)
thoughtfull (adj) troublesome
thrifty (adj) worthwhile
togader, togyder, togyther (adv) together
torned (3 sg pa) returned, reverted
travayle, traueyle (v) labour, work; *traueilid, traueld* (3 pl pa)
tresour(e, tresure (n) treasure
trewe (adj) true
trouth (n) truth
truese, trewes (n) truce

vnder (prep) under
vnderstode (3 sg pa) attended to, gave heed to
vndyde (3 sg pa) destroyed, defeated
vndoynge (n) destruction, ruin
vniuersall (adj) whole, entire, general
vnprofitablyst (adj) most unprofitable
unpurueyed (adj) unforeseen, not provided for
vsed (ppl adj) experienced, accustomed; *vsed to do* practised at, experienced in

valour (n) value
vauntage (n) opportunity, advantage
very (adj) very; true
veryli (adv) indeed, truly
vernicle (n) St Veronica's kerchief, upon which Christ's features were miraculously impressed
vertu (n) virtue

vestment (n clothing, dress
visage (n) face, countenance
vitayle (n) food, provisions
voyde (adj) deserted, unproductive, uncultivated

waged (3 sg pa) hired for military service
ware (adj) aware
warke (n) work
warre, ware (n) war
weyt (adj) wet
whan, when (conj) when
whervpon (adv) upon which
wyll (adv) well
wyst (3 pl pa) knew
wyt (n) thought
worship (n) position of honour, distinction

Appendix: *The Floure of Histories of the Est*

A Note on the Text

This appendix contains from *The Floure of Histories of the Est* (BL MS Royal 18.B.26) the General Preface, the section entitled 'Frere Hayton,' selections from Book Three, and all of Book Four.

The following selections from the Royal Manuscript are reproduced here largely for the purpose of comparison with Pynson's translation. Consequently, scribal abbreviations, excepting those pertaining to numbers, have been accepted throughout and expanded without notice. Scribal 'ff' form has not been preserved. The medial 'z' form is used occasionally by R's scribe for both 'gh' (in 'knight') and 'z' (in 'Sarrazens'), and I have transcribed either way according to its context. Word-division, punctuation, capitalization, and paragraphing follow modern usage. All scribal corrections have been accepted. Obvious scribal errors and omissions have been corrected. Additional emendations are in square brackets.

At several points in Book III, the order of events in R differs from that in P and the original French. R displaces information about the death of Mango Can and his successor, and about the conquests of the three sons of Hottoca Can. Here is a comparison of the relevant French chapters with R and P:

Fr	R	P
XII	172/3–15	34/1–14
	174/21–36	34/14–31
XIII	178/29–37	34/32–35/9
XIV	179/1–23	35/10–36/6
XV	179/24–34	36/7–18
XVI	172/16–173/22	36/19–37/39
XVII	173/23–174/15	38/1–39
XVIII	174/6–20	39/1–10
	175/1–19	39/11–29

[General Preface to BL, MS Royal 18.B.26]

[2r] TO THE HONOUR OF ALMYGHTY GOD and to accomplisshe your high commaundement as towching the passage of an army and hoste of pylgrymes by
Your Highnes blessedly to be purposed and conducted ayenst infideles for
5 the recouery of the Holy Lande (halowed by the mooste precious encarna-
cion, pilgrymage, and passion of Our Lorde Ihesu Cryste, our redemptor –
which lande by many yeres passed hathe ben, and yet is contynued, in the
handes and possession of the auncient enemyes of our faith, the miscreantes
and infideles), here ensuyth a treatie, made vnder correccion, apon the
10 passages of sundrye pryncz and faithfull people of right noble and blessed
memorie, breuely extracted of sundrey histories for precidentes in this
behalf. Diuidet in .v. bokes: wherof the fyrst is of the pilgrymage of Robert,
Duc of Normandye, fadre of William, Kyng and Conquerour of Englonde;
the seconde is of the generall pasage of Crysten pryncz, wherof Godefrey,
15 Duc of Buillon, was chef; the third boke is of the passage of Richard, Kyng
of Englonde the fyrst, called Richard Cure de Lyon, and other; the fourth
boke is of the passage of Edwarde, [2v] Duc of Guyon, son of Kynge
Henry, the third of that name Kyng of Englonde, which after his fadre was
Kyng in lykewyse and named Edwarde the fyrst after the Conquest; and
20 the vth boke is apon the treatie of Frere Haiton, Lorde of Corc, cosyn germayne of the Kyng of Armenye, entitled The Floure of Histories of the Est,
made by commaundement of Pope Clement the vth. Which boke is deuidet in
foure partes: wherof the fyrst is of all the royalmes in Asie, with the
properties and commoditees of the same, and how euery royalme marcheth
25 with other; the seconde partie treateth of all emperoures and kyngz that
were in the same lande of Asie after thencarnacion of Our Lorde vnto the
makyng of that booke, which was made in the yere of Our Lorde .M CCC
vii.; the iii^de boke treateth of the Tartars, how they began, and in how many
partes their seignorie is diuidet (which is next vnto the Holy Lande); and
30 the iiii^th parte spekyth of the passage into the Holy Lande, and how they that
ought to make suche passage shulde byhave theim from the begynnyng
vnto the endyng.

[143r] Frere Hayton

And for the vth partie of this treatis, here foloweth the booke entitled The
35 Floure of Histories of the Land of Asie and other partes of the Orient, the
which Frere Haiton, lord of Corc, cosyn germayne of the Kyng of Armenye,

compiled by commaundement of Pope Clement the Vth in the yere of Our
Lòrde M CCC vii in the citie of Poitiers. And to acomplish your high commaundement I haue translated the same [143v] oute of French into English. In which translacion I muste represent the tyme and state of Asie which
5 was in the said yere of Our Lorde, and speyke of that state presently as
myn auctor did, notwithstondyng the state is muche chaunged in thise CC
yeres nowe past. But otherwise I cannot translate truely, for many causes
apperyng all along in this boke. Which is deuided in iiii partes. Wherof the
fyrst parte declareth of the land of Asie, which is the third parte of the
10 worlde, and deuiseth how many royalmes be in the same partie, and how
euery of the same royalmes marcheth fro other, and what maner of people
do inhabit the same. The secund partie is of the emperoures and kynges
which haue ben in the land of Asie after the incarnacion of Our Lord Ihesu
Criste, and howe longe tyme euery of theim was lorde, and wherof they were
15 lordes, and how they gate the seignourie – as the said Frere Hayton
founde in the histories of diuers nacions of the Este wreton in diuers lettres.
The third partie spekyth of the histories of the Tarters: how they began
and how they gate the landes that they hold nowe, in how many partes is
deuided their seignourie, and who is lord named of that lande which is
20 mooste nygh vnto the Holy Lande. And the iiii^th partie of [144r] this boke
spekyth of the passage of the Holy Lande: how they that oughte to make the
passage to conquere the said land oughte to behaue theim from the begynnyng vnto the ende, after the ordre of the knowleage of the said Frere
Haiton.

25 **[BOOK THREE]**

[164v] **How the Tartars come fyrst in seignourie. capitulo primo.**

The lande and the cuntrey where the Tartars dwellid fyrst is within the
greate mountayne of Belgian; of this mountayne speke the histories of
Alexander, where it maketh mencion of wilde men whiche he founde. In that
30 cuntrey dwelled fyrst the Tartars as bestiall people which had nother faith
ne lawe; and they went from place to place pasturyng beste, and were [165r]
holden vile of other nacions to whom thei serued. Certen nacions of the
Tartars, which were named Margoflz, assembled theimselfes and ordeyned
chieuetaynes and gouernours amonges theimself, and so they grew in
35 noumbres that they departed theimself in vii nacions; and vnto this day they
of the nacions be holden for mooste noble of other. The fyrst of thise

nacions was named Tartare; the secunde, Cangath; the third, Eurath; the
iiiith, Iason; the vth, Sonig; the vith, Mangly, and the viith, Thebeth. And in
the same maner, thise vii nacions dwelled in subieccion of theire neighbours,
as is afore said. After, it come to that an olde pore man which was named
5 Cangius sawe in his slepe a vision; that is to say, he sawe an knyght armed
apon a white horse which cald hym by his name, and saide: 'Cangius, the
will of the immortall God is suche that breuely thow shal be gouernour and
made ruler apon the vii other nacions of the Tartars, the which be cald
Margoflz, and that by the they shal be deliuerd from the seruage wherin they
10 haue ben longe, and they shall haue the seignourie apon their neighbours.'
Cangius arose ioyouslye, [165v] vnderstandyng the wordes of Ihesu Cryste,
and shewde vnto all the Tartars his vision which he had sene. The gentilmen and the people of grete reputacion wold not bileve hym, but mocqued
hym for his saying. But it come to that the night afore the chieuetaines of
15 the vii nacions sawe the white knyght in a vision also, as Cangius had saide;
and commaunded on bihalf of the immortall God that all they shulde obey
vnto Cangius, and do hys commaundementes. Wherapon the chieuetains
afore said assembled the people of the Tartars, and made theim to do
obeysaunce and reuerence vnto Cangius, and that thei shulde make hym
20 their naturall lorde.

**How the Tartars made an emperour apon theim, and cald hym Cane. And of
his commaundement. capitulo secundo.**

After this the Tartars established a sete in the myddes of theire cuntrey, and
they spradde a black clothe of felte, and they made Cangius to sitt apon
25 the same; and the seven chieuetains of the vii nacions lyft hym vp with the
felte, and set hym apon the sete, [166r] and named hym Cane. And after,
they kneled, and all they did vnto hym honour and reuerence as vnto their
lorde. In this tyme ought no man to mervaile, for perauenture they had no
better cloth to sett hym apon, or perauenture they knew not howe to do
30 bettre; but men may merveile in that they woll not change their fyrste
vsage – as yet whan thei woll chose their lorde – which haue conquerd many
landes and royalmes. And I haue ben ii tymes at the eleccion of the emperour of Tartars. Whan thei woll chese theire lorde, thei woll assemble in a
grete felde, and hym that ought to be their lorde they make to sitt apon a
35 black felte, and in the mydell of theim thei sett a ryche sete. And after, they
bryng – the high men and theim of his lignage – and sett hym in the sete.
And after, thei do vnto hym all reuerence and honoure as vnto theire naturall

and soueraigne lorde. And nether for seignourie ne for richesse which thei haue conquered, they woll not chaunge theire fyrst vsage.

After that Cangius was made emperour by comen assent and will of all the Tartars, afore all thinges he wold know yf all the Tartars wolde do vnto
5 hym [166v] obeysaunce. Therapon he commaunded thre thinges. The fyrst commaundement was that all thei shulde beleve and worship the immortall God by whome he was made emperour. And fro that tyme all the Tartars began to bileve and to worship the name of God in all theire workes. The secunde commaundement was that thei shuld stand with theire soueraigne
10 lord ayenst all that bare or might beyre armes. And ordeyned to euery dizaine, which was x men, a capitayne; and to euery x dizaines a capitayne; and x m was a chieuetayne, and they cald the companye of x m men, thoman. After this, he comaunded tne vii chieuetains of the vii nacions and lignage of the Tartars that they shuld lay downe all theire armures and
15 signouries, and hold them content and paid with suche as this Cane wolde yif to theim. The third commaundement which Cangius Cane yaf vnto them semed verry cruell vnto all theim; for he commaunded all the vii chieuetains afore named, that euery of theim shulde bryng his eldest sone afore hym, and whan they had so done, he commaunded that eche of theim shuld
20 smyte of the hed of his awne son – which commaundement [167r] semed to all men felonous and cruell. That notwithstandyng, forasmuche as thise vii chieuetains doubted the people and that they knew that Cangius Cane was made emperour by commaundement of the immortall God, euery of the same vii chieuetains smote of the hed of his awne son. Whan Cangius
25 Cane sawe the will of his people, and had sene that euery of theim had obeyde hym vnto the deth, than he commaunded that all they shuld be apparailed with armures as knyghtes with hym.

How this Cane, Emperoure of the Tartars, was pursued by his enemyes, and saved by a fowle cald an owle. capitulo tercio.

30 Whan Cangius Cane had ordeyned his batailles well and wisely, he entred the land of theim that long had kept the Tartars in seruage, and discomfete all theim in bataill, and all theire landes he put in subieccion. After that, this Cangius Cane went conquering landes and cuntreys, and all went at his awne agrement. And apon a day, as he rode with a few people and en-
35 countred a grete quantitie of his enemyes which [167v] recountred hym very sharpely, Cangius Cane defended hym as well as he myght, but at last his horse was slayne vnder hym. When the people of Cangius Cane sawe theire

lorde entred in the presse, anon thei fledd, and theire enemyes chassed theim and toke no regarde to Cangius, the Emperoure, which was on fote. Whan Cangius Cane saw that, he went hymself into a bush which was therby. And his enemyes, which had the victorye apon hym, began to serche
5 the chase. And as they wolde haue serched this bush where Cangius Cane was hydde, they sawe a fowle cald an owle sittyng apon this bushe. Wherfore they thought that no man shulde be there, and so departed withoute serchyng of this bush, saying that yf any man were in the bush this foule wold not haue sytt there.
10   Whan night was comen, Cangius Cane went oute of the bush, and went to his people. And shewde vnto them all that was fortuned hym in this case, and how his enemyes had lefte theire serching of this bush bicause of the owle syttyng apon the same. The Emperour Cangius Cane and the Tartars yelded [168r] thankynges to God, and fro that tyme forthe thei had in all
15 reuerence this fowle cald an owle. For euery yere he that myght haue a fether of this foule, he was glad to weyre it apon his hed; and as yet the Tartars vse to weyre the fether of this fowle apon thiere hedes.

How the white knyght appered ayen to Cangius Cane. And how he and his people passed the mounte of Belgian. capitulo iiii^{to}.

20 After this, Cangius Cane assembled his people, yaf bataill to his enemyes, and discomfeted theim in bataill; put all theim in seruage, and conquerd all the landes apon that side of the mountaine of Belgian. And so kept theim, vnto the tyme that to hym come another vision as foloweth. He sawe ayen by vision the white knyght, which said vnto hym: 'Cangius Cane, the will of the
25 immortall God is soo that thow shall passe the mountaine of Belgian, and thow shall conquere the royalems and the landes of diuers nacions, and thow shall haue apon [168v] theim seignourie. And for thow shall knowe that I say is apon the bihalf of the immortall God, aryse thow and go to the mounte of Belgian with all thy people. And whan thow shall come there where the
30 see is ioynyng, thow shall descende. And thow and thy people shall knele ix tymes towardes the orient, and thow shall pray the God immortall that he shall shew vnto [the] the way to go. And he shall show vnto the, and to thy people, where thow shall passe.'
    When Cangius was awaked, he bileved in this vision; and anon, he com-
35 maunded his people that thei shuld go to horse, for he wold passe the mounte of Belgian. And from thens thei rode so longe that thei come all to the see syde, and ferther they myght not passe, for thei had no passage more

ne lasse. And anon, Cangius Cane discended of his horse, and made all his people to descende in lyke wise. After, thei kneled towardes the est ix tymes, and praid the almyghty and immortall God that he wolde shew vnto theim way to passe. All that night abode Cangius Cane and his people in
5 prayers, and the next day [169r] after, Cangius Cane and his people sawe that the see was withdrawen from the mountayne ix fote, and had laft a fayre large way. They mervelid muche, and rendred thankynges vnto God. And they passed all towardes the parties of the Est.

And as the histories of the Tartars conteign, after that Cangius Cane had
10 past the mountayne of Belgian, he founde the waters bytter and the lande desert; and so longe to he come into a goode cuntrey, he and his people suffred greate misease. And after that, thei founde good landes and playntyous of all goodes, and by many dayes thei abode in that cuntrey in grete rest. And as hyt pleased God, a grete sekenes toke Cangius Cane. Wherfore he made to come afore
15 hym his xii sonnes, and commaunded theim that thei shuld alwey be of oon will and of oon acorde. And to them he yaue this example; that is to say, he commaunded that eche of theim shuld bryng to hym an arrow. And whan all thise xii arrowes were togader, he commaunded his fyrst son [169v] to breke theim all togader bitwene his handes; and he, assaying so to do, couthe
20 not breke them with his handes. After, he made the seconde son to assay to breke them; so which assaide in like wise, and couth not. And than Cangius Cane disseuerd thise arrowes, and commaunded his yong sone to breke theim singlerly, euery arrow by hymself; and so he brake theim lightly. After this, Cangius Cane turned hym towardes his ii sonnes, and said
25 vnto theim, 'Why might not ye haue broken the arrows so as I commaunded you?' And they answerd, 'Bicause the arrowes were all togader.' And than said Cangius, 'Why then hathe this childe broken theim?' 'Bicause,' said thei, 'that the arrowes were eche of theim by itself disceuerd.' Than said Cangius Cane: 'Even so, shall it come of you. For, as long as ye shal be of oon
30 acorde, your seignourie shall dure euer; and when ye shall be departed and discordyng, anon, your seignourie shall turne to nought, and may not endure.' And many commaundementes and good examples yaf Cangius Cane vnto his sonnes and to his people, the which commaundementes the Tartars kepe yet in grete reuerence. [170r]

35 **How Hottota Cane, sone of Cangius, reigned emperour of the Tartars after his fadre. capitulo v^{to}.**

Whan Cangius Cane saw that he myght not longe dure ne lyf, he made his son named Hottota, which was best and mooste sage, to be lord and emperour after hym, and made all his people to obey and serue hym as theire soueraign and naturall lorde. And after that, this first good Emperour of the Tartars ended his days and passed oute of this worlde. And this Hottata

5 reigned after hym. And forasmuche as the Tartars kneled ix tymes in descendyng to the see at the mounte of Belgian, and that the see was withdrawne fro the same mountaigne by the space of ix fote by the commaundement of God, the Tartars haue euer the noumbre of ix for happy; and he that shall present any thinges to themperoure of Tartars, must present ix

10 thinges of nombr yf he woll haue his present receued graciously.

Hottota Cane, Emperoure of the Tartars after the deth of his fadre Cangius Cane, was a good man, sage [170v] and valiaunt; and his people lovid hym well, and were euer trew to hym. Hottota Cane thought to conquere all the land of Asie; and afore that he was departed oute of the lande where he

15 was, he wold know the power of the kynges that were in Asie, and which of theim was moste myghty – purposing to feight with hym fyrst. For he thought yf he myght conquere the mooste puissaunt of thise kynges, he shulde lightly conquere all the residue of theim. Wherfore Hottota Cane sent a capitaigne sage and valiaunt, named Sebesabada, and sent with hym x

20 M fighting men, and commaunded that thei shuld entre into the land of Asie and see the condicion and state of that land; and if thei founde eny puissunt lord ayenst whome thei shulde not be of power to stande, thei shulde retourne bak. And as Hottota commaunded, it was done and accomplished; for the said capitaine, with thise X M Tartars, entred into the

25 lande of Asie, and sodenly toke the cities and the landes afore thenhabitantes therof might prepare theimself to defence. All the men of armes in theire way they slew, but vnto the other people they did non evill. Horses, harnesses, and vitailles, [171r] thei toke all that them neded, and so ferre they went afore that they come to the mountaigne of Cocas. Fro this mountayne of

30 Cocas men may not passe fro the Depe Asie into Asie the More, withoute the will of the people of a citie which Kyng Alexander made apon the strait of the see there which toucheth this mountaine of Cocas. Thise X M Tartars surprised this citie in suche maner that the inhabitantes had no space ne tyme to defend themself; by reason wherof they toke this citie. And all that they

35 founde, they putt to the swerde, men and women; and after, thei abated the walles to the grounde bicause at their retourne they wold haue no man to disturbe theim. This citie was of olde tyme cald Alexander, but now they call it the Porte of Hell. The renome of the Tartars went ouer all; wherof it come to that the Kyng of Georgie, which was named Ymaims, assembled his

40 hoste and come ayenst the Tartars, and yaf bataill vnto theim in a playne

called Mogan. Longe endured the bataill, but fynally the Georgiens tourned to flight [171v] and were discomfite. The Tartars passed forthe so longe to thei come to a citie in Turquie which is named Arserom, and they vnderstode that the Soldan of Turquie was nigh therby and had assembled his host;
5 wherfore the Tartars durst not passe forthe. And consedering they were not able to recountre the Soldan of Turquie, they retourned by another wey vnto theire lorde, whome thei founde in a citie named Amaleth, and they shewde vnto hym all that they had done and founde in the lande of Asie.

   Whan Hottota Cane had vnderstoud the state and condicion of the land of
10 Asie, he thought that there was no prynce that myght endure ayenst hym; wherfore he cald thre sonnes that he had, and to euery of theim he yaf grete richesse and grete puissaunce of men of armes, and commaunded them that they shuld entre into the land of Asie conquering the landes and royalmes there. And commaunded hys son Iothy that he shuld go vnto the
15 parties of the west vnto the floode of Phison; to his second son, which was named Bacho, he yaf commaundement that he shuld kepe his way towardes the north; and to the yongest son named Cataday, he commaunded to ryde [172r] towardes the southe; in this maner he departed his thre sonnes and sent theim to conquere landes and prouinces. After, Hottota Cane enlarged
20 his host so that oon hed of his hoste held vnto the royalme of Cathay and that other hed vnto the royalme of Tharse. In this partie, the Tartars toke theire letres; for afore that they had no letres, and for this cause the inhabitantes of that cuntrey haue no letres. And so were they all ydolatores. The Tartars bigan to worship the idoles, but alwey thei confessed the God
25 immortall to be more gret and more puissaunt then eny other.

   After this, Hottota Cane yaf vnto his son Bacho XXX M Tartars, which were named Conathy (which is as muche to say as conqueroures), and commaunded that they shuld goo by this way which the X M Tartars afore named had kept, and that they shuld rest in no land vnto they shuld
30 come vnto the royalme of Turquie. And commaunded that they shuld assay yf thei myght feight with the Soldan of Turquie; and yf they sawe that the power of the Soldan were over grete for theim, they shulde abyde without bataill, and call aide of oon of his other [172v] sonnes which were mooste nigh vnto theim. Bacho with his XXX M Tartars went so long that
35 he come into the royalme of Turquie; and there he vnderstode that the Soldan which had chased the X M Tartars afore named was ded, and after hym reigned his son named Siriacadin. This Soldan had grete doubte of the commyng of the Tartars; wherfore he assembled and retayned people of all languages that he myght haue, of Barbaryns and Latyns (which had ii capi-
40 taignes; wherof oon was named Iohn de la Liminate, which was of the isle

of Cipre, and that other was named Boniface of Molins, which was of the citie of Venice).

Whan the Soldan of Turquie had assembled his hoste of all parties, he yaf bataill to the Tartars in a place named Cossodach; grete was this bataill
5 and many slayne apon bothe parties, but fynally the victorye fell to the Tartars. And they entred into the lande of Turquie, which they conquerd in the yere of Our Lorde M CC xliiii; and within lytle tyme after this, Hottota Cane, Emperour of the Tartars, died. [173r]

Guiot Cane reigned after his fadre, Hottota Cane. capitulo vi^{to}.

10 After this Hottota Cane, reigned his son, Guiot Cane; this Guiot Cane lyfed but lytle tyme.

Mango Cane, coson of Guiot Cane, reigned after hym. capitulo vii^{o}.

After this Guiot Cane, reigned as emperour of the Tartars his cosyn, named Mango Cane, which was right wise and valiant; and enough he con-
15 quered of landes and seignourie.

In the yere of Our Lorde M CC liii, my lorde Haiton, Kyng of Armenye of blessed memorie, seyng that the Tartars had conquered the royalme of Turquie, toke counseill to go to the Emperour of the Tartars and to gete his good wyll and amitie. The Kyng of Armenye, by counseill of his barons,
20 sent afore his brother, my lorde Simbatat, constable of the royalme of Ar-meny; which went vnto the royalme of Tartars, vnto themperour Mango Cane, and bare vnto hym many riche presentes, and was [173v] receyued right curtoisly. And he accomplished well the businesses for the which the Kyng of Armenye had sent hym, and there he dwelled iiii yeres or he re-
25 tourned into Armenye. After the constable was retourned and had shewde vnto his brother the Kyng all that he had done and founde, anon, the Kyng appareld hym, and his people, and went secretely by Turquie bicause he wold not be knowen. And founde vii capitaignes of the Tartars which had discomfete the Soldan of Turquie. The Kyng shewde hymself to the Prynce of
30 the Tartars and howe that he went towardes themperour of Tartars, and therapon this Prynce of Tartars yaue vnto the Kyng compeny which con-ducted hym vnto the citie of Molch, where as Mango Cane Emperour of Tartars soiourned. And was right ioyous of the commyng of the Kyng of Armenye, and receuyd hym right honourably, and yaf vnto hym many riche
35 yiftes and grete thankes.

After that the Kyng of Armenye had dwelled certen dayes there, he made
peticions and requestes vnto themperoure of vii thinges. Fyrst he required
that themperoure and his people wolde bicome Cristen, and that they wolde
be baptised. [174r] The seconde, he required that perpetuall pease and love
5 myght be made bitwene the Tartars and Cristen people. The third peticion
was that, in all the landes which the Tartars had conquered and shulde conquere, all churches of Cristiantie, prestes, clerkes, and persons religiouse
shuld be fre from all seruage (and from them to be exempte and deliuerd).
The iiiith request was that this Mango Cane, Emperoure of Tartars, shulde
10 yeue aide and counseill to deliuer the Holy Land from the Sarrasens, and
the same to yeld to Cristen people. The vth request was that the Cane shuld
yeue commaundement to the Tartars that were then in Turquie, that thei
shulde help to distroy the citie of Baldach and the Califfre (which was chief
and techer of the false lawe of Mahomett). The vith request was priuilege and
15 commaundement of power to have aide of thise Tartars which shulde be
moste nigh vnto the royalme of Armenye when he shulde require it. And
the viith request was that all the landes which the Sarrasens had taken which
were of the royalme of Armenye and after were comen to the hand of the Tartars, [174v] or that shulde come, he shulde yeld vnto this Kyng of Armenye
20 frely and quietlye; and in the same maner, that all the landes which the Kyng
of Armenye myght conquere ayenst the Sarrasens, that he myght haue
and holde theim withoute ayen-saying of the Tartars in rest and in pease.
Whan Mango Cane had vnderstoude the requestes of the Kyng of Armenye,
afore his barons and all the courte, he answerd and saide: 'Forasmuche as
25 the Kyng of Armenye is comen from ferre landes into our empyre of his good
wyll, reason it is that we do accomplish his desires. To you, Kyng of
Armenye, we that be Emperour saye that first we shal be baptised, and we
shall bileve in the faith of Criste; and we shall do to be baptised all theim
that be of our household, and all wee shall holde the same faithe which the
30 Cristen men do hold nowe. And to all other we shall yeue counsell to do
the same; but we woll not force theim, for the faith woll not that any be forced
therto. To the secunde request, we aunswer that we woll that perpetuall
pease and loue be obserued bitwene the Tartars and the Cristen people; but
we woll that ye shal be pledge for the Cristen people, [175r] to thentent
35 that the Cristen people shall kepe true and good peas as we shall do ayenst
you. To the third request, we woll that all the churches of the Cristen
people, the prestes, and the clerkes, and all other of what condicion so euer
ther be – seculer or religious, be fre, quiete, and deliuord of all seruage,
and that they be save and kept withoute greve in persons and in goodes. To
40 the iiiith request, as towching the Holy Land, wee say that we shall goo
with good wyll in our owne persone for the reuerence of Our Lorde Ihesu

Criste. But forasmuche as we haue muche to do in thise parties, we commaunde our brother Halcon that he shall accomplisshe that besinesse, and
deliuer the Holy Land from the power of the Sarrasens, and to yeld it to
the Cristen people; and we yif our commaundement vnto Bacho, and to the
5 other Tartars in that cuntrey, that they shall obey vnto our brother Halcon. And, accordyng to the vth request, we shall take the citie of Baldach,
and distroye the Califfre as our mortall enemye. Wee graunte also the vith
request of the Kyng of Armenye to haue ayde of the Tartars; and wee woll
that the priuelege be diuised all at his wyll, and we shall graunte and
10 [175v] conferme the same. And as to the landes which the Kyng of Armenye
requireth to be deliuerd vnto hym, we graunte with good will, and commaunde our brodre Halcon that he deliuer vnto the Kyng of Armenye all the
landes that were of his seignourie; and we yif vnto hym all that he may
conquere apon the Sarrasens, and of our grace esspeciall wee yif vnto hym
15 the castelles which be nigh vnto his land.'

Whan Mango Cane had accomplished all the peticions of the Kyng of
Armenye, anon he did hymself to be baptised by a bishop which afore was
a knight of the kynges of Armenye, and made all theim of his household to be
cristend; and were baptised many men and women. After, he prepared his
20 people to armes, which shulde serue his brother Halcon.

And at last this Mango Cane passed by the see into the royalme of Cathay;
and as he assailed an isle which he proposed to take, thei of this isle sent
oute blak men which entred into the water vnder the vessell wherin Mango
Cane was, and so longe thei abode vnder the water that thei perced this
25 vessell in many places. The water entred within the [176r] vessell, and
Mango Cane hymself toke no hede to the tyme the vessell was full of water
and sanke, and so Mango Cane was drowned.

**Cobila Cane, brother of Mango Cane, reigned after hym as Grete Emperour
of the Tartars. capitulo viii°.**

30 After the deth of Mango Cane, his people made his brother, Cobila, Cane
and Emperour of the Tartars; which kept the seignourie of them xlii yeres,
and was cristend. And made a citie named Ioing, which is gretter then the
citie of Rome; in this citie dwelled Cobila Cane, which was the vth Emperoure
of the Tartars, vnto thende of his lyif. And there muste we leve to speyke of
35 Cobila Cane, and retourne to speyke of Halcon, and of his heires, and of
his workes, and of the thre sonnes of Hottota Cane.

Halcon, brother of Mango Cane, conquerd Perse and the Soldans of Baldach and Halap, and ayded Cristen men. capitulo ix°.

[176v] Whan Halcon and the Kyng of Armenye were departed fro Mango Cane in the citie of Molche, with a grete companye of people thei rode so
5   long that they come to the floode of Phison; and afore that vi monethes were passed, Halcon occupied all the royalme of Perse. And he toke all the landes and cuntreis where the Sarraens cald Assasins dwelled. Which be people withoute faithe and withoute any maner bileve, saving that which theire lord cald the Old Man of the Mountayne techeth theim to bileve; and
10 so muche they be obedient vnto hym that they put theimself to deth at his commaundement. In this land of Sarrasens was a strong castell well garnished of all thinges, which was named Tygado. Halcon had commmaunded a capitaigne of the Tartars that he shuld assege this castell, and that he shuld not departe from the sege vnto the tyme that he had taken it; and therapon
15 the Tartars abode at the sege of this castell withoute departynge by the space of xxvii yeres, and fynally the Sarrasens yelded this castell for defaulte of clothing [177r] and for non other reasons. Whan Halcon entended to take this castell, the Kyng of Armenye toke leve of hym, and retourned into Armenye after iii yeres and an half, hole and mery by the marcy of God.
20   After that Halcon had ordeyned the garde of the royalme of Perse, he went into a plesaunte cuntrey named Soloch, and there he abode very mery in grete rest. Whan the wedder was faire, Halcon rode and asseged the citie of Baldach. And the Califfre was maister and techer of the lawe of Mahomett. Whan Halcon had assembled his hoste, he assailid the citie of Baldach on all
25 parties, and toke it by force; all the men and women which the Tartars founde there, thei put to the sworde. The Califfre was brought on lyve afore Halcon. And all his richesses were founde within Baldach, which was merveill to loke apon. Werfore Halcon commaunded so that the Califfre was brought afore hym, and did all his tresoure to be brought afore the Califfre.
30 And there he said vnto the Califfre, 'Thow knowe that this tresure was thyn.' And the Califfre aunswerd, affermyng the same. And [177v] then said Halcon, 'Thow haste nother made good hoste, ne thow haste not defended thy lande from our puissaunce.' And the Califfre answered that he thought that the old women oonly had ben sufficient to haue deffended that
35 lande. And than said Halcon to the Califfre, 'Forasmuche as thow art maister and techer of the faith and false lawe of Mahomett, we shall do the to be fedde with thise precious richesses which thou haste loved so muche in thy lyif.' And threapon Halcon comaunded so that the Califfre was put into a chambre, and afore hym was putt of his richesses, to thentent he shulde

eyte therof yf he wolde; and so ended the Califfre his lyif in Baldach, a
stronge and a grete citie.

Whan Halcon had taken the citie of Baldach and the Califfre and all the
cuntreys theraboute, he departed his seignourie, and put in euery of them
5 baylifes and gouernours as it plesed hym. And did grete honour to the Cristen people, and the Sarrasens he put in grete seruage. A woman that was
named Descotaton, [178r] which was a good Cristen woman of the lignage of
the thre kynges that come to worship Our Lorde, bilded ayen all the
churches of the Cristen people; and made all the temples of the Sarrasens to
10 be beton downe, and did theim to be putt in so grete seruage that thei
durst not appere.

Whan Halcon, with his people, had rested by the space of a yere in the citie
of Rohays, he commaunded the Kyng of Armenye tht he shulde come to
hym, for he entended to go to deliuer the Holy Lande, and to deliuer it to the
15 handes of Cristen men. Kyng Haiton of blessed memorie was ioyous of
this commaundement, and assembled a grete hoste of horsemen and of
footemen. For in that tyme the royalme of Armenye was in so good a state
that he made XII M horsemen and XII M footemen; and I haue seen that in my
tyme. Whan the Kyng of Armenye was comen, he had parliament and
20 counseill with Halcon apon the fait of deliuere of the Holy Lande. And the
Kyng of Armenye said vnto Halcon: [178v] 'Syr, the Soldan of Halape
holdeth the seignourie of the royalme of Sirie; wherfore, yf wee may take the
said citie of Halap (which is the maistresse citie of the royalme of Sirie), all
the other shal be sore ocupied.' Muche pleased it Halcon, the counseill of the
25 Kyng of Armenye; and therapon he asseged the citie of Halap, which was
of grete strength and well walled. But the Tartars toke this citie by mynyng
vnder therthe, and by other engynes and force, in ix dayes; and the castell, which was in mydell of the citee, defended hitself xi days, and after, hit
was taken. And grete richesse the Tartars founde in the citie of Halap.
30 And so was Halap and all the royalme of Sirie taken in the yere of Our Lorde
M CC lx.

And when the Soldan of Halap, beyng than at Damasce, vnderstode that
the citie of Halap was taken by the Tartars, and how they had taken his
wif and his children, he sawe no better counseill but come to the mercye of
35 Halcon, thinkyng that Halcon for that wolde deliuer vnto hym ayen his
wif and his children and a parte of his land. But Halcon sent the Soldan and
his wyf and children to the royallme of [179r] Perse for that he wolde be
sure of hym. After that, Halcon departed grete richesse vnto his people. And
to the Kyng of Armenye he yaf grete parte, and yaf vnto hym of his landes
40 and of his castelles which he had goten of theim, and specially of them that

were mooste nigh vnto the royalme of Armenye; and the Kyng garnished
them of his people. After this, Halcon sent for the Prince of Antyoche, which
was son-in-law to the Kyng of Armenye, and dyd vnto hym grete honour,
and deliuerd vnto hym all suche landes as he had conquerd of the Sarrasens
5 that were afore of his principalite.

After that Halcon had ordenyd all that was necessarie as touching the
cities of Halape and Damasce, and other landes which he had conquered
ayenst the Sarrasens, as he entended to entre into the royalme of Ierusalem to
deliuer the Holy Lande and to deliuer it to the Cristen people, he sawe
10 commyng a messangere, which shewde vnto hym that Mango Cane his brother
was passed from this worlde, whan the barons of the Tartars sought to make
a new emperour.

And when Halcon had thise nouelles, he was sorofull for the deth of his
brother. And by counseill [179v] of his people he left with oon of his
15 barons, named Garboga, X M Tartars to kepe the royalme of Sirie, and commaunded that all the landes which had ben of Cristen people shulde be deliuerd vnto theim ayen. And after, he tourned towardes the orient, and left
his son named Albaga at Thoris. And from thens departed Halcon, and
come into the royalme of Perse, where newes were shewde vnto hym how
20 that his cosyn Cobila was made emperour; and whan Halcon vnderstod
thise newes, he wente no ferther, but retourned ayen to Thoris, where he
had lefte his son and his meanye. And as Halcon soiourned at Thoris,
newes come vnto hym that Barta (which then held the seignourie that Bacho
held – which was drowned in Almayne in the ryver of Austryche) come to
25 entre into the lande of Halcon. Wherapon Halcon assembled his hoste, and
went ayenst his enemyes, and a greate bataill was bitwene the people of
Halcon and Bartha apon the ise of a riuer overfrosen. And the prese was
so grete of the people and of bestes apon the ise that it brake, and there were
drowned mo then XXX M men; wherfore the parties departed with grete
30 sorowe [180r] for the losse of theire frendes.

Garboga, with whom Halcon had lefte X M Tartars in the royalme of Sirie
and in the parties of Palastine, kept the land in peas, and muche he loved
and honoured the Cristen people, for he was of the lignage of the iii kynges
of the Orient which come to worship the natiuitie of Our Lorde in Beth-
35 lem. Garboga trauaild muche to recouer the Holy Land, but the devel went
and sew a grete discorde bitwene hym and the Cristen people of the
parties of Saitte. For in the land of Belfort, which was of the seignourie of
Saitte, were many townes inhabited with Sarrasens yeldyng tributes vnto
the Tartars; wherof it come that the people of Saitte and Belford assembled,
40 and ran apon thise townes, and robbed theim, and the Sarrasens they

slew and toke prisoners. A nevewe of Garboga was in this cuntrey; which ran after thise Cristen men with a few in company of horsemen; and as he blamed thise Cristen men for that they had done, and wolde haue taken from theim theire pray, some of thise Cristen men ran apon hym and slew hym.
5 And when Garboga vnderstode that the Cristen men of Saette had slayne his nevewe, [180v] he rode with all his people and come to Saiette, and all the Cristen people that he founde there he putt to the sworde. But allweys the people of Saiete flee vnto an isle; by reason wherof few of theim were ded. Garboga made to be beton downe grete parte of the walles of the citie, and
10 neuer after that he had truste ne faith in the Cristen people of Sirie, ne they in hym.
In this tyme that Barta moved werre ayenst Halcon, as afore is expressed, the Soldan of Egipt assembled his hoste and come vnto the cuntreys of Palastine, into a place that is named Aymaloch. And fought with the Tartars;
15 which myght not abyde the power of the Soldan, but fled. And their chieuetayne, which was named Carboga, was slayne in the bataill. The Tartars which escaped fro this bataill went into Armenye. And than the royalme of Sirie tourned into the power of the Soldan of Egipt, except certeyn cities by the see coste which Cristen men helde. Whan Halcon Cane
20 had knoleage that the Soldan of Egipt was entred into the royalme of Sirie and that he had chased and slayne his people, he assembled his hoste, and sent vnto the Kyng of Armenye, and to the King [181r] of Georgie, and also to the Cristen men of the parties of Sirie, that they shuld prepare them-self to goo with hym ayenst the Soldan of Egipt. And whan Halcon Cane
25 was all redy to entre into the royalme of Sirie, a greuous sekenes toke hym wherof he dyed within xv dayes; and so was distourbed the voiage of the Holy Land by the deth of Halcon Cane.

Iothy, the fyrst son of Hottota Cane. capitulo x°.

Iothy, the fyrst sone of Hottota Cane, rode towardes the west with all his
30 people that his fadre deliuerd vnto hym, and conquerd the royalme of Turquesten and of Perse the Lesser. And come to the flode of Phison, and founde suche goode and plentious cuntreys of all goode comoditees that he dwellid in that land in peas and rest, and was multiplied in grete richesse. And vnto this day the heires of the same Iothy holde the seignourie
35 of this land. And vnder theim be ii brethern tenantes of this seignourie; wherof oon is named Chaphar, and that other, Tothay – which lyf in rest and peas.

Bacho, the secunde son of Hottota Cane. capitulo xi°.

[181v] Bacho, the secunde son of Hottota Cane, with his people which his
fadre deliuerd vnto hym, rode towardes the parties of the northe so longe
5 that he come to the royalme of Cumayne. The Kyng of Cumaine assembled his
people and recountred the Tartars by bataill, but finally the victorye fell
vnto the Tartars. And the Cumans fled vnto the royalme of Hungarie, and
vnto this day they be cald Cumans, habitantes in the royalme of Hungarie.
After that Bacho had chased the Cumans oute of the royalme of Cumanye, he
10 entred into the royalme of Roussie, and conquerd the lande of Gereze and
the royalme of Burgarie. After that, he rode vnto the royalme of Hungarie,
and there founde some Cumans, which he toke. After that, the Tartars
come towardes Alemayne and by the Duchie of Austry. The Tartars purposed
to have passed by a brygge there, but the Duc made the brigge to be kept,
15 and so myght not the Tartars passe overr there. And whan Bacho saw that he
myght not passse by this brigge, he and many of his people trusted theire
horses, and put theimself in aventure to swymme [182r] ouer the ryver; and
were drowned he and mooste parte of his people. And whan the Tartars
that were not entred into the ryuer sawe that theire lorde and suche people
20 as entred with hym were drowned, thei retorned with grete sorowe and
grete hevynesse to the royalmes of Roussie and Cumayne. And after that, the
Tartars neuer entred into Almayne. The heires of this Bacho as yet do
holde the royalmes of Corasme, Cumaine, and Roussie.

Chacaday, the third son of Hottota Cane. capitulo xii°.

25 Chacaday, the third son of Hottota Cane, with his people which his fader
deliuerd vnto hym, rode towardes the southe, and come towardes the
parties of Inde the More. And founde landes desertes and barayne the which
he myght not passe, but loste muche of his people and of his bestes. After
that, he turned towardes the west, and come towardes Iothey his brother, to
30 whome he shewde all his aventures. Iothy receved well his brother and
hys companye, [182v] yaf vnto theim parte of his conquestes, and so thise ii
brethern and theire heires contynued so in good peas. And he that is
nowe lorde of thise landes, that is to say at the said tyme of compilyng of this
booke, is cald Beretath.

35 The power of the Tartars. capitulo xxi°

The Grete Emperoure of the Tartars which now holdeth the seignorie is

named [201v] Thamor Cane, and he is the vi[th] emperoure; and in the
royalme of Cathay he holdeth the siege of his empire in a grete citie named
Ioing, the which his fadre made. The puissaunce of this emperoure is
grete, for he hymself may more than all the other prynces of the Tartars. The
5 people of this emperour be holden for more noble, and thei be more ryche
and better of all thinges garnished then any other be; for in the royalme of
Cathay be grete habundaunce of all riche thinges. And after hym ther be
iii other kynges of the Tartars which haue grete puissaunce, and all thei
bayre reuerence to the Grete Emperour and obedience to his iugement.
10 The fyrst of thise kynges is named Capar; another, Tottay; and the third,
Carbanda.
    Capar holdeth the seignourie of the royalme of Turqueston, and he is the
grettest of the land of the Emperour. This Kyng, as men say, may bryng to
bataill CCCC M horsemen, and thise be men of grete prowesse and hardi-
15 nesse, and they haue grete habundaunce of good harnesse and of good
horses. Somtyme the people of themperoure make werre apon Capar; and
gladde thei wolde be to take his land, but he defendeth hymself vigorously.
The seignourie of Capar hathe ben of oon lorde, [202r] notwithstondyng his
brother Tottay holdeth oon grete partie of his land.
20   Tottay, Kyng of the Tartars, holdeth the seignourie of the royalme of
Cumayne, and holdeth his sege in a citie which is named Sarra. This Tottay
may bryng to bataill V CC M horsemen, as men say. They be not so valiant
in dedes of armes ne in bataill as be the people of Capar, howbeit they haue
better horses and better harnesse. And they haue sometyme werre with
25 the Kyng of Hungarie, and somtyme thei discorde amonges theimself; but as
now Tottay holdeth the seignourie in peas and rest.
    Carbanda holdeth his power in Asie the More, and he holdeth his sege in
the citie of Thoris. He may bryng to bataill aboute CCC M men of armes
horsed, and they be people of diuers nacions; riche thei be and well gar-
30 nished of all thinges, so that they haue no nede of Capar ne of Tottay.
Which make werre ayenst hym many tymes, but this Carbanda defendeth his
land wisely. Carbanda medeleth not to make werre to any man but to the
Soldan of Egipt, to whom his auncetoures haue made werre. And alwey the
afore named prynces Capar and Tottay wold put Carbanda oute of his
35 seignourie, but [202v] they haue not the power, notwithstandyng that they
be more puissaunt of landes and of seignouries and of men also.
    And this is the reason how Carbanda defendeth his land fro the puissaunce
of his neighboures. For Asie is diuided in ii partes: oon is cald Asie the Depe,
and that oher, Asie the More (and in that partie dwellith Carbanda). There
40 be iii wayes oonely by the which men may entre fro Depe Asie into Asie the

More: oon way is by the which men go fro the royalme of Turqueston vnto
the royalme of Perse; that other way is by the bought which gothe nygh by
the citie which Alexandre made, named the Port of Hell; that other way is
towardes the Grete See cald Mare Maior, and it passeth by the royalme of
5 Dabcas. By the fyrst way the people of Capar may not entre into the land
of Carbanda withoute perell and grete misease, for they may fynde no pasture for theire horses by many dayes iourneys; for this cuntrey is drye
and desert, and so, afore that they might come to good landes, theire horses
shuld be ded for hungre and misease, and a few of enemyes myght dis-
10 comfett a grete hoste passing by this way. By that other way towardes the
bought, the people of Tottay may haue entre into the [203r] lande of
Carbanda duryng vi moneths of the yere in the wynter tyme. But Albaga did
to be made, by a iourney in length, listes, diches, and other trenches in a
place named Ciba; and euer there be men of armes which kepe thise pas.
15 Mony tymes thise people of Tottay assay to passe priuely, but they may
not, for they must passe by a playne cald Mongan. In this playne, and
specially in the tyme of wynter, is allwey assemble of oone maner of fowles
which be as grete as fesauntes; and they haue fayre plumage, and be cald
seysserath. Whan the people entre into this playne, thise fowles flye awey
20 and passe by the said lystes towardes the playne of Mongan. Then they
that be deputed to kepe this place know anon the comyng of theire enemyes
by the commyng of thise fowles, and therapon they garnish theimself to
kepe the cuntrey. By that other way towardes Mare Maior they dar not entre;
for by that wey they muste entre within the royalme of Dabcas, which is
25 garnished of people and of strong holdes. And by this maner Carbanda and
his auncestres haue defended theire landes from the grete puissaunces of
theire neighboures. [203]

The cust[u]mes of the Tartars. capitulo xxii°.

And nowe we shall saye somthing of the maners and custemes of the Tartars.
30 The Tartars haue many diuersities from other people of maners and cus-
tumes, and it is paynfull to rekenne all theire diuersities. The Tartars bileue
and name God simplicitie, and say that God is immortall, and thei putt
God afore all thiere workes; and other reuerence they do not to God, nether
by fastynges, ne by prayer, ne by affliccions, ne by other good dedes. The
35 Tartars repute it no synne to slay a man, and, yf the brydle were in the throte
of the horsse, they thinke that they haue synned dedly. They repute
lecherie no synne, for they haue many wyffes. And for vsage, after the deth

of the fadre, the son shall take for his wyf his modre-in lawe; and the
brother the wyf that was his brodres wif; and they bedde with theim. Thise
Tartars be good men of armes, and to theire lorde they be obedient more
than other people be. Theire lorde yeueth vnto theim no wages ne pay-
5 mentes, but he may take all that they haue yf he woll. Nether for hoste ne for
rydyng theire lord is not bounden to yeue vnto theim anything, but they
must lyf [204r] apon chasse and of pray which they gayne apon theire enemyes.
Whan they shall passe by a cuntrey where they knowe is scarscetie of
vitailles, they bryng with theim grete plentie of vitailles, of bestes and kyne;
10 and they lyf by mylke and flessh. The Tartars be quyk and deliuer people
in dedes of armes on horsebak, but on foote they be lytill worth (for they
cannot go on foote). Whan they be ordeinyd to feight, they vnderstonde
anon the wyll of theire capitayne, and knowe what they haue to do; wherfore
the chieftens gouerne lightly theire people with lytill travaill.
15 They haue grete wyttes in takyng of castelles and townes, and seke all
theire avauntage ayenst theire enemye in bataill, and they haue no shame
to departe fro the bataill or sege and to do other thinges for theire profyttes.
The Tartars haue this avauntage of other people: for yf they be in a felde
assembled to fight ayenst theire enemyes, yf it please theim thei feight; and yf
20 the bataill please theim not, the enemyes may not feight ne assemble to
theim to theire avauntage. And therfore the bataill of Tartars is perillous and
mortall; for in a lytill bataill of Tartars shall mo people be slayn and wounded
than in a muche gretter bataill of other people. And for theire bowes and
arrowes they know [204v] theimself well to medle. Also, whan the Tartars
25 be discomfet, they flie all togaders surely. And it is a perillous thing to folow
or to pursue after theim; for in fleyng thei slei men and horses with their
arrowes shotyng backwardes, for they shote as well backwardes as for-
wardes. And yf they see that their enemyes followe the chasse folyshly, they
retourne anon apon theim. Many tymes it hathe comen to, that they which
30 chased the Tartars haue ben discomfeted. The hoste of Tartars is of no grete
moustre ne apparence, forasmoche as thei goo all togader surely; wherfore
M Tartars seme not to be V C men.
Also they be of fayre maners to their hostes, and gladly they dispende
theire vitailles curtoisly; and woll that the same be done to theim ayen, or
35 elles they woll take it by force. The Tartars can well conquere estraunge
thinges, but they can not kepe theim; for better they love to be in tentes
and in the feldes then to abyde in townes. Also they be covetous and willing
to take other mennys goodes, and they can not kepe their awne, ne they
woll not spende. Also, whan the Tartars be in companye of other people so
40 that thei be the more feoble, thei shewe theimself curteis and humble; and

yf thei be the more strong [205r] parte, they shew theimself oulteragious and
fiers. Also, for their profyte the Tartars woll lightly lye. But in two thinges
thei dar not lye; that is to say, in saying that he had done actes or had
prowesse of armes or valure in enything yf he dyd it not, ne also denye his
5 evil dede yf he dyd it. And that other, afore the lorde or afore the iugge they
dar not denye the trowth, and yf it were to be condempned to lose theire
lifes. And so this sufyseth to speyke of the Tartars.

[BOOK FOUR]

[Of iiii thinges to be concidred afore that weres be moved. capitulo primo.]

10 [206v] Reason requyreth that he that woll move werre ayenst his enemyes,
he ought to concidre iiii thinges: fyrst, he oughte to haue iuste quarell or
occasion to move werre; the secund is that he ought to loke apon his power,
yf he be sufficient in dispence and in all other thinges to comence werre,
mayntene it, and to finish it; the third is that he ought wisely to serche
15 thentent and condicion of his enemyes; the iiiith is that he ought to see that
he begynne werre in tyme conuenient.
    And I, Frere Haiton, by the commaundement of our mooste Holy Fader the
Pope, ought to spek of this mater; and after, verely to say that Cristen
people haue iust cause and resonable to move werre ayenst the Sarrasens
20 and the foule sect of Mahomet. For they haue ocupied the heritage of
Cristen men, that is to say, the Holy Lande, the which God hathe promysed
vnto the Cristen men; and they hold the Holy Sepulcre of Our Lorde Ihesu
Criste, which is the begynnyng of the Cristen faith; and for the grete iniuries,
effusions of blode, and the grete shames which the miscreantes haue done
25 vnto the Cristen people in tymes past; and for other diuers reasons which
were to longe to acompte. [207r] To the seconde partie and reason, I say
that no man ought to be in doubte. For the holy Church of Rome, which is
lady and maistresse of all the worlde, hathe well power by the grace of
God, with the aide of the kynges and prynces, Cristiantie, and of the true
30 people of Criste crossed, to deliuer the Holy Sepulcre and the Holy Land
from the power of the Sarrasens; the which they withholde and occupie for
our synnes.
    And to the third and the iiiith reasons, that is, to knowe the state and con-
dicion of his enemyes, and to chose the tyme, place and season conuenient
35 to move werre, it behoueth me to speke more at large. For, even as to a
goode phisicion it belongith to knowe the cause of the maladye wherof he

woll yeue remedye and heyle, in likewise it belongith to a good duc to enquere the condicion, thentencion, and the state of his enemyes, to thentent he may his werres the more wisely begynne, maynteyne, and conduct
vnto thende. Vnto a good and wise duc ought no thing to be hydde in fait
5 of werre ayenst his enemyes; for the thinges purueyd be not wont to greue,
but thise dispurviaunces many tymes trouble the corages [207v] of people
– and namely in dedes of bataill, where men haue no place ne tyme to stande
ayenst the perilles which ther be all redy apparailed. In all other workes
men may better put amendment then in any fait of bataill, for anon there the
10 payne ensueth. And for a more clere vnderstondyng we woll traite of the
fait of the passage of the Holy Lande, and of the condicion and state of the
lande of Egipt, of Babilone, and of the puissaunce of enemyes of the faith
of Criste.

The power of the Soldan and the condicion of the people of Egipt. capitulo
15 **secundo.**

The Soldan which now holdith the seignourie of the royalme of Egipt and of
Sirie is named Melcuaser, and is Cumant of nacion. The host and the
chiualrie of Egipt be folkes of diuers parties and of estraunge londes; for the
people of the cuntrey borne be worth nothing in dedes of armes, nother
20 on foote ne on horsebak, nether by see ne by lande. The power of the host of
the Soldan of Egipt is litle of footemen, but of horsemen it is grete; and the
mooste parte of theim be esclaues sold and boughte, [208r] which the evill
Cristen men bryng into that lande of Egipt to gayne money by. Other ther
be which haue be taken in bataill and constreyned, but the esclaues which be
25 solde be holden for mooste dere, and mooste they be honoured; wherfore
many of theim make theimself to be solde, bycause their lorde shulde holde
theim the more dere. The Soldan of Egipt is alwey in grete suspeccion and
in grete doubte of his people; for they be of suche maner that they loke alwey
to vsurpe the seignourie, and by that reason many soldans haue ben
30 murdred. The hoste of Egipt may be about XX M knyghtes, and of theim be
some good men of werre and good feighting men, but the mooste parte of
theim be of no grete price. Whan the Soldan goothe with his hoste, he dothe
bryng grete quantitie of somages and of camelles charged. They haue good
horses for men of armes and good mares to renne; rouchins and mulates they
35 haue few; theire horses may not awey with grete travaill, but they haue
nede of grete kepyng. The hoste of Egipt is alwey redy at commaundement of
the Soldan, for all they dwell in the citie of Kayre.

The condicion of the hoste of Egipt is suche: euery man of armes [208v] hathe his wages which amounteth no more but vnto C x florences, and an horseman is bounden to kepe iii horses and a camell for his sompter; and whan the Soldan bryngith his people out, yf he woll, he yeueth vnto
5 theim of his speciall grace somthing more. Also the Soldan departeth his soldiours, and yeueth theim to kepe and gouerne to his barons, which be cald admiralles. To some baron he yeueth C men; to another, CC, or mo or fewer, after that he woll honour and avaunce oon more then another. For yf the Soldan yeue power vnto oon admirall to hold C or CC knightes, he
10 shall yeue vnto hym for all the soldioures as muche as it shulde amounte in some holly, after the rate afore expressed. And by the said ordonaunce the Soldan hathe grete defaulte of his seruice. For thise admiralles, which oughte to serue with C or CC knyghtes, do bye esclaues with their money; and to theim they yeue horses and harnesse, and put theim in seruice for
15 men of armes, and they receyue for theim the paymentes for theire wages. Or elles they seke men of lytle price, and to theim they yeue somthing, and leene horses and harnesses, and thei receyue for theim theire paymentes, and all the remanent they put in their purses. Wherof it cometh that in grete quantitie [209r] of suche folkes shal be founde a small nombre of
20 valiaunt men.

The power of the Soldan in Sirie. capitulo tercio.

The puissaunce of the Soldan in the royalme of Sirie may be aboute V M knightes, which haue theire lyvyng ordeneyd apon the rentes of the landes. Also, there he hathe grete quantitie of Beduins and Turquemans, which be
25 stronge people. And they be grete aide vnto the Soldan, namely whan they go to asege in all landes; for they woll go withoute wages, oonly for to gayne any thing, to defende the land or to go in bataill. But the afore seid Bedins and Turquemans shall do nothing for the Soldan by compulsion, ne withoute grete allowance. And yf the Soldan constreyne theim thei flie
30 from hym; the Turquemans shall to the Tartars, and the Bedins to the desertes of Arabie. Also, the Soldan hathe sergeauntes on foote of the cuntreys of Morlebeth and aboute the Mounte Liban and in the land of the Assasins; and he shall haue aide of theim to assege a citie or a castell and to kepe the land in theire cuntrey. And from theire cuntrey they shall not goo for the Soldan
35 to no partie, ne he may not constreyne them, [209v] for the stronge moun- taynes that be where they dwell. The people of the Soldan of Egipt is en- gegneus to take cities and castelles, and in diuers maners they enuade the

landes; for by arbalesters, engynes, stones, mynes vnder therthe, fyre that may not be quenched, and by other maners, they take landes lightly withoute grete perill.

How the Grekes loste the seignourie of Egipt. capitulo iiii^{to}.

5 The Emperour of Grece was wont to holde the seignourie of Egipt, and gouerned the lond by dukes and officialles which he sent thether euery yere to geder the rentes of that land. And so dured the seignorie of the Grekes in the land of Egipt vnto the yere of Oure Lorde V CC iiii. And than they of the land of Egipt myght not suffre the greuances which the
10 Grekes did vnto theim; wherfore they yelded theimself to the Sarrasens, and made apon theim a lorde of the ligne of Mahomet, and they named hym cailif. And all theire lordes were named califes. And they of the ligne of Mahomet held the seignorie of Egipt CCC xlvii yeres. After that, thise Sarrasens loste theire land, and Mendiens which be cald Cordyns occupied
15 the seignorie [210r] of Egipt, as we shall deuise herafter.

[How the Sarrasens loste the signourie of Egipt. capitulo v^{to}.]

In the yere of Our Lorde M liii the Kyng of Almaney, then Kyng of Ierusalem, of blessed memorie, assembled his hoste in all the landes of Ierusalem, and entred into Egipt, and conquered many townes and landes, as it is conteigned
20 all alonge in the boke of the conquest of the Holy Lande. The Calif, seyng that he myght not resiste ayenst the power of Cristen men, sent his messangers to the Soldan of Halap named Saraton, which kept the lawe of Mahomet and which thought to haue grete quantitie of tresoure of the Calif. And he with grete puissaunce of men of armes come in aide of the Calif, and they did so
25 muche that they chassed the Cristen people from the riche and delectable land of Egipt. And the power of the Calif was litle. The Soldan vsurped the seignourie, and toke the Calif, and put hym in pryson; and after, he enuaded the lande of Egipt with grete strength, and put it in his subieccion, and made hymself soldan and lorde of Egipt. This Saraton was of the nacion of the
30 Corasmins, and was the fyrste lorde of Egipt of hys nacion. [210v]

How Salhadin, after his fader Saraton, was Soldan of Egipt. capitulo vi^{to}.

After the deth of Saraton, his son named Salhadin was named soldan of Egipt. And so grew the power of this Salhadin that he discomfetid the Kyng

of Ierusalem and toke the citie by force, and toke many other landes of the
Cristiantie, as it is conteyned in the boke of the conqueste of the Holy Lande.

**The son and nepneue of Salhadin kept the seignorie of Egipt after his deth.
capitulo vii°.**

5 After the deth of Salhadin, his brother and his nepneue, oone ayenst another,
kept the seignourie of Egipt vnto the tyme of the soldan which was named
Melettasala. And he was Soldan of Egipt the tyme that the Tartars toke the
royalme of Cumane. This Soldan of Egipt herd tell howe the Tartars solde
grete chepe of the Cumans which they had taken; and sent by see many
10 marchauntes, and bought of thise Cumans grete nombre of yonge people.
And they were brought into Egipt. Melettasala did theim to be norished,
and much he loved theim, and did theim to be taught [211r] to ryde and to
were harnesse, and muche he trusted in theim and kept theim nigh vnto hym.

Howe the Cumans slewe theire lorde Melettasala, Soldan of Egipt, and
15 **vsurped his seignourie. capitulo viii°.**

In the tyme that Saint Loys, Kyng of Fraunce, passed ouer see and was taken
prysoner by the Sarrasens, the afor said Cumans (which had ben bought
and sold) slewe theire lorde Malettasala, and made lorde oon of theimself
which was named Turqueman. And by that reason, the Kyng of Fraunce
20 and his brother, which were in the pryson of the Sarrasens, were the more
lightly redemed and deliuerd from pryson. In this maner the Cumans
bigan to haue seignorie in Egipt. This ligne of Cumans is cald Capsch of the
parties of the Orient.
  And after a lytle tyme another of the same esclaues which was named
25 Cothos slew the said Turqueman, and made hymself soldan, and he cald
hymself Melomees. This Melomees went vnto the royalme of Sirie, and
chased Ginboga and X M Tartars which Halcon had lefte to kepe the same
royalme. [211v] And as sone as he was retourned into Egipt, another of
thise Cumans named Bandocdar slewe this Melomees, his lorde, and made
30 hymselff soldan, and he was cald Meldaer.
  This Meldaer was wyse and a valiaunt man of armes, and by hym grewe
muche the power of the Sarrasens in the royalmes of Sirie and Egipt. And
he toke by force the noble citie of Antioche, and many other cities and londes
which the Cristen men kept afore, in the yere of Our Lorde M CC lxviii.
35 And to the royalme of Cumane he did grete domages. In the tyme of this
Bendocdar my lorde Edward, Kyng of Englond, passed the see, and the

Soldan thougnt to cause hym to be slayne by an assassin; and by this assassin
the Kyng was wounded with a knyf envenemed, but by the grace of God
he was well made hole. And after, this Soldan dyed apon a poyson that he
dranke in the citie of Damasce.

5   After his deth was made soldan his son named Lecsart, which held the
seignourie of Egipt but a litle tyme; for another Cumane named Elsye chassed
hym oute of his seignorie of Egipt, and made hymself soldan. And ths Elsye
was he which asseged the citie of Triple, and toke it by force in the yere of
Our Lorde M CC $\overset{xx}{\underset{iiii}{}}$ ix.

10   In the yere then next [212r] ensuyng the said Elsye assembled all his power
and went to Babiloine, entendyng to assege Acres. And apon a day as he
went into a fayre place to ease hymself, oone of his seruauntes (which he
trusted muche, and whome he had made constable of his hoste) yaf vnto
hym dedly venem to drynk; wherof he dyed anon. This constable occupied
15 the seignourie, but the other Sarrasens ran apon hym and cut hym in
peces. And after was made soldan oon that was son of the said Elsye, named
Meleccasseraph; which toke the citie of Acres, and chassed oute the Cristen
people from the lande of Sirie in the yere of Our Lorde M CC $\overset{xx}{\underset{iiii}{}}$ xi.

And whan this Meleccasseraph was comen ayen into Egipt, as he went on
20 huntyng apon a day, oon of his seruauntes slew hym in a wode. And
anon this seruaunt was cut in peces by the other Sarrasens. And after that,
was made soldan he that now is Soldan of Egipt, named Melcuasser afore
named. And forasmuch as this Melcuasser was verry yonge, there was yeuen
vnto hym a tutour, which was of the nacion of the Tartars, named Gin-
25 boga. This Ginboga chassed the said enfant Melcuasser, and left hym at the
Crac of Monriall; and after, he toke the seignourie, and made hymself
soldan, and was named Mellecchadell. In the tyme [212v] of this Melecchad-
ell was so grete defaulte of vitailles that all the Sarrasens had died of
hungre yf evyll Cristen people had not brought vnto theym vitailles enough
30 for couetice of gayn. After this, come newes of the commynge of the Tartars;
wherapon Ginboga assembled his host, and went vnto the royalme of Sirie
to defende that lande ayenst the Tartars. This Ginboga honoured muche
theim which had ben Tartars and kept them next vnto hym. And of that had
the Cumans grete envye; wherapon, as Ginboga retourned into Egipt, the
35 Cumans putt hym out of his seignorie, and of oon of themself thei made
their lorde, which was named Lachin (which after was named Melemanser).

This Lachin wold not slea Ginboga bicause he wolde be his fellowe, but yaf
vnto hym a land which is named Sarta. And after he yaf vnto hym the
seignourie of Haman, but he wold not suffer that Ginboga shulde dwell in
40 Egipt. This Soldan Lachin abode iii yeres at the castell of Kayre withoute

departyng, for the doubte that he had of his folkes, sauf oon day that he
descendet to the playne. And they playing at a play which thei cald the
Solle, the horse of this Lachin fell vndre hym and brused his legge. After, the
same Soldan Lachin apon [213r] a day plaid at the chesse, and had sett his
5 sworde by hym; and oon of his seruauntes toke the same sworde, and slew
this Soldan. And anon his felowes ran apon hym, and cut this seruaunt in
peces. After that, the Sarrasens were in grete discorde to make a soldan, and
fynally they accorded and put in the seignourie Melecuasar afore named,
whom Ginboga had left at the Crac of Monreall. This Soldan was he whom
10 Casan discomfited in bataill, and yet he is Soldan of Egipt.

Pardon me though I speyke to longe of the Cumans, which be esclaues
bought and sold, and of the soldans of their lignage; for the cause is to
shew that the Sarrasens may not abyde longe but that suche aduersitie shall
come vnto theim, for the which they may not go oute of Egipt ne go with
15 host into other landes.

The boundes and properties of the royalme of Egipt. capitulo ix°.

The royalme of Egipt is riche and delectable; and it is in length apon xv
iourneys, and in brede apon thre iournayes. And it is as an isle; for apon
two partes it is enuironed with desert and sand, and apon that other parte is
20 the see of Grece. Toward thest [213v] it is more nigh vnto the land of Sirie
then eny other land; verely, bitwene that oon royalme and that other is well
the way of viii iourneys, all in sande. Towardes the west it costith with a
prouince of Barbarie calde Darta, and bitwene that and Egipt be well xv
iourneys of desert. Towardes the southe it costeth with the royalme of
25 Nubie which is Cristen (and they be all blacke for the grete heyte of the
sonne), and bitwene that land and Egipt is of wey, all in sande, well xii
iourneys. In the royalme of Egipt be v prouinces: the first is cald Saith; the
secunde, Meser; the third, Alexandre; the iiii^th Richic (and that cuntrey is
enuironed of the see); and the vth is named Damiette. The maistresse citie of
30 the royalme of Egipt is calde Kayre, and it is sett nigh vnto an auncient citie
which is named Meser. And thise ii cities be apon the riuage of the flode of Nile.

Which floode is verrey profitable, for it dewes and waters all the landes
where it passeth by, and it maketh the landes plentiouse and abundaunt
of all goodes. The floode of Nile hathe good fish plentie, and it beryth grete
35 nauys, for it is grete and depe. And in all thinges the floode of Nile myght
be praysed aboue all other [214r] yf it were not that it kept oon maner of
bestes which be as dragons that deuoure men and horses within the water

or apon the shore, and thise bestes be named cocalz. The floode of Nile
groveth oon tyme of the yere; and begynneth to grove in the moneth of
August, and cotynueth growing vnto the fest of Saint Michell. And whan it is
as muche as it may grove, the people of the cuntrey lette renne the water
5 by conducttes and by esclusees ordeyned to enewe and water all the land;
and so standeth the water apon the landes xl dayes, and after that the
land dryeth, and the people sowe and plant. And all good thinges growe in
the same lande by that same wateryng oonly; for in this lande it nother
renyth ne snoweth enything, and it is herd to knowe somer fro the wynter.
10 Also thenhabitantes of the lande haue sett in myddes of the floode of Nile,
in a lytle isle which is afore the citie of Meser, a pilloure of marbre, and they
haue made markes in the same pillour. And after that the water shall grove
thei shall well knowe yf they shall haue habundaunce and plentie or elles
scarestie that yere, and after that they sett prises apon thinges. The water
15 of the floode of Nile is holsome to drynke; verely, when men take it oute of
the floode, it is over hote, [214v] but whan thei put it in vesselles of erthe,
it becometh clere, colde, and holsome.

In the royalme of Egipt be ii portes of the see; wherof that oon is Alexandre,
and that other, Damiette. In Alexandre may well arryve shippes and galees,
20 and that citie is stronge and well walled. The water that men drynke in
Alexandre cometh by conductes fro the floode of Nile, wherof thei fill their
cisternes and haue enough; other water haue they non wherby they may
lyf. Then they that myght put from theim the water which gothe by the same
conductes, thei shulde put them to grete misease, and thei myght not
25 longe endure; otherwise it shuld be herd thing to take Alexandre by force.
The citie of Damiette is apon the floode of Nile, which of old tyme was well
walled. But it was taken two tymes by Cristen men: oon tyme by the Kyng of
Ierusalem and by other Cristen men of thest cuntrees, and another tyme
by Saint Lowes, Kyng of Fraunce. And for that cause, the Sarrasens haue
30 abated the walles, and transposed it farder fro the see; and they haue
made nother wall ne fortresse, and they call that the Newe Damiette; and the
olde Damiette is all desert. Of thise portes of Alexandre and Damiette the
Soldan [215r] hathe grete encrees and grete goodes.

The land of Egipt rentith grete habundaunce of sucre and of all good
35 thinges. Wyne they haue but lytle, but that they make is verry good and
fressh; Sarrasens dar drynke no wyne, for it is defended theim in theire lawe.
Flesh of moton, pultrie, and wilde foule, they haue enough; they haue
fewe beofes; they eyte the flesh of camelles. In the royalme of Egipt be some
Cristen people dwelling which they call Kepty, which hold the sect of
40 Iacobyns; and they haue in thise parties many fayre abbayes, the which they

hold in fraunchesse and in peas. Thise Kepties were the mooste auncient
habitantes of the land of Egipt, for the Sarrasens bigan to enhabit in that land
long after they had the seignourie. The thinges which be not founde in the
lande of Egipt, ne the Egipcions may not fynde but they be brought vnto
5 them fro other cuntreys, be iron, stele, and the esclaues wherof they
encrees theire hoste. Of thise thinges haue they grete nede; for withoute
thise they may not longe endure. In all the royalme of Egipt is not a citie ne
a castell walled; but oonly the citie of Alexandre, which is verrey well walled,
[215v] and the castell of Kayre, which is not verry stronge. Verely in that
10 castell dwelleth the Soldan, and of all the land of Egipt it is susteyned, kept,
and defendet by the chiualrie. Then, after that the hoste of Egipt shulde
be discomfite, the land shuld lightly be conquerd withoute perill.

**The tyme devised conuenable to move werre ayenst miscreantes, enemyes
of our faith. capitulo x^{mo}.**

15 Shortly than I say that I may say thise wordes *'Ecce nunc tempus acceptabile.'*
For verily it is tyme conuenient and acceptable to move werre ayenst
thenemyes of the Cristen faith; nowe is tyme conuenable to yeue aide to the
Holy Land, the which hathe ben longe tyme in seruage of the miscreantes;
nowe is tyme conuenable in which the corages of true Cristen men oughte to
20 embrace the passage of the Holy Land, to thende that fro the handes of
enemyes may be deliuerd the Holy Sepulcre of Our Lorde which is the begynnyng of our bileve. We haue not had in days past so conuenable a tyme as
nowe, as by His pytie [216r] He hathe shewde vnto vs in many maners. Fyrst,
God allmyghtye and marcifull hathe yeuen vnto vs a shepard mooste holy,
25 and mooste Cristen Fader, and full of all vertues; which, after that he was sett
in the Sege Apostolique, desirously bothe day and nyght he studied howe
he might socoure the Holy Lande biyonde the see, and how the Holy
Sepulcre of Our Lorde might be deliuerd from the miscreantes and from theire
power (which blaspheme the name of Criste). And for that cause, men may
30 well bileve fermely that God hathe tourned His mercifull eyne to loke
apon the Holy Land, and to hym hathe yeuen in erth his redemptour that
is our Holy Fadre the Pope. In the tyme of whome, by the mercy of Our
Lordé, the holy citie of Ierusalem, which is and hathe ben holden longe
by our synnes vnder the seruage of thenemyes, shal be deliuerd and
35 shal be broughte into theire former fraunchesse and power of Cristen
men.

Thexortacion of Frere Haiton vnto Cristen prynces to entreprise the voiage of the Holy Land. capitulo xi^{mo}.

[216v] Now is tyme acceptable and conuenable in the which God hathe shewde vnto vs clerely that the Holy Land shal be deliuerd fro the power of
5 his enemyes. For by the grace of God all the kynges and prynces of Cristiantie be nowe in good estate and peasable amonges theimself; thei haue no werre ne discorde as they were wont to haue somtyme. Then it semeth that God almyghtye woll deliuer the Holy Land. Also all Cristen people of diuers landes and of diuers royalmes by faith and by deuocion be redy to
10 take the crosse and to passe ouer see in the aide of the Holy Land, and to put therapon bodyes and goodes in the reuerence of Our Lorde Ihesu Criste vigorously and with good will.

Nowe is tyme conuenable and acceptable which God hathe shewde vnto Cristen men; for the puissaunce of thenemyes of the faith of Crist is
15 minyshed by the warres of the Tartars, by the which they were discomfeted and loste their folkes withoute nombre in battaill. Also, as for the Soldan which nowe reigneth in Egipt, he is a man of no value and of no bountie. On that other partie, all the prynces of the Sarrasins which were wont to yeue [217r] aide vnto the Soldan be all ded and distroyed by the power of the
20 Tartars; and oon was oonely remaynyng, which was named Soldan of Meredin, which is late tourned to the seruage of the Tartars. And for that cause, in this tyme withoute perill and withoute grete trauaile may be socoured the Holy Lande and may be goton the royalmes of Egipt and of Sirie; and with that, as it is said, may the puissaunce of thenemyes be
25 confounded lightly in this tyme present better and more easily then euer it myght be in tyme past.

Also the tyme is conuenable the which God hathe shewde vnto Cristen people, in that the Tartars haue offred to yeue aide vnto them ayenst the said Sarrasens; and for that reason Carbanda, Kyng of Tartars, hath sent his
30 messangers, offeryng to put all his power to confounde thenemyes of the faith of Crist. And in this tyme, namely for the aide of the Tartars, the Holy Land may be recouerd and the royalme of Egipt conquered lightly withoute perill. And for that cause, it were conuenient that Cristen men yaf their socoures to the Holy Land withoute longe abydyng, for longe tarying draweth
35 to hym grete perill. [217v] For that Carbanda is nowe frende and woll not fayle; and there myght come another in his place which myght hold the sect of Mahomet, and which shuld accorde hymself with the Sarrasens so that it might tourne to grete perill to Cristiantie and of the Holy Lande.

Howe Frere Haiton declareth vnto the Pope the prosperitees and aduersites that may fall to thenemyes of the faith. capitulo xii°.

Afore Your Reuerence, Holy Fader, I say and confesse that I am not of sufficient connyng to counsell so grete a worke as is the busynesse of the
5 passage over see into the Holy Lande. But, for that I woll not renne in the payne of a childe inobedient, it behoueth me to obey vnto Your Holynesse and vnto your holsome commaundementes (ayenst which it belongith not to eny good Cristen man to do). Then, fyrst requeryng [pardon] of that I say more or lesse, I shall say myn advise after my lytill knowleage, saving alwey
10 the bettre counseill of wise men.

To the honour of Our Lorde Ihesu Criste, by whose mercy I hope to accomplish this litle compilacion or werke, I say, to thende [218r] that the Holy Lande may be goten with the lesse trauaile, it is byhouefull that the Cristen men do entre into the said land, and that thei enuade theire enemyes, in
15 suche tyme speciallye when their enemyes shal be troubled by eny aduersitie. For yf the Cristen men woll do that in tyme that the enemyes be in good prosperitie, they may not accomplish theire dedes withoute grete perill and grete trauaile; wherfore we shall devise surely what is the prosperitie and what is the aduersitie of the enemyes. The prosperitie of thise enemyes may
20 be in that whan the Sarrasens haue a soldan and a lorde valiaunt and sage, suche as may withoute drede of rebellion or treason of his people hold and kepe his seignourie; another prosperitie of enemyes may be whan they haue ben longe tyme in peas and withoute werre of the Tartars or of other people; also whan in the royalme of Sirie they haue a good yere and
25 habundaunce of whete and of other goodes; also whan by see and by land the wayes be sure and open, and the thinges wherof thenemyes haue nede may be broughte vnto theim fro estraunge cuntreys withoute lett or disturbance; also whan the Sarrasens haue [218v] peas or trues with the Nubiens and the Beduins of the desert of Egipt, if they make no werre ne
30 brigandie; and whan the Turquemans and the Beduins which dwell in the royalmes of Egipt and of Sirie be obedient vnto the Soldan of Egipt. By thise afore said prosperitees the power of thenemyes shuld grove so longe that it shuld be no light thing to distroye theim.

By the contrarie, aduersities may come to thenemyes in many maners; that
35 is to say, whan the miscreantes rebell and slea theire soldan, as they haue done or this tyme and do well many tymes. For after that this lignage of Cumans began to haue seignourie in Egipt, ix haue ben ordeyned soldans

and lordes apon theim. And of the ix soldans which haue ben in Egipt, non escaped, that afore his dayes ne hathe ben slayne: that is to saye, Turqueman, Cochas, Lashin, and ii other, were distroyed by poyson; and Bendocdar and Elsye, Ginboda and Melecasseraph, were exiled. And this Melcuaser,
5 which is nowe soldan, was oones chassed fro the seignorie, and nowe he dwellith in balance abiding an [219r] evill ende.

Also to thise enemyes may come aduersitie; that is, whan the flode of Nile encresseth not so muche as it may watter theire landes as nede is, for then the Sarrasens of Egipt shulde haue scarstie and hungre. And that is not longe
10 ago sith it was so and that thei had all died for hungre, yf false Cristen men had not for couetise and fals gayne brought vnto theim vitailles enough. And whan suche thinges fall, thise enemyes must nedes grove into grete pouertie, sell their horses, and mynysh their people; and by that reason they shulde haue no power to departe oute of Egipt ne to go into Sirie. And it is
15 of necessitie that euery man must bryng with hym oute of Egipt as much as he must haue nede of for viii dayes, for hymself, his meanye, and for his bestes; for he shall fynde nothing but gravell and sand in viii iourneys. Than he that lakketh an hors or a camell may not departe from Egipt to go into Sirie, and by this maner the Soldan shulde be so distourbed that he myght
20 not come to socoure the miscreantes in the royalme of Sirie. Also, whan thise enemyes haue ben longe in the werres, grete aduersitie myght [219v] come vnto theim yf the portes of the see were so kept, that nothing myght be brought into theire land of suche thinges wherof they haue mooste nede: as iron and esclaues, and other thinges which thei may not haue but yf
25 they be brought from estraunge landes. For withoute thise thinges thei may not longe endure. Also, when Beduins or the Nubiens move werre ayenst the Soldan, he shulde by that werre be so distourbed that he myght not departe from Egipt ne go into Sirie. Also, whan the land of Sirie hathe defaulte, and an evill yere is there, other by drynesse or by werres of the
30 Tartars or in any other maner; for yf the royalme of Sirie shulde fayle in rentes, the hoste of Egipt might not come to abide in Sirie. For from Egipt, ne from eny other lande, thei may nothing bring into Sirie, and by that reason the hoste may not departe from Egipt. Then, whan it shuld so be that thise enemyes shuld haue eny of thise aduersitees, thei shuld be so distourbed
35 that thei myght not departe from Egipt to come into Sirie. Then the Cristen men myght lightly occupie the royalme of Ierusalem, and might make ayen the cities and the castelles withoute greuaunce, and do garnissh theimself in suche maner [220r] that thei shuld not doubte the power of theire enemyes after.

The fourme of begynnyng of werres ayenst the miscreantes, after Frere Haiton. capitulo xiii°.

After that we haue resonably deuised of the prosperities and aduersities which may come to the enemyes of the faith of Criste, we shall say in this
5 partie of the begynnyng of the passage of the Holy Lande. To me it semeth, for the suretie and profite of a passage generall, that at the begynnyng certen noumbre of men of armes, bothe horsmen and footemen, to knowe the power of thise enemyes were sent afore; and it is myn advise that for this present tyme shuld suffise the nombre of M knyghtes with x galees and III M
10 footemen. And apon thise folkes wolde be a chieuetayne sage and valiant which with theim shuld passe ouer see and gouerne theim; and thei to arryve in the isle of Cipre or in the royalme of Armenye, as to theim it shulde seme best to do. And after, withoute abydyng, to do by counseill [220v] of the Kyng of Tartars, requyring of hym ii thinges: oon, that Carbanda
15 shulde defende by all his lande that nothing shuld be had thens into the lande of thise enemyes, and another, that he shulde sende messangers and of his men of armes to the cuntreys of Meleture that they shuld wast and ouerrenne the lande of Halap. After that, our pilgrymes and thei of the royalme of Armenye and of Cipre, by see and by lond, shulde move werre
20 and enuade vigorously the landes of thise enemyes, and to trauaile them-self to kepe the see cost in suche maner that nothing shuld come by see to the socour or relief of thenemyes. Also our Cristen men may garnish the isle of Cocose, which is in a good place for theire galees to aryve, and ther may they do grete damages to theire enemyes. Verely the maner to begynne the werre
25 and to enuade the landes of thise enemyes, I leve it to the wise capitayne which shall entreprise this werkes; for his estate and the condicion of his enemyes must change counseill, and werk wisely by the counseill of wise men which shal be present att the seid busynesse. And the profites that may come of this first passage breuely I shall devise herafter. [221r]

30 **The profites and auauntages that may grove to the pilgrymes by the fyrst voiage ayenst theire enemyes. capitulo xiiii°.**

This fyrst passage may be so ordred that thise enemyes shal be so trauailed by the aide of the other Cristen men which be in the parties of the Orient, and by the Tartars also, that thei shall haue no rest, and thei shall suffre grete
35 annoyce and grete damages. For yf by the Cristen men and the Tartars

were moved werre ayenst the Soldan of Egipt by see and by land of the
royalme of Sirie, it behoved that the Soldan shuld send to kepe and defend
theim which be nigh the see cost, and all other which myght be enuadet
or in perill. And yf the Tartars moved werre in the parties of Meletur in the
5 land of Halape, it behoued that the people of the Soldan shuld come well
xxv^{ti} iourneys long, and thei that shuld come fro Babilone to do that seruice;
in a short tyme thei shuld be empoueryshed and shulde lose theire horses
and theire harnesse, and thei shuld be so trauailed that they myght not
dure. And in iii or in iiii chaunges so made, thise [221v] enemyes shuld lose
10 theire goodes and shuld haue grete damages. Also, by the fyrst passage
thise enemyes myght be muche troubled; for with the arriuage of thise x
galees of the fyrst passage, with the aide of theim which might be arriued
fro the royalmes of Armenye and of Cipre, the landes of theire enemyes might
be all overronnen, and the galees myght retourne in sauftie vnto the isle of
15 Corcorsse. And yf the Soldan wolde kepe and defende the said landes, it
behoved hym that he come in his awne persone with all his power from
Babillone into Sirie, and with people sufficient to yeue aide to all the landes
which be nigh vnto the see cost. In thissue fro the royalme of Egipt to
come into Sirie shuld be to the Soldan a thing perillous and damageous:
20 perillous, for treason of his people; damageous and annoyous, for by the
enuasions of Cristen men thei myght be so troubled that thei shuld haue no
power to auaunce theimself; also damageous, for he shulde consume and
waste all his treasoure (and with grete payne it is to be bileved the grete
quantitie of money which it behoueth that the Soldan and his folkes dis-
25 pende att all tymes whan he dothe issue from the land of Egipt to come [222r]
into Sirie). Also, by the said galees the portes and the wayes of the see
cost may be kept in suche maner that vnto theire enemyes nothing shuld be
brought wherof thei had nede to haue oute of estraunge cuntreys, as afore
is said; also thise enemyes shuld lose the rentes which thei haue of the portes
30 of the see, which amounte vnto grete goodes and tresore.

    Also, yf it come to that thenemyes were troubled by any aduersitie so that
thei myght not departe fro Egypt ne yeue aide vnto theim of the land of
Sirie, then the pilgrymes of this first passage, with the aide of other Cristen
people of the Orient, might well redresse the citie of Triple. And in Mount
35 Liban be inhabitantes, Cristen people, good sergeauntes aboute XL M, which
grete aide shuld yeue vnto the pilgrymes; the which be themself many
tymes rebelle, and haue done grete damage vnto the Soldan and his folkes.
And after that the citie of Triple were made and fortified, the Cristen
people might hold it and make it stronge, vnto the commyng of the generall
40 passage, and thei myght take all the cuntrey theraboute and holde the

countie of Triple. And that myght tourne to grete ease of the people that shall come with the passage generall, for so thei shuld fynde the porte apparailed where [222v] thei myght surely arryue.

Also yf it come to that the Tartars shuld conquere the royalme of Sirie and
5 the Holy Land, the Cristen men of the fyrst passage shulde fynde theim-self redy to receyue the land of the Tartars and to garnishe and kepe the same. And I, which knowe enough the willes of the Tartars, bileve fermely that all the cities and landes which the Tartars shuld conquere apon the Sarrasens, with good will thei wolde yif theim vnto Cristen men frely and
10 quietly; for the Tartars may not abyde in that cuntrey for the grete heyte which is there in the tyme of somer. Than it shuld be well that the Cristen men held the landes and kept theim; for the Tartars neuer feight ayenst the Soldan for couetyse to geyte landes ne cities, but thei fight for that the Soldan hathe ben alwey their enemye and hathe done vnto theim more greuaunce
15 and damage then any other (namely whan thei be in werres ayenst their neighbours). And for thise reasons aboue seid, I bileve that the nombre aboue expressed, that is to say, M knyghtes, x galees, and III M footemen, shuld be enough and suffice for the first passage. And me semeth that in thise begynnyng ii tymes so muche people shuld not do so much [223r] as
20 thei shuld do, and that were but multiplicacion of exserpenses.

Also, by the fyrst passage may come iii other profittes. For after that the pilgrymes of the fyrst passage hadd abiden oon season in the parties of byyond the see, and had knowen the condicion of the land and the maners of their enemyes, they might adresse and advertice the other that shulde come in
25 the passage generall. Also take we it soo that the Tartars, for the werres amonges theimself or for other cause, may not or woll not yeue aide vnto the Cristen people ayenst the Sarrasens, and that the Soldan and his people were in theire prosperitie, and that it were no light thing to conquere the Holy Land and it to deliuer fro the power of enemyes; Your Holy Faderhod,
30 knowyng the condicion of the Holy Land and seyng the power of the passage generall, it may better haue counseill and advertisment by this fyrst passage apon that which it behoveth to do. And the generall passage then may attende the tyme and season good and conuenable to passe, and by that may be eschewed all the annoyes and the perilles that may come. [223v]

35 **Howe it is deuised that the Pope shulde write vnto the Georgiens and Nubiens for aide of the Holy Lande. capitulo xv^{mo}.**

Also pardon me Your Holynesse that I may say ii other wordes. Oon is that

Your Holynesse do wryte vnto the Kyng of the Georgiens, which be Cristen
and which more then other nacions be deuoute vnto the pilgrymages and
to the saintuaries of the Holy Lande, that they shulde yeue aide vnto the
pilgrymes to recouer the Holy Land. And I bileue fermely that for the honour
5 of God and for the reuerence of Your Holynesse thei shuld gladly accom-
plissh your commaundement, for they be deuout Cristen men and people of
power grete enough; and they be valiant men of armes and neighboures to
the royalme of Armenye. Also, that Your Holynesse woll wryte ayen to the
Kyng of Nubiens, which be Cristen and were conuerted by Saynt Thomas
10 in the land of Ethiope, commaundyng theim that they shall move werre to the
Soldan and his people. And I beleue fermely that the afor said Nubiens,
for the honour of Our Lorde and for the reuerence of Your Holinesse, shuld
move werre to the Soldan and to his folkes, and wold do [224r] vnto theim
annoyance and damage to theire powers; which shuld be grete distourbance
15 to the Soldan and his people. And the same letres may be sent vnto the
Kyng of Armenye which shuld do them to be translated in theire language,
and he shuld send theim by good messangers.

Howe iii maner of wayes be diuised wherby to passe into the Holy Land.
capitulo xvi°.

20 Deuoutly and faithfully haue I shewede after my lytle knowleage that
which behoveth to folowe at the begynnyng of the passage to aide the Holy
Land; herafter woll I obey vnto the commaundement of Your Holy Faderhode apon that that bihoueth to the passage generall ouer see.
The passage generall may be taken thre wayes. Oon is by the way of
25 Barbarie, but that way I leve to the counseill of them which knowe the
condicion of that cuntrey. Another is by the way of Constantynoble, that is to
say, by the way which held Godefroy of Buillon and other pilgrymes of
that tyme. And as I beleue, the passage generall myght lightly go vnto [224v]
the citie of Constantynoble. But passing by the Brace of Saint George and
30 goyng by Turquie the way shuld not be sure, for the Turquemans, which be
Sarrasens, inhabit in Turquie. Verely, the Tartars may deliuer this way,
and so may they ordeyne that the land of Turquie shuld bryng vitaill enough
for the hoste of pilgrymes att resonable prices. And that other way which
is knowen to all men is by the see.
35 Then, yf the passage generall shuld passe by the see, it is necessarie that in
all the portes of the see be apparailled shipps and other in all thinges
sufficient to passe; and it behoueth that at oone terme named all the pil-

grymes in season conuenable be sufficiently apparailled to take shipping
and to passe togeder. And thei may arriue in Cipre to rest and refresh theimself and their horses of the trauaill of the see. And after that the passage
generall shuld be arriued in Cipre and had rested certen dayes, yf the pil-
5 grymes of the fyrst passage had made stronge the citie of Triple or some
other citie apon the see cost in Sirie, the generall passage myght arryue there,
and that shuld be to theim grete ease. And [225r] if the pilgrymes of the
fyrst passage had not made stronge eny citie in the land of Sirie, it bihoved
that the passage generall kept his wey by the royalme of Armenye in this
10 maner: that is to say, that the pilgrymes at the royalme of Cipre so yeuing
vnto theim and their horses rest shulde abide there vnto the fest of Saint
Michell, and than they may go surely into the royalme of Armenye. And ther
thei shall fynde all that thei shall haue nede of; verely, thei may abide in
the land of Thersoth easely for that which they shall fynde there (as grete
15 plentie of waters and of pastures for their horses). And fro the land of
Turquie, which is nigh vnto theim, they shall haue vitailles and horses and all
that thei shall nede, and fro the land of Armenye also. And thei may dwell
in rest all the wynter in the said land of Armenye. Att the new tyme and
spring of the yere, the hoste of pilgrymes may go by land vnto Antyoche
20 (which is from Armenye a iournay), and by shippe they may go oon partie by
the see and arriue at the porte of Antyoche, and so shuld be neighboures
the host by land and the host by the see.

   After that the Cristen men shall haue taken the citie of Antyoche, the
which by the helpe of God they [225v] shall sone take, the pilgrymes may
25 rest in that lande for a tyme, and they may ouerrenne and take the landes of
their enemyes which be theiraboute; and with that they may knowe and
lerne the condicion, beyng, and will of theire enemyes which be theraboute.
And in thise parties of Antyoche be habitantes Cristen people enough,
which be good men of werre and which anon shall come into the host of
30 pilgrymes and may do theim good seruice. After that the pilgrymes departe
from Antyoche, thei may go by the see coste vnto the citie of Liche, which is
their mooste shorte and the best way, and the hoste of Armenye may
folowe nigh after the hoste by land. Verely, nigh vnto Magart at the arriuage
of the see is a pas muche annoyous for grete noumbre of people to pass.
35 And if it come to that the enemyes had kept that pas by suche wise that the
pilgrymes might not passe, our people withoute perill might retourne into
Antyoche. And they might go by the way towardes Chesare vp by the banke
of the flode cald Renel; and by this way the hoste shuld fynde plentie of
pastures and good waters and the landes of theire enemyes garnished with
40 vitailles and of other good thinges, [226r] wherof the hoste may haue grete

ease. And by this way our folkes may goo vnto the citie of Hamam, whiche is a riche citie, and which the Cristen men myght take lightly. And if it come to that the enemyes wold defend the said citie bicause it is riche, and if they come to the bataill ayenst the Cristen men, they shuld haue grete auaunt-
5 age to feight in that place, and lightly thei shulde discomfet their enemyes.

And yf the Cristen men might oones discomfite the hoste of the Soldan, they shuld not fynde after any man ayenst theim, and thei might go right to the citie of Damasce; which thei shuld take, or elles thei of the citie wolde yelde theim by appoyntment. For after that the Soldan were discomfite,
10 they of Damasce might not holde, but they shulde yeld theimself with good willes, saving their lyfes as thei did to Halcon and to Casan after that thei had discomfeted the Soldan. And after that the Cristen men had taken Damasce, they shuld conquere vigorously the remanent. And yf the enemyes eschewde the bataill, the Cristen men myght come right to Triple in iiii
15 dayes iourneys from Damasce, and thei may make and repaire ayen the citie of Triple; [226v] and with that the Cristen men which be in Mounte Liban shuld yeue grete aide to the pilgrymes. Then, yf the Cristen men held the citie of Triple, thei might conquere the royalme of Ierusalem with the helpe and grace of allmyghty God.

20 **Howe the Cristen men and the Tartars may be conducted ethir host from other. capitulo xvii°.**

In the company of the Cristen men is myn advise that the noumbre of XX M Tartars may do grete ease and grete profite to the Cristen men ryding by the cuntreys; for by doubte of the Tartars the Beduins and the Turquemans
25 dar not approche the hoste of Cristen men. Another thing, the Tartars shuld geyte grete vitailles for the hoste of Cristen men, and cause theim to come from fer londes for some gayne. Also by the Tartars, thei may en-quere and knowe the condicion of theire enemyes; for the Tartars be light to renne here and there, and they can well entre by night and by day as thei
30 will. Also, in fait of bataill and takyng of cities and townes the Tartars may be right profitable, for they be verrey wise in suche purposes. [227r] And yf it com to that Carbanda, or other in his place, with people come for to entre into the land of Egipt, then it were good to escewe and kepe the hoste ferre along fro the Tartars. For the Tartars woll not folowe the will of the Cristen
35 men, and the Cristen men may not folowe the willes of the Tartars, which be horsed and ryde verry hastelye, and also thei may not folowe bicause of the footemen. Also, the Tartars, whan they thinke theimself in power and

strength, they be verry oultragious and prowde, and thei may not suffre withoute doyng oulterage vnto the Cristen people, which thing the Cristen men may not suffre; wherof might sourde esclaundre and hate bitwene theim. But apon that thing men may putt good remedye: that is to sey, that
5 the Tartars shall go by way of Damasce, as they haue done and haue ben accustomed to do, and the Cristen men shall go right vnto the parties of Ierusalem. In this maner, that oon beyng ferre from that other, bitwene the Cristen men and the Tartars good peas shuld be kept in good amitie, and the puissaunce of thenemyes shuld be confounded soner by thise ii hostes
10 then by oon.

Also, another [227v] thing is to be remembred vnto Your Holynesse: that is, to wytt, that wisely be kept the counseill of Cristen men, which in tymes passed haue not ben kept; wherfore thei haue suffred grete annoyances and their enemyes therby haue escewede grete perilles, and by that meane
15 they haue founde the maner to put the Cristen men fro the accomplishment of their desires. And, howbeit that the renomme of the passage may not be kept counseill but that thrugh all the world vniuersally it must be knowen, yet all that may tourne no profite to thenemyes, for aide may non come vnto theim from eny partie. And in many maners the counseill of the Cristen
20 men may be kept secrete, makyng semblant to do oon thing and therapon to do another. And for that that the Tartars may not kepe their counseill, many tymes it hathe tourned theim to grete annoyance. For the Tartars haue suche maner that in the fyrst mone of the yere, which is Ianuarii, thei take counseill of all that they woll do that yere. Than, yf it come to that
25 they woll move werre ayenst the Soldan of Egipt, anon their counseill is knowen of all men; and the Sarrasens do it to be knowen [228r] vnto the Soldan, and therapon the Soldan garnisheth hymself ayenst theim. And the Sarrasens can well kepe their awne counseill, which hath ben to theire profite many tymes. And this sufficeth as nowe to say apon the fait of the
30 passage of the Holy Lande.

The wordes of the auctour to the Pope. capitulo xviii°.

After all this, I pray humbly that Your Holynesse benignely receyue this which of my deuocion I haue wreton apon the passage of the Holy Lande. And to that which I haue said more or lasse, be it putt vnto your correccion,
35 for I haue not the hardiesse to counseill so grete a werke as the passage of the Holy Land yf it were not by the commaundement of Your Holy Faderhode. Which, after that he was sett in the sege pastorall by the purviaunce

of God, with all his hert hathe studied disirously and procured and treated
howe the Holy Land which was dewed with the precious blode of Our
Lorde Ihesu Criste shuld be deliuerd fro the power of the miscreantes. And
by that reason, he hathe cald all the kynges and prynces of Cristiantie to
5 his [228v] counseill, to thende that they may counseill and advertise apon the
passage of the Holy Lande. And howbeit that God allmyghty and mercifull hathe shewde vnto vs by verrey apparences that he woll deliuer the said
Holy Lande fro the seruage of the miscreantes in the tyme of Your Holy
Faderhode, we ought all to pray humbly that longe lyf, good fortune yeue
10 vnto you he that lyfeth and reigneth in *saecula saeculorum.* Amen.

So endeth the boke of the Floure of Thistories of the Parties of the Orient
(compiled by the religious man, Frere Haiton of the ordre of the Premonstre, somtyme Lord of Corc, cosyn germayne of the Kyng of Armenye) apon
the passage of the Holy Land biyonde the see, by the commaundement of
15 our Holy Fadre the Apostle Clement, the vth of that name, in the citie of
Poitiers. The which boke, I, Nicholl Falcon, wrote fyrst in Frenche as the
said Frere Haiton said it of his mouthe withoute note or examplaire; and fro
Roman translate it into Latyne in the yere of thencarnacion of Our Lorde
M CCC vii in the moneth of August.

TORONTO MEDIEVAL TEXTS AND TRANSLATIONS

General Editor: Brian Merrilees